Here's what the experts have to say about *4-Wheel Freedom: The Art of Off-Road Driving*:

4x4 Power **magazine:** "One book to have in your 4xlibrary is *4-Wheel Freedom*. This easy-to-understand book uses tons of photos and illustrations to teach you basic driving techniques for snow, water, hills, and other adverse or adventuresome conditions."

Mark Cox, Director, The Bridgestone Winter Driving School at Steamboat Springs: "Brad DeLong has hit a home run with this book. *4-Wheel Freedom* leads the reader step by step through all aspects of off-road travel, with a wealth of pertinent information for beginners and seasoned off-road adventurers alike."

Harold Pietschmann, President of The Adventure Company—Professional 4x4 Training and Expeditions: "*4-Wheel Freedom* is America's most valuable 4x4 book. Everybody who owns a 4x4 should read it. It answers all those nagging 'What if . . .' questions and creates true 4-wheel freedom."

Del Albright, BlueRibbon Coalition: "If there ever was a handbook or a 'bible' for off-road/four-wheel drive enthusiasts, Brad DeLong's book, *4-Wheel Freedom* is it. It achieves a comprehensive overview of four wheeling that makes it a necessity for all off-road drivers."

Anthony J. Scotti, President, Scotti School of Executive Protection and Evasive Driving: "An excellent job of simplifying complicated topics. The book has all the information anyone would ever need or want to know about utility vehicles. An excellent book!"

Harry Lewellyn, "The Professor of Off-Road," Ecological 4-Wheeling Adventures: "With 14 chapters and four appendices, it is the most modern, up-to-date, comprehensive book available . . . an admirable job."

4-WD & Sport Utility **magazine:** "A mini encyclopedia about the art of four-wheeling . . . Five separate chapters cover driving off the paved path and provide information worthy of any 4x4 training course in the country. The chapter on winching is more comprehensive than some the owners' manuals we've seen . . . Our impression of *4-Wheel Freedom* is we wish we had written this book."

Curt Biberdorf, *Fort Riley Post*, Fort Riley, Kansas: "DeLong's personal anecdotes praising four-wheel drives and cautioning drivers about the dangers are a welcome addition . . . Entertaining by itself or as a practical guidebook in the sport of off-roading, *4-Wheel Freedom* is right on track."

Bill Burke, Bill Burke's 4-Wheeling America: "Well-thought out and researched . . . highly readable . . . lots of hints and tricks to help the reader become more self-reliant . . . I am recommending this book to my students as part of their curriculum."

Keith Hanson, owner Hanson's Garage, Orofino, Idaho. Jeep, Chrysler, and Eagle dealer serving the inland northwest: "I grew up in 4-wheel drive country and have driven and sold 4x4s for over 20 years. Brad's book introduced me to many aspects of 4-wheeling I had never even heard of. The book is easy to read and understand and there is something for everyone, whether you are a beginner or have been around 4x4s all your life."

Matt Young, *Ducks Unlimited* magazine: "An indispensable source of information for off-road driving enthusiasts. This encyclopedic work covers everything a 4x4 owner needs to know, from selecting a winch to driving techniques to the principles of ecologically sound four-wheeling."

4-WHEEL

FREEDOM

To my family—Irene, my loving wife, who shares the adventures and spirit of this book. My kids, Michelle, Monique, Stephanie, and Jonathan, trying to make sense of this world we're leaving them. And our dogs: Hershey, our gentle golden mix, and Sadie, our sturdy young yellow Lab. Their greatest pleasure is just being with us, whether we're snuggled together in our log home or at a secluded campsite in a cedar grove on the banks of a mountain stream. To Bailey, our wiry, wily English pointer pup, whose goal in life is running as hard as he can to nowhere in particular, just finding joy in the journey. And to Arthur, our old man, part terrier, part poodle, who left us at the age of 18, going strong to the end, teaching us that keeping up with the younger dogs keeps you alive and healthy for a long, long time.

4-WHEEL
FREEDOM

THE ART OF OFF-ROAD DRIVING

Brad DeLong

PALADIN PRESS • BOULDER, COLORADO

4-Wheel Freedom:
The Art of Off-Road Driving
by Brad DeLong

Copyright © 1996, 2000 by Brad DeLong

ISBN 0-87364-891-9
Printed in the United States of America

Published by Paladin Press, a division of
Paladin Enterprises, Inc.
Gunbarrel Tech Center
7077 Winchester Circle
Boulder, Colorado 80301, USA.
+1.303.443.7250

Direct inquiries and/or orders to the above address.

Visit our Web site at: www.paladin-press.com
Front cover photos: top right by Knut Akseth;
bottom left by Bill Burke

CONTENTS

ACKNOWLEDGMENTS

A lot of people deserve thanks for helping me write this book. My wife, Irene, was there during the many hours of writing, photography, and research. My son, Jonathan, while still an uninhibited and indestructible teenager, expanded my notions of 4-wheeling by showing me what a lifted Toyota pickup can really do. My brother, Jim, an attorney in Washington, D.C., continues to teach me a lot about the tug-of-war between environmentalism and the protection of property rights. He has written his own book on these issues called *Property Matters: How Property Rights Are Under Assault and Why You Should Care* (Free Press).

My thanks to the many knowledgeable 4x4 dealers and salespeople who take the time and trouble to learn about the products they sell. Special thanks to Keith Hanson, one of the owners of the Hanson Garage in Orofino, Idaho, who gave me much useful advice on off-roading in general and Jeep products specifically. Thanks also to Todd DeBerg, a world-class Jeep mechanic who works for Keith and who has upgraded my '87 Wrangler. Todd has spent many hours with the Wrangler and me in the woods, teaching me the mastery of rocks, mud, and hills.

My appreciation to the service department at Barnett-Thompson Chevrolet in Orofino. They share off-road tips with me so I don't have to learn the hard way. They keep my K-Blazer going.

Thanks to Harry Lewellyn for his unsurpassed expertise, which he shares with us in his newsletter, *Ecological 4-Wheeling*. Thanks to Tony Scotti, who teaches evasive driving techniques at his school in Medford, Massachusetts, and at other sites around the world. I'm grateful, also, to Mark Cox, who heads up the Bridgestone Winter Driving School in Steamboat Springs, Colorado, for advice on handling a rig on snow and ice. Thanks to Scott Thornsberry for teaching me about both computers and Toyotas and for encouraging this book.

I received invaluable advice and instruction from off-road gurus Bill Burke, who showed me what the slick rock of Moab was all about, and Harold Pietschmann, who taught me the intricacies of the Rubicon. My friend, Hummer owner and enthusiast Knut Akseth, who learned his extensive off-roading skills during his service in the Norwegian army, shared his expertise and his Hummers with me. Kristian Akseth, Knut's son, kindly shared his mechanical engineering knowledge with me and helped this edition be more accurate in its description of the physics of differentials, traction, torque, and steering. I kept the discussions as straightforward as I could to make the book as readable and enjoyable as possible. Any inaccuracies remaining are entirely my responsibility.

Warn Industries engineer Tom Telford kindly took the time to share some of his winching knowledge and experience with me, which I certainly appreciate.

My gratitude goes to my friend, author and adventurer Ragnar Benson, for inspiring this book in the first place and helping make it happen. Thanks to the Clearwater National Forest Service people for guiding us around the beautiful Idaho wilderness and to the BLM people in Boise and Salt Lake City for maps and other advice. Thanks to my staff for their help in preparing the manuscript and the photos and for mailing the book out to the off-roading public.

And, last but certainly not least, my gratitude to Jon Ford, Peder Lund, and the rest of the staff at Paladin Press for being so supportive and easy to work with and for turning this book into a useful vehicle for advancing the wonderful sport of off-road recreation.

WARNING

Off-highway and off-road driving can be extremely dangerous. Don't attempt the techniques described in this book until you complete a personal hands-on course of instruction from a fully qualified and experienced off-highway driving instructor. The author, publisher, and distributors of this book disclaim any liability whatsoever for any injuries or damages of any type incurred by a reader or any other person as a result of using or attempting to use information contained within this book. Information in this book is presented only for academic, informational, and entertainment purposes.

PREFACE

PREFACE TO THE FIRST EDITION

This book is about freedom and self-reliance. About using ecological principles to gain access to a world of trees and streams, rugged hills, meadows and mountains, deserts, and wetlands. About staying safe on icy roads. About reaching the full potential of America's love affair with the automobile.

It's about male and female bonding and family bonding. About smelling pine trees, listening to birds at first light, and feeling the gentle early morning mist on your face. About sitting with someone you love, watching the colors of a mountain sunset get painted on the sky.

It's about 4-wheeling.

PREFACE TO THE SECOND EDITION

Actually, this book is about a lot more than 4-wheeling and the wonderful world of backcountry recreation. It's about preserving one of the basic freedoms that made this country strong—the freedom of mobility. Americans regard the freedom to move about this great land as one of their basic rights. But unless we learn to do so in a responsible manner, carefully minimizing the impact we and our vehicles have on the environment, more and more regulations and land closures will diminish our access to remote areas.

This book is about using your 4x4 to enjoy the great outdoors with respect for wildlife and the environment. Because of the success of the first edition of *4-Wheel Freedom*, we've decided to develop a new second edition, expanding some of the explanations of the various 4-wheel drive systems available and adding many more tips and tricks for negotiating challenging terrain. For several reasons, we decided to eliminate the specifications of the various SUVs available: they change so rapidly that they're out of date before we publish them; current specs are regularly published in several of the 4x4 and automobile magazines and on the 4x4 web sites; and dealers can furnish you with the exact specs of particular vehicles you're interested in. Also, by leaving out the specs, we've been able to reduce the cost of the book, making it more accessible to more people.

Please mention *4-Wheel Freedom* to your friends. Enjoy the book, use your 4x4 to enjoy the backcountry, and *Tread Lightly!*

WHO NEEDS THIS BOOK?

When Bob and Pat Collins decided their little 1987 BMW 325 wasn't giving them enough room for groceries, kids, and other cargo, they joined the millions of Americans who spice up their lives with a sport-utility vehicle. Every year in the United States, close to two million new vehicle buyers choose sport-utility vehicles (SUVs). In 1998, cars accounted for only 52% of light vehicle sales. Light trucks (SUVs, pickups, and vans) were 48%.

A sport-ute typically has a closed cargo space, except for the classic Jeep and a few other models. Originally a two-door vehicle, four-door models are much more common today. The subcompact version is called a "mini-ute." A sport-ute also goes by the name of SUV, 4x4, 4by4, or just plain 4by. There's some confusion with the small ATVs, or "all-terrain vehicles," which are also 4x4s and go "4-wheeling." Some magazines call SUVs "mall-terrain vehicles," since the vast majority of SUV owners, 95 percent by some estimates, never take their machines off-road.

WHAT THIS BOOK TEACHES YOU

This book teaches the art of 4x4 driving and gives a taste of the challenges accompanying it. Using ecological 4-wheel driving principles, it shows what's possible and suggests teachers for direct hands-on experience. It describes various distinctions among available SUVs and helps you decide which rig fits your needs. You'll learn what questions to ask 4x4 salespeople, and these same salespeople will learn how to answer questions from their potential clients.

Use the glossary in Appendix A to get better acquainted with some of the 4-wheeling terms. Appendix B gives you a general idea of the various SUVs and 4-wheel drive systems available, and Appendix C tells you where to find stuff—resources for maps, instruction, books and magazines, equipment such as tires and winches, global positioning systems, and organizations that encourage ecological motorized off-road recreation.

There are facts in this book for people owning their very first 4x4, and there are tips even the most experienced 4-wheelers can use. Readers familiar with 4-wheeling can skip around in the book, going to the parts that describe crawling over boulder-strewn trails that wind through thick forests or traveling through the purple pastel swirls of the high desert; climbing steep hills to breathtaking views of canyons, streams, and forests; driving on remote snow-packed roads winding among glazed trees sparkling in the winter sun toward hidden ski areas, tucked back where you can go only with a 4x4; winching your way out of a trail that's a little too muddy or a gully that's a little too steep; or

Figure 1. The author's wife, Irene, and Hershey contemplate the Clearwater River Valley.

simply finding a place where you can be alone for a little while.

The world of 4-wheeling and off-road recreation takes some getting used to. If you're just beginning, don't be intimidated by the terms, equipment, or maneuvers that may seem a bit technical or even risky. Just absorb what you feel comfortable with. Skip around in the book to pick and choose information according to your own comfort level.

If you come across a term or description of equipment that's not clear, just absorb the part that makes sense to you. It'll probably be discussed in more detail later on in the book. You can also check the glossary (Appendix A) for a more complete definition. You may want to jump ahead to the technique chapters first, then go back and pick up a more thorough understanding of 4-wheel drive systems. It's up to you. Four-wheeling is fascinating and fun. The main goal of this book is for you to enjoy learning about it.

4-WHEELING FOR WORK AND FUN

Who needs this book? People who want to know more about 4-wheeling so they can be safer and have more fun. People who carry kids. A family with a dog (or two, or three, or four). Anyone who uses a vehicle for recreation—camping, fishing,

skiing, boating, scuba diving, surfing, hunting, snowmobiling, or just hiking in the hills. People who use their rig for work—farmers, outfitters, law enforcement officers, search and rescue personnel, ranchers, employees of the National Forest Service or National Park Service, businesspeople, Bureau of Land Management (BLM) employees, salespeople, realtors, doctors, loggers, the military, videomakers, hospitals, sports teams, nurses, blood banks, lawyers, painters, contractors, plumbers, and many more.

It's for people who want to take three or four passengers with them comfortably, along with a generous amount of cargo in a closed compartment. Anyone who wants the comfort and convenience of a sedan but wants a vehicle that travels slippery roads more safely than a passenger car and can master terrain a sedan or van just can't maneuver. People wanting a vehicle doing all the above, plus towing a trailer, boat, or camper in the bargain.

This book is for anyone who has to drive in snow or ice, travel off the asphalt from time to time, or just wants to have fun.

It is for anyone who absolutely must get through.

4-WHEELING FOR SELF-RELIANCE

A family who owns a sport-utility vehicle can say, "We depend on ourselves. In an emergency, we

Figure 2. SUVs and pickups in a small-town parking lot.

Figure 3. Sport-utility vehicles and pickups parked on a single block in San Francisco's posh Pacific Heights. 1) Blazer. 2) Grand Cherokee. 3) Another Cherokee. 4) Ford pickup. 5) Another Ford pickup. 6) Trooper. 7) Bronco. 8) Jeep CJ-7. 9) Another Trooper.

have the means and training to transport ourselves away from danger and into safety. We can escape hurricanes and floods, forest and grass fires, and the aftermath of earthquakes, taking the back trails to avoid highways clogged with passenger cars.

"When that means crossing rough terrain, fording flooded roads, and escaping across fields and through forests, we can do it. We have the plan. We have the means. We have prepared."

Pat and Bob Collins weren't interested in hard-core off-roading. They wanted to camp and needed a vehicle for relatively unimproved country. They joined the organization "Tread Lightly!" even before they chose their 4by to learn more about 4-wheeling. They bought some BLM and Forest Service maps to get an idea of where to go.

They decided on a used rig, choosing a 1998 Jeep Cherokee. Saying good-bye to their BMW, they drove home

in a white 4x4. Bob still drove to work in his restored 1981 Porsche. He'd had that car since college and law school, and he wasn't about to get rid of it. Pat accepted that. The car came with the marriage.

Bob is an in-house attorney for one of the large St. Louis financial firms, and Patricia works in administration at one of the universities. They live with their two young boys, Brandt and Robert Junior, in a comfortable home in Webster Groves. Staying within their means is important to them, and a used Cherokee made sense.

The week after buying the Cherokee, Bob got a couple of videos on 4-wheeling, which they watched together. Pat shopped for sleeping bags. Soon after, on a particularly warm morning in early summer, loading the Cherokee with basic vacation luggage, they started off on a simple driving vacation. They planned a westerly drive across the plains, taking their time as they swung through

Colorado, ending up in Yellowstone National Park for five days. They didn't plan any off-highway travel this trip, but plans can change.

Getting off to a late start, they drove through light rain, staying in a motel outside Kansas City the first night. Watching TV that evening, they noticed that there'd been severe thunderstorms in the western part of Kansas, with hail the size of light bulbs around Sharon Springs and Tribune. The forecast called for a few scattered thunderstorms the next day, but the sky would clear for the Rocky Mountain part of their trip.

They slept late the next morning, taking advantage of the chance to rest. After eating a leisurely breakfast in the restaurant next door, they headed west on I-70 again.

They soon hit their first thunderstorm. Rain poured so hard off the windshield the wipers barely helped, and wind buffeted the Cherokee from side to side. The rain let up, but the sky was still so black it looked like night. Driving on past Topeka, Abilene, and Salina, they left the freeway and headed south to spend the night with some old college friends who lived east of Great Bend.

They formed a small convoy, second in line to a Lexus sedan, an Audi behind them. Then came an old rusty pickup, probably a Ford and probably originally brown (Bob couldn't tell for sure), followed by a semi hauling a big open trailer looking like it contained gravel. Headlights on, they moved across the plain toward weather the color of charcoal.

Brandt and Robert Junior were restless in the backseat, agitated by the odd gloom and the stroboscopic flashes of lightning, coming more frequently now. The wind came again, like huge hands tossing the Cherokee back and forth, threatening to hurl it into the deep, wide ditch to their right. Beyond the ditch, in the unnatural gloom, the fields of grain were like restless windswept seas.

The rain started again, sheets and sheets of water, with the wind slamming it against the windshield like a wrecking ball. Bob shifted the Cherokee into full-time 4-wheel drive and slowed down until they were about 50 yards back behind the Lexus, barely able to make out its taillights through the darkness and the torrents of water. Abruptly the rain stopped, but the wind continued to smash them from side to side. The air was clear, crystal clear, and the Lexus ahead stood out in sharp relief, like a cardboard cutout in a child's pop-up book. Suddenly, a few hundred yards ahead of the Lexus, moving steadily toward them along the highway was a swirling, trembling black funnel bouncing against the asphalt, snapping and sucking up telephone poles, fence posts, and gates.

"My God, it's a tornado!" Bob shouted.

Pat screamed, "It's coming right toward us!" The boys started to cry, terrified by their parents' fear.

Seeing it at the same time, the Lexus driver jammed

Figure 4. 4x4s in their element.

Figure 5. Hitting the cross-country trails in Idaho's Ponderosa State Park.

on his brakes and fishtailed back and forth across the highway just as the front edge of the funnel caught him. Slamming him first to the side of the road, it lifted him 20 feet in the air, like a ball in a giant juggler's hand, then lowered him into the ditch on the right. The car rolled to the bottom, ending up on its side.

"Jesus!" Bob said, part profanity, part prayer. He had to do something. Anything. He twisted the wheel to the right, heading sharply toward the ditch. Images from the 4-wheeling video somehow materialized: "Angle across a gully so you won't hang up the front or rear bumper on the slope and to have a better chance of your frame clearing the lip." Something about approach angles and departure

Figure 6. A police Jeep Cherokee in Idaho.

Figure 7. A Hummer rigged out for fire fighting.

angles and breakover angles. They were too fast for thoughts—just flashes—because the tornado was on them.

He turned the wheel to angle less sharply into the ditch, moving fast and dropping with a bone-jarring bounce as the left rear wheel caught air, the Cherokee's frame scraping the lip but breaking free. Crossing the bottom, he slammed the transmission into low and started up the far side, feeling the funnel tugging at them, trying to twist them out of their path. The Cherokee slowed, losing traction in the mud near the top. Bob flashed on the videos again—"Going up a slippery hill in 4-wheel drive, turn your steering wheel quickly from side to side to give your front wheels more bite." That did it. They cleared the far rim, still rocking violently from side to side as the edge of the twister tried to suck them up.

"Oh, God! Don't let there be a fence!" Bob silently prayed. Prayer answered, sort of. The Cherokee easily ran over a rotten fence post and snapped three strands of rusty barbed wire. They were in the field, the edge of the funnel still pulling at them. Bob quickly twisted the wheel, wrenching the Cherokee away from the snarling black cloud, driving a hundred yards into the soft new grain. Shifting into part-time 4-wheel drive to get better traction in the shallow mud, he swung the rig around and stopped, facing the highway. He was trembling, holding the wheel hard with both hands to steady himself. Pat was hyperventilating but tried to control her breathing as she turned to calm the boys.

They were okay, pale and wide-eyed, seat belts in place. "Thank God we had the boys buckled in," Pat said, remembering the jolting drop into the ditch. They could see the funnel moving down the highway a few hundred yards away, veering off across the fields, tracking steadily toward the northeast. The Audi had tried to follow their Cherokee

across the ditch but didn't have enough clearance to make it. It hung up on the near side, pitched down into the ditch with the rear wheels off the ground. The twister caught it and hurled it back onto the highway in a series of slamming bounces that left it looking like it had been in the final heat of a demolition derby.

The old pickup, with more clearance and experience than the Audi, made it across the ditch and into the field. A grizzled old farmer, still wearing a battered straw hat, climbed out and walked around shaking his head. He'd driven that old pickup through more rocks and mud than most 4-wheelers would see in several lifetimes, and he'd seen a lot of twisters at a distance, but this was the first time one had challenged him close up. And he made it. Not my time yet, he thought.

The semi was caught just before the funnel veered off the road and had jackknifed across the highway, but at least it was still upright. The trailer, moments before containing tons of gravel, was completely empty. Its driver, a woman, was on her CB calling for help.

Bob drove back onto the highway, this time shifting the T-case into 4-wheel low and easing the Cherokee at an angle down the ditch and up the other side, heading toward the Lexus, lying door-down with the underside of the car toward them. Smoke was drifting from the engine compartment. Jumping from the Cherokee, Bob grabbed a fire extinguisher from under the front seat and ran toward the Lexus, noticing the rain again, large soft drops splashing on his face and hands. He discharged the fire extinguisher into the underside of the engine compartment and ran around to peer through the windshield. No one was moving inside the car. It looked like there were four people, still strapped in with their seat belts. The weird torque of the twister hadn't deployed the air bags.

5

The semi driver came running up, a large crowbar in her hands. She jumped from the side of the ditch onto the side of the car and smashed the driver's door window open. "Damned electric windows!" she exclaimed. "I hate 'em. Even if those people could move, they couldn't roll down the windows to get out." She removed the pieces of shattered glass with gloved hands. "This'll get glass on 'em," she said, "but it's better than burning to death if that fire gets started." Smoke was still wafting from the engine compartment.

Wriggling through the broken glass and into the car, she turned off the ignition. Supporting the groaning driver on her shoulders, she cut the seat belt with a pocket knife. Other cars had arrived by now, with people running up to help. They pulled the driver from the Lexus. The semi driver popped the hood release and climbed back out. Using her crowbar, she pried the hood open and several people directed fire extinguishers toward the engine. Other people checked the Audi, but the man and woman inside hadn't made it. The rescuers directed their efforts toward the survivors in the Lexus.

No longer needed, Bob walked back to the Cherokee, smelling the fresh grain, the rain splashing on his face and hair. Now that the adrenalin rush was gone, his knees were

Figure 8. The Dodge Durango has superior towing capacity. Full-time 4WD is available.

shaky. Pat and the boys, standing beside the rig, were none the worse for wear. "Well, dear," she said, turning toward him and putting her arms around him, "anything else you want to do to break in our new 4by4?"

BASIC 4-WHEEL DRIVE

GETTING STARTED

Once you are deeper into the pastime of 4-wheeling, you can do some pretty exciting stuff. You can negotiate the tooth-rattling, bone-jarring Rubicon Trail in California, explore abandoned mining settlements deep in the Arizona desert, climb the rocks of the breathtaking top-of-the-world Continental Divide trail running across Utah, Colorado, and New Mexico, or drive the slick-rock trails around Moab, Utah. You can test your skills and luck by entering off-road competitions, like the Baja 1000 race or the gruelling week-long Transylvania Trophy in the western Ukraine, winching up hills in the shadow of Dracula's castle. You can try out for the privilege of representing the United States in the Olympics of 4-wheel driving, where you drag a Land Rover Discovery across 1,000 miles of waist-deep mud and parched desert sand to compete for the coveted Camel Trophy.

But a lot of the most experienced 4-wheelers around have never entered a race or other competition, have never gone on a Jeep Jamboree, and don't even think of themselves as off-roaders or 4-wheelers. They're the men and women who use their 4bys every day to get a job done—fetching a calf lost in a rocky draw, slogging across a muddy expanse of rugged grazing land to repair a fence line, or clawing their way up a steep forested hill to deliver a repaired starter to a stalled skidder at a logging site.

They learned "wheelin" from their fathers, uncles, and brothers, from their mothers and sisters. They're Idaho loggers, Maine outfitters, and Montana ranchers. They're West Virginia miners, Everglades guides, Texas cattlemen and women, and kids carting 4-H calves to county fairs all across our land. They're 4-wheelers because it's in their blood, and the skills are second nature to them now. They don't write books and don't teach courses because they take their skills for granted, and if you ask them what they know, they're puzzled by your ignorance because they think everyone knows this stuff. When you ask them what spare parts you should bring along off-road, they say, "You worry too much."

But when you get them talking about the places they've been and how they've gotten there and back, you learn more in 10 minutes of conversation than you can pick up in several hours from books, magazines, and videos. They're the heartbeat of 4-wheeling, the reason the sport exists in the first place, because their fathers and grandfathers brought the quarter-ton military truck back from the battlefields of World War II and put the Jeep to work in the United States.

I'm assuming most readers of this book want solid information about 4-wheel drive vehicles and what 4-wheeling is all about. We'll start off with basic facts and build from there, but if you come to a paragraph that's more basic than you need, skip ahead.

7

THE BASIC 4-WHEEL DRIVE RIG

A lot of people think of a "rig" as a semi-tractor trailer—an 18-wheeler—but in the country, your "rig" is whatever vehicle you happen to be driving. It can be a beat-up Volkswagon bug; a Cadillac El Dorado; a Jeep, Blazer, or Land Cruiser; any pickup truck; a massive semi-tractor trailer; a logging truck; or just about anything. In this book, a "rig" means a 4-wheel drive vehicle, whether it's a pickup truck, an open Jeep, or a sport-utility vehicle such as a Chevy Tahoe, Ford Explorer, Jeep Cherokee, Hummer, Geo Tracker, or RAV4.

SO WHAT IS A 4x4 ANYWAY?

A 4-wheel drive rig is also called a "4by4" ("4x4" or simply "4by"). The origin of the term 4x4 goes back to World War II and means any four-wheeled vehicle with all four wheels under power. A 4x2 is a four-wheeled vehicle with two wheels under power, either the rear two or the front two. A 6x6 is a vehicle with six wheels on three separate axles, all under power.

When you step on the gas of the typical passenger car, you're applying power to just two of the four wheels. A 4-wheel drive rig has additional parts in the drivetrain, giving you the option of applying power to all four wheels at once.

The drivetrain is what makes a car or truck go. In the usual 2-wheel drive car, it includes the engine, the transmission, the driveshaft, the differential, the rear axles, and the rear wheels (Figure 9).

The Engine

The engine creates the power, and the gasoline (or diesel fuel) exploding inside the engine's cylinders causes a shaft (the crankshaft) inside the engine to rotate. This rotating shaft turns gears inside the transmission.

The Transmission

The transmission is a metal box under the car with a series of gears inside it. The gearshift lever inside the car connects to these gears. The gears let you choose how much power to apply to the back wheels. When starting out, you need more power to get rolling, so you use low gear. Low gears are large gears moving at low speed to create more power. When zipping along the freeway, you need less power and more speed, so you use high gear or overdrive.

The terms *low gear* and *high gear* can be a little confusing if you're not used to looking at the mechanical side of driving. Low gear means low speed but the most power, and high gear means high speed but less power.

With a manual transmission, you move the gearshift lever yourself to change the gears from low (starting out) to high (zipping along), and you use the clutch between each change. With an automatic transmission, you just put the lever in D for drive and the transmission automatically moves through the gears, or ranges (low to high), for you.

The Driveshaft and Differential

The gears in the transmission rotate the driveshaft, a long shaft running under the car between the transmission and the back wheels. The driveshaft goes into the differential. This is another type of gear box that sits under the car between the back wheels. It's round, about the size of a pumpkin, which is what the gears inside it are called in 4-wheeling slang.

The gears in the differential turn the rear axles, which are the two shafts that turn each back wheel. The gears in the differential also let the back wheels turn at different speeds, which is necessary when turning a corner. The inside wheel has to travel more slowly than the outside wheel. If rigs didn't have differentials, every time you turned a corner or went around a curve, the inside tire would drag and scuff on the pavement, and the tires would wear out in a hurry.

Avid 4-wheelers fool around with their differentials a lot. They change the size of the gears inside, depending on whether they want more power or more speed. If they put larger tires on their rig, they have to deliver more power to the back wheels to drive the larger tires. They do this by changing the differential gears. This is one of the things 4-wheelers mean when they talk about "changing the gear ratios."

That's the drivetrain of a basic 2-wheel drive car or truck with rear-wheel drive. Sometimes the transmission sends the power to a differential between the two front wheels instead of the back wheels. This makes the car a front-wheel drive vehicle. In these cars, the front wheels both steer and drive the car. There are pros and cons of rear-wheel drive versus front-wheel drive, but the basic fact is this: in a 2-wheel drive vehicle, only two wheels power the car—either the back wheels or the front wheels.

THE 4x4 DRIVETRAIN

A 4x4 lets you move a lever and choose to apply power only to the two back wheels or to all four wheels at once. In other words, you can drive in 2-wheel drive (2WD) or in 4-wheel drive (4WD). You can choose 4WD because there are extra parts in the 4by drivetrain. These are a transfer case, a front driveshaft, and a front differential (Figure 10).

The transfer case (commonly known as the T-case and occasionally written X-case) is another box of gears under the car, more or less behind the transmission, that adds power to the front wheels. This happens when the 2WD/4WD lever is moved inside the rig. (Some vehicles switch between 2WD and 4WD with a button or dial instead of a lever.) Gears move in the transfer case, transferring power from the transmission to all four wheels. A second driveshaft, the front driveshaft, connects the gears in the transfer case with the gears in the front differential. The front differential lets the two front wheels turn at different speeds when they're under power turning corners.

Some rigs now have full-time 4WD, without the 2WD option. More about these later.

TRACTION AND POWER

If two wheels can move a vehicle along perfectly okay, why would anyone want to apply power to all four wheels? Two reasons: traction and power.

Traction means how well a rig sticks to the road. When driving on dry paved highway, the tires have good traction (assuming you're sane and don't drive on bald tires with cords standing out). But when driving on snow, ice, wet pavement, or loose gravel and dirt, the tires have poor traction. With only two wheels driving the vehicle, the chances are good the rig will slip and slide without moving forward. There's also a greater chance of going into a skid and sliding off the road.

By shifting into 4WD in a poor-traction situation, you have less chance of both the front and back wheels sliding at once. There's a better chance that at least two of the four wheels have good traction, giving you a safer ride.

The other reason to use 4WD is power. Climbing a steep hill off-highway, you have a better chance of making it when all four wheels are driving you up the hill. This is also true when climbing over large rocks on a rough trail.

Most transfer cases have two ranges of 4WD—high and low, abbreviated Hi and Lo. High range—4WD Hi or 4-wheel Hi—gives higher speed but less power. It's the 4WD range you use most of the time. Most modern 4x4 rigs can be shifted into 4WD Hi while you're driving ("shifting-on-the-fly"). Low range—4WD Lo or 4-wheel Lo—gives greater power but moves at a low speed.

Shift the transfer case into 4WD Lo for super pulling power up steep hills, especially when hauling a trailer, or when crawling over large rocks. Remember, 4WD Lo is the low gear, low speed, greater power range of the transfer case. 4WD Hi is the high gear, high speed, lesser power range.

LOCKING FRONT HUBS

The hubs are the plates at the ends of the axles that hold your wheels on the vehicle. Some hubs, called locking hubs, can be locked or unlocked. When unlocked, they allow the wheel to turn freely on the axle ("freewheeling"), and the axle doesn't turn. When driving in 2WD with the rear wheels pushing the vehicle, it saves gas and avoids wear and tear on the rig if the front wheels can just freewheel. The front axles, front driveshaft, and the gears in the front differential can just sit quietly without dragging on the drivetrain.

Putting the transfer case into 4WD won't do any good if the front hubs are unlocked and the front wheels are freewheeling. The front hubs must be moved from the unlocked to the locked position before the front wheels can provide drive for the vehicle. This can be done manually or automatically.

Manual hubs require stopping the rig, getting out, and turning a bar on the hubs to lock or unlock them (Figure 11). Some avid 4-wheelers want manually locking hubs because of the greater control it gives them. For instance, when a rig has to be towed by another vehicle, if the driveshafts keep turning, the T-case and transmission can be damaged. This is because oil doesn't circulate adequately inside these parts when the engine isn't running. The turning driveshafts keep the gears in the T-case and transmission turning, too, and the lack of oil soon causes the gears to seize.

Towing the rig with its manual hubs unlocked allows the wheels to freewheel without turning the driveshaft. This keeps the gears in the T-case and transmission from turning and protects them from damage. If manual hubs are installed to take the hassle out of towing the rig, they need to be on the rear wheels, too, so neither the front nor the rear driveshaft will turn. It's not hard to do this on a Jeep,

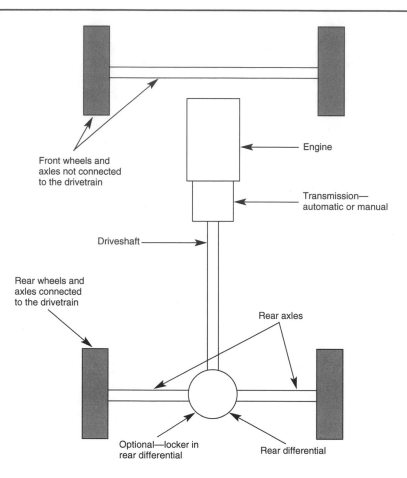

Front wheels and
axles not connected
to the drivetrain

Engine

Transmission—
automatic or manual

Driveshaft

Rear wheels and
axles connected
to the drivetrain

Rear axles

Optional—locker in
rear differential

Rear differential

Figure 9. The basic 4x2 drivetrain.

but it's not practical for larger 4x4s because too many modifications would be required.

The average sport-ute owner considers the manual locking and unlocking process to be a nuisance, and it's unlikely you have a rig with manual unlockable hubs on even the front two wheels, let alone all four wheels. This means you must be very careful when you're having your vehicle towed. Be sure to follow the manufacturer's instructions carefully to avoid damaging the transmission and T-case. Depending on the rig you own, towing it can be quite complicated. It might involve disconnecting a driveshaft or transporting the vehicle on a flatbed truck or trailer so no wheels turn. Make sure anyone offering to tow your rig knows what he's doing.

If you do have manual locking hubs, anticipating snow, you can stop and lock your hubs before you're in the white stuff and then keep your T-case in 2WD until the flakes start to cover the road. At that point, shift the T-case into 4WD and you have power at all four wheels because you've already locked the

hubs. There's some wear and tear on the front of the drivetrain in 2WD when the front wheels aren't freewheeling, so when the road clears and you shift back into 2WD, the front hubs need to be manually turned back to the unlocked position.

Most newer sport-utes have the automatic variety of locking hubs (Figure 12). With these, shifting into 4WD puts power to the front axles, and this force automatically locks the hubs. You don't have to get out of the vehicle to lock and unlock them, but some rigs have to be stopped completely to shift into 4WD and engage the automatic feature of the locking hubs. The '95 Isuzu Trooper and Rodeo are like this. Once engaged, the rig can be shifted between 4WD and 2WD while moving, just as if you'd stopped and locked manual hubs. To disengage the automatic hubs when the road clears, the rig must be brought to a stop, shifted into 2WD, and backed up 10 or 20 feet. This unlocks the hubs. The '96 Isuzu 4x4s have a more convenient system, but the tradeoff is more wear and tear on the front drivetrain in 2WD because the front wheels never freewheel.

In fact, most sport-utes don't use locking hubs

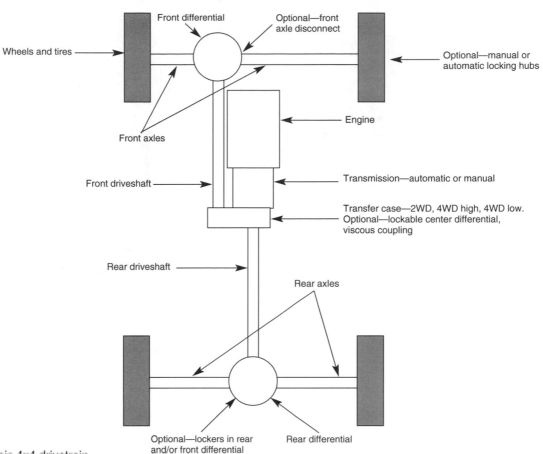

Figure 10. The basic 4x4 drivetrain.

now. They use other means of applying power to the front wheels, such as a front-axle disconnect system, which lets part of the front drivetrain rest in 2WD.

You can install aftermarket automatic or manual locking hubs on a rig. Aftermarket equipment is put on a rig after it's brought home from the auto dealer. It is usually made by a company other than the automobile manufacturer. Equipment put on at the factory, including factory options, is OEM stuff—original equipment manufacturer. Warn Industries sells aftermarket automatic hubs, for example. Warn hubs automatically lock when shifting into 4WD while moving. Shifting back into freewheeling 2WD still requires stopping the rig and backing up.

4-WHEELING FINESSE

Using 4WD requires finesse. Be careful about four things.

1. *Watch out for overconfidence.* 4WD is so effective in maintaining traction and moving a rig along, it's easy to forget that the road is slippery.

Getting distracted on a slippery road for even a couple of seconds can make you skid and spin out, especially if you hit a patch of black ice. (Black ice is frozen water on a road that looks dry. It's dangerous because you can't see it.)

And don't forget—4WD only helps you go; *it doesn't help you stop!* Your brakes stop you. If you are moving along on a snowy road in 4WD and suddenly need to slow down, as soon as you lift your foot off the gas, your traction slowing down isn't any better than you would have in 2WD. There may be a little more slowing from engine compression by being in 4WD, but not much.

Anticipate the need to slow down or stop to give you plenty of time for your brakes to work. Even in 4WD, you've got to use good braking technique—downshifting to let engine compression slow you down, hard steady pressure for ABS brakes, and pumping for standard systems without allowing the wheels to lock and slide. See Chapter 11 about driving on snow and ice where we talk about braking technique.

Figure 11. Manual locking hubs on the front wheels of a '92 Ford F-150 pickup.

Figure 12. Automatic locking hubs on the front wheels of an '89 V6 Montero.

Four-wheel drive helps you drive up a slippery hill safely, but it won't keep you any safer going down than without it. On slippery roads, *slow down*, with or without 4WD. How do I know this? Because I've been there.

On a picture perfect winter evening a few years ago, Irene and I were driving back home after a day of riverbank steelhead fishing. We'd caught our limit and were finally beginning to warm up as we moved along the hills and curves of the snow-packed road. The icy boughs of the big pine trees glistened and sparkled, swaying in the setting sun.

Our Tahoe moved along briskly. Hey! We had 4-wheel drive! We drove into shadow as we climbed a steep hill, maintaining our pace on brand-new snow tires, studded and center-siped. We crested the hill, came into the sun again, and headed down toward a left-hand curve a few hundred yards away, still moving briskly. Hey! We had 4-wheel drive!

The thin film of water on the sun-warmed snow had frozen again as the approaching evening had dropped the temperature. I touched the brakes lightly, preparing for the curve. Nothing. Nada. Nichts. No traction, 4WD with studded tires or not. We were heading into the curve as I felt the rear wheels lose it first, swinging toward the outside of the curve.

I desperately tried to steer into the skid, but what started as a rear wheel slide in a split second turned into wild 360-degree skids, twice around. If there had been a

cliff on the outside of that curve, you wouldn't be reading this particular book now. But God had decided to give me a lesson, not a sentence, and we ended up in a deep, rocky ditch against a low bank covered with trees and boulders.

We were intact, and so was the rig, more or less. Still shiny side up, no tires were blown, and our skid plates had protected our transfer case and oil pan from the jagged rocks. The oil-pressure gauge said the engine was okay. We got out and surveyed the situation. We were high-centered on a large rock, and the right rocker panel was dented, but I deserved at least a little damage for being dumb.

We were on a back road deep in the forest, miles and miles from help. We got to work and cranked up the rear bumper with the Hi-Lift jack, raising the rig's frame off the rock. Throwing a bunch of small rocks under the jacked-up wheel, we lowered the Blazer onto the makeshift ramp, which kept the frame clear of the rock.

Unwinding the cable out of the winch on the front of the rig, we threw a nylon tree strap around a large pine about 50 feet away and double-lined the cable through a shackle block. We cautiously winched the rig toward the road until we could drive the rest of the way out of the ditch in 4WD Lo.

It was well into the dark of the evening by the time we packed up our gear, turned off our flashlights, and climbed back into the rig. As we headed home again, Irene said, "You know, I was just getting ready to suggest that maybe you ought to slow down a little."

2. *Be careful about driving on dry pavement in 4WD.* This is hard on a rig and wears out tires in a hurry. Four-wheel drive is designed to be used on surfaces that are at least a little unstable, like dirt or gravel roads, so the wheels can slip a little. Driving in 4WD on a surface with perfect traction causes the front and back wheels to work against each other, which strains the drivetrain and tires.

In some rigs with full-time 4WD or all-wheel drive, driving in 4WD on dry pavement is fine. In others, you shouldn't use 4WD at all on hard, dry surfaces. Check with the dealer or manufacturer of your rig to find out how much wear and tear results from using 4WD on dry pavement.

A Jeep Cherokee with Selec-Trac has two selections in 4WD Hi—part-time and full-time. In part-time 4WD Hi, you shouldn't drive on dry pavement at all. In full-time 4WD Hi, you can get away with it. You might want to use full-time 4WD when running into scattered patches of ice and snow on otherwise dry pavement.

3. *Don't shift into 4WD low range while moving.* This can severely damage the transfer case. *Stop* before moving the transfer case lever to 4WD Lo. Most 4WD vehicles require that you push in the clutch (if you have a manual transmission) or shift into neutral or park (with an automatic transmission) before shifting the transfer case to 4WD Lo. In some rigs, you can get away with shifting into 4WD Lo while moving slowly (2 or 3 mph), but it's safer to make a habit of always coming to a complete stop before shifting into 4WD Lo.

4. *Don't corner too fast.* Remember, a 4x4 has a higher center of gravity than most 2-wheel drive cars, especially with taller tires or lifters added to raise the rig and get more clearance over the ground. Going around curves and corners, it's a lot easier to skid or even roll over in a 4x4. It's not built to take corners as fast as a highway car. It's built to get you where you're going reliably and safely.

chapter three

MORE ABOUT 4-WHEEL DRIVE

EXPLORE THE OPTIONS

Why learn more about different 4-wheel drive configurations? Because the knowledge will help you choose a rig that's correct for you. Working with salespeople who deal mostly with passenger cars can be frustrating unless you're able to guide them as they demo a 4x4. The information in this book will help you do that. If you happen to be one of those salespeople, use this book to familiarize yourself not only with the products you're selling but also with those of the competition. You'll be way ahead of the game when it comes to answering your potential customers' questions.

This knowledge will also allow you to use your sophisticated and expensive machine to its fullest potential. It will give you confidence as you explore your rig's off-road capability.

MAXIMUM TRACTION

Four-wheel drive delivers power to all four wheels at once. Maximum traction comes with all four wheels locked together, all turning with the same power and at the same speed. In fact, there are options available that will do just that—locking all four wheels together to get you out of an especially slippery spot. The Mercedes Gelaendewagen provides this capability as standard equipment, and

the Toyota Land Cruiser provides it as a factory option. But you can't drive like this for very long because of the trade-offs.

The Outside Wheel Versus the Inside Wheel

Driving in completely locked 4WD all the time quickly wears out the tires, since the inside wheel can't turn more slowly when turning a curve or corner. Instead, it scuffs off a layer of rubber around every turn. Turning is difficult with the outside and inside wheels locked together, and it puts a lot of wear on the drivetrain.

Strain and wear are avoided by using a differential to connect the outside and inside wheels so they can rotate at different speeds. Remember, the differential is the round gear box that transfers torque from the driveshaft to the axles. Each driving set of axles has a differential between them. If the vehicle has rear-wheel drive, the differential sits between the rear wheels. If it's front wheel drive, the diff sits between the front wheels. If the rig has four-wheel drive, there is a diff between both the front wheels and between the rear wheels.

The differential balances the power, or torque, between the right and left axle connected to it, sending an equal amount of torque to each axle all the time. However, when a vehicle enters a turn, the complicated arrangement of gears inside the diff

15

allows the outside wheel to speed up and the inside wheel to slow down. The inside wheel slows down the same amount the outside wheel speeds up.

Suppose a car traveling 50 mph in a straight line down the road enters a curve and the outside wheel has to speed up to 60 mph to get around the curve. The inside wheel will slow down to 40 mph.

Suppose this same vehicle suddenly hits an icy patch, and one of the driving wheels loses all traction and starts spinning. This sudden loss of resistance means that less turning force, or torque, is being applied to the spinning axle. Since the differential balances the torque between the two axles, the other wheel with traction gets less torque, too—so much less that it doesn't have the power to move the vehicle forward.

If the driver doesn't change the engine speed, so the driveshaft is still trying to move the vehicle forward at 50 mph, then the stopped wheel with traction will obviously be traveling 0 mph (a decrease of 50 mph from its previous speed), and the spinning wheel will be turning at a rate of 100 mph (an increase of 50 mph), even though it can't develop enough traction to drive the rig forward.

A standard torque-balancing differential is called an "open" differential.

Front Wheels Versus Back Wheels

Besides the wear caused when the inside and outside tires are locked together, there's also wear caused by the front and back wheels fighting against each other. Driving in 2WD, the front and back wheels don't turn at quite the same rate. The front wheels of a vehicle have to travel farther than the rear wheels when going around a curve. This is because the rear wheels track inside the front wheels. Therefore, the front wheels have to go faster than the rear wheels to get around the curve. If the front and rear driveshafts are locked together in 4-wheel drive, then this difference in front and rear wheel speed can't occur, and the front and rear parts of the drivetrain fight against each other. On slippery surfaces in 4WD, the tires slip and slide, relieving the strain, but on dry pavement they wear rapidly and there's strain on other parts of the drivetrain as well.

To relieve the wear that occurs when the front and back wheels fight against each other, some 4x4s have a third type of differential inside the transfer case. An example of this is the full-time 4WD selection in a Jeep Cherokee's Selec-Trac T-case. This allows the front and back driveshafts to rotate at different rates, so the front and back wheels can also turn at different speeds. This relieves wear, but traction loses out. With either the front wheels or the back wheels slipping, torque will be largely transferred to the slipping set. The other set of wheels that still have traction may not get enough power to move the rig.

Four Layers of Traction

To overcome these trade-offs, 4x4 designers and aftermarket manufacturers offer different options. These include full-time 4-wheel drive, part-time 4-wheel drive, and locking rear or front differentials.

Full-time 4WD. Full-time 4-wheel drive lets all four wheels move at different speeds. There's a differential between the front wheels, another between the rear wheels, and a third in the transfer case between the front and rear driveshafts. This allows independent rotation between the right and left wheels and between the front and rear sets of wheels.

Some 4x4s use a system called viscous coupling in the T-case to transfer power to the wheels that still have traction when one or more wheels are slipping. The front and rear driveshafts are linked through a silicone compound that becomes stiffer as it heats up. A spinning driveshaft heats the silicone, transferring torque through the other driveshaft to the set of wheels that still have traction. The new Jeep Grand Cherokee uses a hydraulic disc arrangement called the Gerodisc or Gerotor in both the T-case and the front and rear differentials to create a very sophisticated 4WD system. Ford and GM use an electronic clutch in their 4WD systems to accomplish full-time 4WD. In 4WD low range, most rigs with these systems lock the T-case completely for greater traction.

Some vehicles with full-time 4WD also have a part-time 4WD setting as well as 2WD, like the Cherokee's Selec-Trac. Others don't have part-time 4WD, a 2WD selection, or a low-range selection in 4WD. The Olds Bravada and the Subaru Legacy Outback are in this category. Neither has a 2WD or 4WD low-range setting; they have only full-time 4WD Hi. Some manufacturers call this arrangement all-wheel drive or permanent 4-wheel drive.

Part-time 4WD. Part-time 4-wheel drive has no differential in the T-case, so in 4WD the front and rear driveshafts move at the same speed all the time. The front and rear wheels both are driven with the same amount of power. This improves traction. Locking the T-case differential means that with one

Figure 13. This under-the-hood compressor serves two purposes—it furnishes power to the ARB locker in the rear differential and supplies pressure to air your tires back up after you've mushed through mud or sand.

or even both rear wheels spinning on a slippery surface, both front wheels still have power and move the rig, or vice versa. With the front wheels spinning, the rear wheels move the vehicle. A number of 4x4s have part-time 4WD, along with 2WD and 4WD Lo selections. The Chevy Blazer and Tahoe, Toyota 4Runner, Kia Sportage, Ford Bronco, Jeep Wrangler, and many others all have this type of system.

With front and rear wheel sets locked together, don't use part-time 4WD on dry pavement because of the increased wear on the tires and the rest of the drivetrain. Even using part-time 4WD off-road can create tension between the front and rear wheels that can persist even after shifting back into 2WD on dry pavement. If the rig seems to be handling strangely back in 2WD, pull over and stop. Then back up 20 or 30 feet. This will relieve the strain.

Binding up the drivetrain on part-time 4WD vehicles can occur with manual locking hubs, if your rig is equipped with them. When you try to unlock the hubs to return to 2WD, you may find that you can't move the lever on the hub to the unlocked position. If this happens, jack up each front wheel so it's clear of the ground. This will relieve the tension, and you should be able to unlock the hubs.

Lockers and posi's. Rigs without a differential in the T-case or with a locked T-case differential (part-time 4WD) still have a traction problem with one front wheel and one rear wheel spinning on a

slippery surface. The slipping wheels can be on the same side of the rig or can be on opposite corners. When wheels in opposite corners slip, Harry Lewellyn, the Southern California professor of 4-wheeling, calls this "diagonal teeter-totter."

To overcome this problem, the engineers gave us locking differentials, called *lockers*, which lock together the right and left wheels on the front or rear. They also created limited-slip differentials called *posi's*. GM first called the limited-slip device Posi-traction. The term posi has become a generic term for all limited-slip differentials, which allow some motion between the right and left wheels.

Lockers. Let's talk about lockers first. With a locker engaged, the differential doesn't function and both wheels turn at the same speed because they're absolutely locked together. If one wheel doesn't have traction, the locker doesn't let it spin at a different rate from the other tire on the axle. Torque is delivered to the wheel with traction, and the rig moves ahead. The Mitsubishi Montero comes with an optional locker for the rear differential. The Toyota Land Cruiser provides optional front and rear locking differentials, and they are standard equipment on the Mercedes Gelaendewagen. Lockers and limited-slip differentials can also be purchased as aftermarket equipment. (See the resource list in Appendix C.)

Some lockers are manually controlled and

Figure 14. This Hummer uses brake/throttle modulation to increase the torque to the wheels with traction and get it out of the ditch. Newer models use TorqTrac4 (TT4) electronic traction control (ETC). (Photo by Hummer owner Knut Akseth.)

some are automatic. The manually controlled ones, like the ARB air locker, have a switch on the dash that let you either lock the differential completely (the "locked" mode) or leave it functioning normally (the "open" mode). With the rear or front differential completely locked, you absolutely must not drive on anything but slippery surfaces unless you enjoy watching the cords on your tires come into view at a rapid rate.

A totally locked differential also interferes severely with steering. With the lockers engaged on a dry surface, the rig tends to go straight ahead. This is even more so with a locking differential on the front axle as well as the rear. Driving around a curve with a locked differential can easily make the rig skid uncontrollably. Even using a locker when driving straight can cause the rig to be thrown abruptly to one side, especially when accelerating on a slippery surface.

Losing traction with an open, unlocked differential allows the wheel without traction to spin freely. The other wheel doesn't spin, and because it isn't spinning, it resists sideways motion and provides at least a little directional stability. The rig tends to go straight, even with one back wheel slipping. This directional stability is lost with the wheels locked together across the differential. With both locked wheels losing traction, both wheels spin, and neither resists sideways motion. The spinning wheels pull the

rig toward one side or the other, depending on the sideways slope of the surface and centrifugal force if you're going around a curve at the time.

Use a manual differential locker only at slow speeds and only for serious lost traction in mud, snow, or ice. Use it also for rock crawling and hill climbing, where you need maximum torque and traction at low speeds.

Other lockers are automatic, like Eaton, Lock-Right, and Detroit Lockers. The driver doesn't control them—the motion of the wheels does. An automatic locker senses a spinning wheel and locks the differential so both wheels get torque. An automatic locker locks the right and left axles together with the rig traveling straight and automatically unlocks when going around a curve. This type of locker can make the rig hard to handle in a curve, especially when not applying the gas smoothly and steadily.

Posi's. With either a manual or automatic locker in locked mode, nearly 100 percent of the torque is transferred from the slipping wheel to the wheel that still has traction. A limited-slip differential (a posi) limits the slip of a wheel without traction but provides only partial torque to the wheel with traction. A limited-slip differential handles like a standard open differential, so a posi is a reasonable trade-off. It has somewhat less traction than a locker but better handling characteristics. You can order a limited-slip rear differential as a factory option on many 4x4 sport-utes as well as on most 2-wheel drive passenger cars. The Auburn Gear posi and the Detroit TrueTrac are aftermarket examples. Some 4-wheelers recommend using a posi in front and a locker in back. But steering on a slippery surface can get a little squirrelly with a posi in front if one wheel or the other suddenly grabs traction, throwing the front of the rig to the opposite side.

Electronic Traction Control (ETC). Some manufacturers use a traction control system called "electronic traction control" or "ETC." This system transfers torque from a slipping wheel to a wheel with traction by using the antilock braking system (ABS). When the ETC system senses a wheel spinning, it uses the ABS to brake the spinning tire. With the spinning wheel braked, torque is partially transferred to the wheel that has traction. This is the opposite of what the ABS usually does. It usually takes the brake off a sliding locked wheel. ETC is used on the Range Rover models, on the Mercedes M-Class SUV (where it's called the "Electronic Traction System" or "4-ETS"), and on the new Hummer models (where it's called "TorqTrac4" or "TT4").

The Australian ARB locker. On my '94 K-Blazer, I went with the Australian ARB air locker on the rear differential. On my '87 Wrangler we upgraded to heavy-duty Dana 44 front and rear axles and installed an ARB locker in both the front and rear differential. This gives me true locking diffs. The ARB locker operates from an air compressor mounted under the hood and allows me to push a button on the dash and leave the differential totally locked or totally unlocked. The locker is disengaged when no longer needed. The differential is completely open for normal driving in 2WD or 4WD and locked completely when needing maximum traction for getting out of a stuck spot or for rock crawling and hill climbing.

The ARB setup also provides a powerful way to reinflate your tires after airing down. Attaching an air hose to the underhood compressor airs you up faster than the average cigarette-lighter-powered air pump (Figure 13).

THE WEAK LINK

The combination of a locking T-case and locking differentials can deliver tremendous torque to just one or two wheels. The torque of the engine is focused away from the slipping wheels to the wheels with traction. However, the drivetrain is designed to have the engine's torque divided among the four wheels. If only one or two wheels have traction, they may be receiving more torque than that part of the drivetrain can withstand.

Something's gotta give, so lockers, or even limited-slip differentials, can dramatically demonstrate the weak points in the drivetrain. With three wheels sitting without traction on slippery ground, it's easy to break an axle as you put torque to the single gripping wheel while pushing a rig to the max to get over a large rock or log or to get out of thick mud. That's the cause of the icy feeling in your stomach as you hear that sickening snap. Your front axle is especially vulnerable with a locker on your front differential. A front tire may lose traction and spin for a couple of seconds as it tries to grip the face of a boulder. When it suddenly grabs, the front part of the drivetrain may not absorb the sudden shock, and a front axle or the front driveshaft gives and winds up like one of those corkscrew pastries.

You can also break a U-joint, gears in the differential, or hubs. With serious rock crawling, you may have to beef up the rest of the drivetrain, especially the axles, to take full advantage of lockers.

CLIMBING TREES

Let's look at how some of the available sport-utes put their T-cases and differentials together. One high-end rig, the Lexus LX 470, has full-time 4-wheel drive with no 2WD option. It has high and low range in 4WD. It has a computerized anti-skid system called VSC (vehicle skid control) which works with the electronic traction control (TRAC) and the ABS to maintain as much stability as possible. However, Lexus emphasizes that the VSC system is no substitute for caution and common sense.

In 4WD low, the center differential is locked, and you can push a button and lock both the front and rear differential as well. In this configuration, you could probably climb a tree.

The LX 470 also has a variable height control. You can lower the vehicle two inches to allow easier entry and exit, and you can raise it four inches above normal height to gain more ground clearance over obstacles on rough trails. When vehicle speed reaches 20 mph, the vehicle drops back down to normal height automatically to lower the center of gravity for maximum stability.

Figure 15. The Jeep Grand Cherokee with the sophisticated Quadra Drive Gerotor 4WD system.

The Range Rover 4.0 SE and 4.6 HSE are also at the high-end. These 4x4s have permanent 4-wheel drive with viscous coupling in the T-case. There is no 2WD option, but there is low range in 4WD. They use electronic traction control to transfer partial power from a slipping wheel to a wheel with traction.

Those wanting to push the upper limit of high-end could choose the Mercedes Gelaendewagen ($130,000 and up), which has standard locking front and rear differentials as well as a locking T-case.

The high-end AM General Hummer uses a T-case like the part-time/full-time 4WD Selec-Trac that Jeep uses, except the Hummer doesn't use the 2WD option; it uses 4WD all the time. The T-case can be locked for more traction and 4WD Lo is available. The Hummer uses Zexel Torsen differentials, which are a type of limited-slip differential. "Torsen" stands for "torque sensing," and these devices are known as "torque-biasing" differentials. When a wheel loses traction, previous models require the driver to activate the locking action by applying the brake. Then, while pressing the accelerator, he or she slowly releases brake pressure, using the brake sort of like a clutch. This is called "brake/throttle modulation." Newer models use electronic traction control ("TorqTrac4" or "TT4") instead of brake/throttle modulation. We'll look more at the Hummer in Chapter 8 on rocks and ravines.

The midrange-priced Mitsubishi Montero has full-time 4WD with viscous coupling in the T-case, but in 4WD Hi the T-case can be locked to provide more traction. It can be shifted back and forth between 2WD and 4WD on-the-fly, and it has a manually activated fully lockable rear differential available as an option.

A Jeep Grand Cherokee equipped with Quadra-Trac has permanent 4WD. There is no 2WD option, but low range is available in 4WD. A Gerotor in the T-case transfers power between the front and rear driveshafts and Gerodiscs are an option in the front and rear differentials. Jeep's Selec-Trac 4WD system in a Cherokee gives it a lockable T-case so you can drive in full-time 4WD, part-time 4WD, or 2WD. Four-wheel drive Lo is also available. The Dodge Durango can be ordered with the same T-case, to give both part-time and full-time 4WD.

TRANSMISSIONS—MANUAL OR AUTOMATIC?

Most of the high-end sport-utes come only with an automatic transmission. Some of the mini-utes and mid-range 4x4s come only with manual. Others offer a choice. There are pros and cons with either.

An automatic transmission is easier to use and gives less worry when maneuvering over rough trails. It gives the advantage of feathering the throttle with your right foot and the brake with your left when rock crawling.

A manual transmission gives more control and lets you choose the exact gear you want when starting out or traveling over rocks or hills. It lets you crawl over rocks using only the starter motor and 4WD Lo. It gives better engine compression to slow the rig down when traveling down steep hills, forward or backward.

Advocates of manual transmissions believe they're less likely to break and less likely to leave you stranded in the backcountry. Advocates of automatics point out that manuals need clutches, and clutches can break, leaving you just as stranded. (Unless, of course, you've mastered clutchless shifting, which is an art form all its own.)

A rig with a dead battery offers more options for getting started again with a manual transmission. Jump-starting is the most convenient way, but it obviously requires another vehicle or a second isolated battery in your own rig. It also requires an intact starter motor. A manual transmission lets you get the vehicle started by pushing it or coasting downhill, even with a broken starter and dead battery. With an automatic, if you can't jump-start it, you're out of luck.

You may be able to get a manual rig started even without another rig to provide a live battery or a push. It takes at least one other person. Put the vehicle in 2WD and jack up a rear wheel. Turn on the ignition, put the transmission in second gear, and push in the clutch. The second person turns the jacked-up rear wheel by hand. When it's going as fast as possible, he shouts, "OK!" and you pop the clutch out and feed some gas. This sometimes works. The rear wheel can also be turned by wrapping a rope around it several times, then pulling hard and fast on the rope to spin the wheel. Just be sure your buddy turns the rear wheel in a forward direction.

If you are just getting started with off-road experience, it's probably better to go with an automatic, simply because there's enough to learn without having to worry about when and how to shift. Someday, when you decide to equip a Jeep CJ-7 or Wrangler for serious off-roading, you might swap in a small-block Chevy V8 engine, install a heavy-duty T-case (perhaps an NP 205) along with stronger-than-stock axles (maybe Dana 44s front and rear), put an ARB locker on the rear and a TrueTrac posi on the front, and lift it over 35-inch (or larger) aggressive mud tires. If you're that serious, you'll probably want a manual transmission.

SAFETY AND ECONOMY

In some respects, sport-utility vehicles are safer than passenger cars and vans. The midsize and full-size 4x4s offer considerable protection because of their weight alone. Their 4WD capability gives better traction on wet or snowy roads, and 4WD offers a lot more resistance to hydroplaning on wet roads than does 2WD. This is because a driven wheel cuts through the film of water and gets back down to the road surface. On dry pavement, a vehicle with full-time 4WD has several advantages over a 2WD vehicle. When all four wheels are under power, tracking, cornering, and stability are improved, and acceleration is more efficient.

Until recently, auto manufacturers haven't had to conform to the same safety standards when building sport-utes and pickups as when building passenger cars. The crash-worthiness of light trucks is being improved.

Rollover potential is greater in sport-utes and pickups than in passenger cars because of their higher center of gravity. Drivers of these taller vehicles have to keep this in mind and avoid sudden swerves that place high lateral G (gravity) forces on the rig. A sport-ute should be loaded with heavy items on the floor, not on the roof rack, to keep the center of gravity as low as possible.

Until recently, sport-utes didn't even come with air bags. The manufacturers were afraid they might inflate accidentally when off-roading. This concern was not insurmountable, however. Chrysler's Jeep division solved the problem and brought out an air bag for the Grand Cherokee, and other manufacturers soon followed suit.

Most SUVs now come equipped with air bags, at least for the driver's side, and many have one for the passenger as well. However, it's now recognized that air bags can harm or even kill people as well as save them. It's absolutely essential that you fasten your seat belt and shoulder harness if you have an air bag in front of you. If you don't, and if you're thrown forward in a crash, you may be in the zone of the deployment of the air bag when it inflates at 200 or 300 mph. The force of the air bag can snap your head and neck backward, causing spinal fractures with paralysis or death. Children and smaller women are especially susceptible to air bag injuries. Smaller children should be belted up in the rear seat. Older children riding in front must fasten the seat belt and shoulder harness. Smaller individuals should not drive with the seat in a forward position that puts them into the air bag's zone of deployment.

If your vehicle is equipped with air bags, you have to be careful when driving off-road. Although you may want to pull the seat way forward when driving on hills to make sure you don't lose contact with the pedals, or slip out of the restrictive shoulder harness and place it behind you, leaving only the lap belt fastened, either one of these maneuvers may place you in the zone of deployment of the air bag. If you collide with a large rock or tree, and the air bag deploys with you in a forward position, you could be seriously injured. I personally favor equipping all vehicles with a switch that allows us to turn off the air bags in certain situations.

Gas mileage is another consideration. To perform well off-road and tow a decent load on the highway, sport-utes need powerful engines. The 255 horsepower Chevy Vortec 5.7 liter V8 or the 235 horsepower Grand Cherokee 4.7 liter V8 are examples of fine engines that really do the jobs a sport-ute needs to do. These current V8s use sequential fuel injection, which improves economy substantially. Sport-ute fuel economy needs to be tweaked a lot more because of federal corporate average fuel economy (CAFE) standards. Meanwhile, those wanting maximum economy should buy a lightweight passenger car with a small engine. Adventurers requiring a rig they can depend on in all sorts of tight places should get a sport-ute.

One thing I really like about highway driving in a full-size sport-ute is sitting high. You get a good look at what's going on. I was coming back from Tahoe on I-80, just past Sacramento, heading west into the setting sun, planning to exit at Vallejo and take 37 across the top of the Bay to Marin. The speed limit at the time was 55, but the four swollen lanes of traffic were moving at the usual late Sunday afternoon pace—70 mph. If you wanted to go 55, you'd have to drive on the shoulder! I was next to the outside lane, moving along behind a compact Toyota pickup. An old white Chevy Impala was ahead of him.

I have to admit that I was violating the rule that says you need two seconds of travel time between you and the vehicle ahead of you. I was about one second behind the pickup, which is pretty much standard spacing for traffic on I-80 on a Sunday afternoon. (The collective attitude of the steel herd seems to be, "Whatever you do, don't leave enough room for anyone to squeeze into your lane in front of you.")

The Toyota started to drift back toward me just a little (maybe 68 mph) because the Impala in front of him had slowed slightly. To maintain my 70 mph pace, I decided to swing into the outside lane and gradually pull past the Impala. I checked my side mirror and did a quick head check—the lane was clear. Just as I nudged the wheel to begin my drift to the left, the Impala's brake lights came on! I could just see them over the top of the Toyota's cab. I cut the wheel sharply left to clear the Toyota just as he jammed on his brakes. Then, free in the outside lane, I jammed on my brakes, anticipating the Impala, who swerved over into the outside lane, across my path, bouncing and lurching onto the left shoulder. I passed him as he drifted to a stop on the gravel in the median strip. Why he decided at that moment that he needed to brake suddenly in 70 mph traffic and swerve without warning across the outside lane, I'll never know. Flat tire? Didn't look like it. Medical emergency? Maybe, though the four people inside looked pretty healthy.

I do know that if I'd been lower to the ground in a smaller vehicle, I wouldn't have seen the Impala's brake lights come on before the Toyota braked, and my rig would have ended up in the bed of the Toyota pickup. Lessons: ride high and pay attention to the two-second rule. Especially at 70 mph.

chapter four

CHOOSING A RIG

ARE YOU HAULING PEOPLE OR STUFF?

What do you want your 4x4 to do? If you've got a 4by now, you've made these choices already. If you're thinking about buying one, here are the considerations.

A PREOWNED RIG

When shopping for a used 4x4, make sure your deal includes the right to have the rig inspected by an experienced independent 4x4 mechanic before you put your money down. If the rig you're thinking about has had hard off-road use, you need to find out up front. You'll be disappointed, angry, and poorer if you buy it and discover later that the frame is bent, the transmission's shot, and the engine provides only a fraction of the power you need, or that the rear differential and wheel bearings have been hopelessly corroded because the rig's been used to back a boat trailer into the water regularly without proper maintenance.

You're about to make an important investment. Get some professional help to be sure you get the fun and satisfaction you deserve. It's a red flag if the seller makes it difficult for you to have the vehicle inspected by your own mechanic or tries to sweet-talk you out of it. If that happens, find another seller and another rig.

WHAT ARE YOU HAULING?

Are you hauling people or stuff? Most people buying a 4x4 these days want to haul both. They're looking for a sport-utility vehicle—a closed vehicle with a roomy cargo area in the back that will carry five people (two in the front bucket seats and three on the rear bench seat). SUVs allow folding the backseat forward to make more space for more cargo. In some, the back of the rear seat is split, which is a better arrangement (Figure 16). Part of it folds to carry more cargo, still allowing one or two people to ride on the rear bench on the unfolded part. Some SUVs can add extra backseats to carry two or three more people in the cargo compartment, for a total of six or seven passengers plus the driver. Roof racks are available for carrying baggage on the top of the rig.

Full-size SUVs. GM offers the Chevy Tahoe or GMC Yukon, the buslike Chevy Suburban or GMC Yukon XL, the GMC Yukon Denali, and the Cadillac Escalade. Ford has the Expedition, the Lincoln Navigator, and the barnlike Excursion. Toyota provides the Land Cruiser, and Lexus has the LX 470. Land Rover has the Range Rover 4.0 SE and the 4.6 HSE. The Hummer is at the high end of this category. The new Dodge Durango, with its optional 5.9-liter 245 horsepower Magnum V8 engine, probably fits best in the full-size category.

Midsize SUVs. The Nissan Xterra is a new entry. You can also buy the Chevy Blazer or its corporate twin, the GMC Jimmy or Envoy. Also in this class are the Ford Explorer (or its corporate twin, the Mercury Mountaineer), the Honda Passport or Isuzu Rodeo (similar rigs with different nameplates), the Isuzu Trooper, the Jeep Cherokee and Grand Cherokee, the Land Rover Discovery Series II, the Mitsubishi Montero and Montero Sport, the Nissan

Pathfinder (or its upgraded corporate twin, the Infiniti QX4), the Olds Bravada, the Toyota 4Runner, the Lexus RX300, and the Mercedes M-Class in either the V6 ML320 or the V8 ML430 version. Subaru has the Forester and the Outback and BMW is marketing their entry, the X5, as an SAV, a "sports-activity vehicle." The Honda CR-V could be included in the midsize category. The Kia Sportage bridges the midsize and mini-ute classes.

Mini-utes. These are the smallest SUVs, also being called *cute-utes* by the marketing gurus. The standard is the Jeep Wrangler, upgraded in 1997. Its roots go all the way back to World War II, and it's hard to beat as a trailworthy vehicle, even in its stock version. The Land Rover Defender 90 is no longer available new in the US. It's hard to fit much cargo in any of these rigs when carrying two or more people.

The Chevrolet Tracker, Suzuki Grand Vitara, Honda Amigo, and Toyota RAV4 are standards in this class. Honda also offers the unusual VehiCROSS. If you want a compact rig to maneuver through urban sprawl but also need off-road capability without a huge amount of cargo space, look at the mini-utes.

Whatever model you choose, consider investing in an alarm system. According to insurance reports, in 1998 the top 10 vehicles most likely to be stolen in the United States included the Cherokee/Grand Cherokee in fourth place. Full-size Ford and Chevy pickups were also in the top 10 nationally. The top 10 in individual cities included the Suburban, the 4Runner, and the Wrangler.

If you will be hauling more stuff and fewer people, you may want to choose a 4x4 pickup truck. Lots of cargo fits in the rear open bed, and the rig still carries one or two passengers along with the driver in the cab. If you need to carry more people than that, buy an extended cab pickup with a rear bench seat. If you want, you can buy a camper shell to enclose the open bed.

TRAILERS

Full-size sport-utes and most midsize SUVs can haul a decent-sized boat trailer or camper. When hauling a sizable trailer, a rig with a longer wheelbase offers better stability. You will also need a heavy-duty engine and such tow-package options as an oversize radiator, transmission cooler, heavy-duty power steering pump, heavy-duty brakes, beefed-up suspension, and more powerful gear ratios in the differentials in addition to the frame-

Figure 16. A split rear seat lets the rig carry three or four people along with extra stuff.

mounted receiver and hitch. It's best to have the tow package put on as a factory option by the manufacturer; it's hard to add all the stuff you need as aftermarket accessories. In fact, in some rigs without a factory option tow package, the electrical wiring harness is too light weight to allow adding a tow package later. If you try to tow anything substantial with one of these vehicles, you'll burn out the wiring. For heavy hauling, consider a three-quarter-ton Suburban or a three-quarter or one-ton pickup. Most standard sport-utes fall in the quarter- or half-ton category.

If you will be hauling a trailer any significant distance over rough off-road trails, limit its size to Class I, which is less than 2,000 pounds fully loaded. Neither your rig nor a big trailer stands up for long under heavy off-road pounding. In fact, a small trailer won't stand up well either unless you beef it up. Replace the factory bolts with heavier-duty bolts and locking nuts. Replace lightweight aluminum fenders with steel fenders welded in place, located high enough so you can put oversize tires on the trailer to increase ground clearance. Fitting your trailer with the same size tires and wheels as your rig saves having to lug along a specific spare tire for the trailer.

Be sure the coupling hitch on the trailer fits the ball on the rig's hitch. Dropping a 2-inch trailer coupler over a smaller ball is just asking for the trailer to come detached from your rig, especially traveling over rough trails. Even with a proper match of ball and coupler, use two safety chains to tether the rig and trailer together, in case the hitch fails en route.

If you'll be using a mini-ute or smaller midsize 4x4 to haul a Class I trailer loaded close to the 2,000 pound limit, it's best to equip the trailer with electric brakes. Make sure the wiring harness furnishes the trailer with proper taillights, brake lights, and turn signals.

Load the trailer so it's balanced with slightly more weight forward. The tongue of the trailer (the narrow part that projects forward and holds the socket that connects to the ball hitch on the rig) should put about 10 to 15 percent of the trailer's weight onto the rig's hitch. A trailer with a gross weight of 2,000 pounds, for instance, should be applying about 200 pounds to the hitch. If your trailer is loaded with too much weight toward the rear, it will be hard to control because it will tend to sway back and forth across the lane. Loaded with too much weight forward, it pushes the rear of the towing rig down, creating steering problems and forcing the headlights' aiming point too high.

If you will be towing an expensive boat on a trailer over rough country, consider protecting the boat by customizing the trailer's suspension. A boat can be torn up a lot by the pounding it takes riding on the miserable springs most trailers have. Consider adding heavier springs and shock absorbers to the trailer to safeguard your valuable investment.

We'll discuss trailering more in the "Rear Hitch and Trailers" section of Chapter 7.

WHERE ARE YOU GOING?

Whether you are buying a sport-ute or you already own one, you're probably going to be taking advantage of off-highway trails you just couldn't negotiate in a passenger car or van. Most of the current sport-utes offer plenty of highway comfort combined with reasonable off-road capability. The Bureau of Land Management (BLM) has classified its trails according to difficulty (which we discuss more in Chapter 5). A stock sport-ute should be able to handle Type II trails, which consist primarily of unpaved roads. To handle Type III trails, add some additional hardware to the rig you already own or buy a rig with Type III capability in mind.

If your main priority is gnarly off-roading while carrying just two or three people besides yourself, look at a vehicle with a short wheelbase and open cargo area like the classic Jeep (now remodeled into the Jeep Wrangler). Its World War II ancestor, the quarter-ton military truck, stirred up public interest in 4-wheeling. By the way, the word Jeep is

now copyrighted by the Chrysler Corporation and can legally be applied only to Chrysler products, except for the Mitsubishi Jeep, which can be sold in Japan. (Mitsubishi licensed the name directly from the Willis Corporation, the main manufacturer of Jeeps during World War II. The copyright on the term Jeep passed to American Motors when it acquired Willys and then to Chrysler when AM became part of that company.)

Just remember, the lower and longer your rig, in general the more problems it will have off-road. There are some advantages to a longer wheelbase, such as better traction across short patches of mud, ice, or slippery rock. In a long rig, when your front wheels enter the mud, the rear wheels still have traction. When the rear wheels enter the mud, the front wheels are out of it, digging in and pulling you forward. But you will have more challenges getting over boulders and logs, more challenges making the approach on and off hills, and more trouble driving through water.

The rougher the country you're traveling in, the higher and shorter the rig needs to be, without sacrificing overall stability.

IF MONEY'S NO OBJECT

As we the public demand more and more luxury features on sport-utility vehicles, the prices rise. Most of the midsize vehicles will be in the $30,000-40,000 range. Some will creep into the $40,000-50,000 range as more options are added. The Mercedes ML 430 with its V8 engine is in this range. Some are less, such as the Nissan Xterra and the Jeep Cherokee, which start at $20,000-25,000 for the 4x4 models.

If you want to move into a full-size SUV, the cost will vary from the $35,000-40,000 range for a Suburban or Dodge Durango, through the $40,000-50,000 for a Toyota Land Cruiser, and into the $50,000-70,000 level for one of the Range Rover models or the Lexus LX 470.

If you're totally rich, you'll probably look at the imported Mercedes Gelaendewagen that goes for over $130,000, available in the United States through Europa International in Santa Fe. A switch to disable the ABS for off-road use along with three locking differentials (front, back, and T-case) makes it a great off-road rig, if you don't mind dragging a very expensive vehicle around on the rocks.

If you don't care about quiet highway comfort but want to go anywhere in the world a 4x4 can go, buy the military's current favorite, the AM General

25

Hummer, a high-riding workhorse. Hummer, or HUMVEE, is the nickname of the acronym HMMWV, which stands for High Mobility Multipurpose Wheeled Vehicle. This amazing rig can pass through narrow trails that would squeeze the doors off a full-size Chevy Tahoe, Ford Bronco, or Toyota Land Cruiser, in spite of being almost 10 inches wider than these other rigs. How? A Hummer's stability lets you put one set of wheels high up on one side wall of the trail and drive through on edge! All you need are guts and around $80,000-100,000 for the enclosed wagon model, depending on the options. AM General has improved the internal acoustics, but it's still pretty noisy on the highway. Its off-road potential is hard to beat because of the tremendous power the engine generates at low speeds. The Hummer's optional 6.5 liter Turbo-Diesel engine puts out grinding torque of 430 lb-ft. at a relatively low engine speed of 1,800 RPM, ideal for rock crawling. (An engine's rotational force is called torque, measured in what the engineers call pounds-feet, abbreviated lb-ft.)

THE IDEAL SPORT-UTE

The ideal off-road sport-ute doesn't exist, but if it did, based on current technology, it would probably have the following features. When you're choosing or modifying your own SUV, you can pick and choose from these ideal options.

The drivetrain starts with a powerful but economical engine, probably a V8 with sequential fuel injection, which runs on regular unleaded gas and gets 26/22 miles per gallon for highway/city driving. I'd opt for a 4-speed automatic transmission, but a manual transmission is available for hard core 'wheelers who wouldn't crawl rocks or climb hills in anything but. The automatic transmission should let you choose which gear you want to be in, similar to the Autostick in some Dodge passenger cars. This helps on slippery surfaces because you can start out in second or even third. Starting out in low can overpower the driving wheels, causing them to spin.

The T-case should provide full-time 4WD, either with viscous coupling or the new gerotor coupling available in the Jeep Grand Cherokee's Quadra-Trac II T-case.

The ideal rig has traction control, either through electronic traction control now available on many vehicles, such as the Range Rover models, the Mercedes M-class vehicles, the Lexus LX 470, and the

Figure 17. The '96 Chevrolet 4-Door Tahoe. The dual rear panel doors are standard; a tailgate/lift-glass option is available.

Hummer, or through the Gerotor differentials available as the Quadra Drive system on the Jeep Grand Cherokee Limited model. Ideally, the front and rear differentials should be lockable for maximum traction, such the system provided on the Lexus LX 470. The ideal rig would have 10 to 15 inches of ground clearance, possible because of offset geared hubs (like the AM General Hummer, sometimes called portal axles), which allow the axles to enter the hubs of the wheels above their centers.

To allow easy towing, it would be helpful to have hubs on all four wheels that can be unlocked so they can freewheel. This greatly simplifies the towing procedure and avoids the risk of towing a rig the wrong way, with serious damage resulting.

This ideal rig comes with light truck (LT) all-terrain tires. A *tow package* is a standard feature, with a rear Class III frame-mounted hitch receiver, heavy-duty shocks, heavy-duty brakes, a transmission cooler, and a heavy-duty radiator. It has frame-attached mountings for an optional front winch and a front hitch receiver. It comes with skid plates protecting its underbelly.

Safety features include dual next generation (less forceful) air bags for the driver and front passenger, including side impact bags, that can be switched off when necessary, head restraints (head rests) on all seats front and back, and, of course, seat belts and shoulder harnesses. Optional heavy-duty seats with five-point seat belts and shoulder harnesses are available. Crash test performance is at least equal to the safest passenger cars, both for direct frontal impacts (the government's testing program)

Figure 18. The mid-size Lexus RX 300.

and offset frontal impacts (the insurance industry's testing program). Roof-crush resistance is sufficient to protect the occupants in case of a rollover.

The rear seat folds forward for more cargo space, but the back of the seat is split, so you can still carry three or four people along with added cargo. The ideal rig has running boards or nerf bars to allow easier access and to protect the rocker panels. An optional removable third seat is available, allowing the rig to carry seven or eight passengers. The spare tire can be mounted on an optional outside rear swing-away carrier or can be carried under the rig in such a way that the ground clearance isn't diminished. (The four-door Chevy Tahoe does this, using an extended cab pickup frame.) Having the carrier on the rear is probably better in case you have to get at the spare when you're stuck hub-deep in mud.

The suspension should be aimed toward improving off-road ground clearance. Many sport-utes these days have independent front suspension (IFS) or even four-wheel independent suspension. This means each wheel can move up over obstacles by itself without tilting the rest of the car. This improves the on-highway ride, too, by causing less swaying when going around a curve or turn. However, there's a big downside to IFS when traveling off-road. When an independently sprung wheel goes over a big rock, it doesn't lift the differential over any other rocks lying around, which may result in damage to the differential.

Without independent suspension, the two front wheels or two rear wheels are attached to each other through a rigid axle housing with the differential in the middle. When one wheel goes over a large rock or log, it tilts the whole axle assembly and lifts the differential higher off the ground, improving clearance. For vehicles intended for serious off-road travel, nonindependent suspension is better. The trade-off is a little less comfortable highway ride.

Other options include an internal system for airing the tires up and down, such as the Hummer's central tire inflation system (CTIS), and a system for changing the height of the vehicle above the ground , like the Range Rover's or Lexus LX 470's electronic air suspension system.

This ideal rig comes in three basic sizes: a full-size model like the Chevy Tahoe, Lexus LX 470, or Dodge Durango; an even larger model like the Chevy Suburban; and a midsize model such as the, Nissan Xterra, Toyota 4Runner, or Jeep Cherokee and Grand Cherokee. And the price? About $30,000 to $50,000, depending on the size and options selected.

And the price? About $25,000 to $40,000, depending on the size and options selected.

SOMETHING FOR EVERYONE

The 4WD techniques in this book apply to the entire spectrum of sport-utes, from high-end rigs to economical mini-utes, as well as to rigs that have already been beefed up with skid plates, winches, lifters, and mondo tires. First-time sport-ute owners can use these ideas to graduate to the experienced 'wheeler category. There are a few ideas in here that even the dustiest, muddiest, most hard-core rock crawler can use the next time he or she hits the dirt.

And don't tell the 4-wheelers, but a lot of the off-road techniques in this book don't even require 4-wheel drive. You can get a long way off the beaten path by taking it slow and easy in the family car, especially if it's equipped with a limited-slip differential and decent LT all-terrain tires and it's packing a portable come-along winch and Hi-Lift jack in the trunk.

But right now we're concentrating on sport-utes and their owners, present and future, who haven't been there—yet—and haven't done that—yet.

Maybe as you read this book, you're deciding what you really want to do with your rig is fit it out with a winch, skid plates, a rear locker, and good LT tires. Then, early some fresh spring morning, you set out with an adventurous friend or loved one, shifting into 4WD where the pavement ends, picking a distant peak and heading for it along a dirt trail, slick from yesterday's rain. Follow the

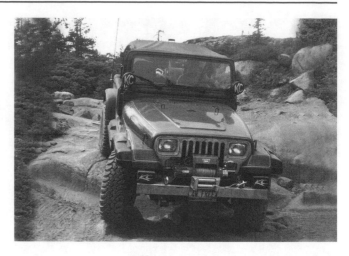

Figure 19. The Mercedes M-Class "All Activities Vehicle." It comes as the V6 ML 320 or the V8 ML 430.

Figure 20. The Jeep Wrangler is one of the most trailworthy 4x4s. This is the author's rig on the Rubicon Trail, modified with Mopar fuel injection for the 4.2L in-line six engine, 4.56:1 Dana 44s with ARB air lockers front and back, a Dana 300 T-case, an NV 4500 transmission, 4" of suspension lift and 1" body lift, 35" BF Goodrich mud-terrain tires, and a Warn 9,000 pound winch. It has a Premier under-the-hood welder, dual Optima batteries, and an R & M Specialty Products under-the-hood hot water shower.

trail through the tall trees, breathing in the fragrance of the forest, the dirt path gradually blending into the forest floor, becoming two shallow ruts heading up an impossible-looking slope. In 4-wheel Lo, you climb as far as you can, then get out, chock the wheels, and break out the winch.

Throwing a nylon strap around a tree 30 yards up the hill and attaching a D-shackle and the shackle block pulley, you double-line the winch cable back to one of the tow hooks attached to the frame of your rig. Working your way up the hill, stopping every 4 or 5 feet to rechock the wheels, you look back frequently to take in the spectacular view unfolding below you. You throw a tarp over the cable to contain it if it breaks, winching the rig up the hill, tree by protected tree.

With the trees getting smaller near the top of the peak, you throw a tow strap around several of them, attaching your double-lined cable to the nylon loops. The slope flattens near the top and, getting back in your rig, you clear the rim in 4-wheel Lo, operating the remote switch lead through the driver's open window. You reel in the winch cable, and drive into the clearing. It's on a small,

flat bench near the top of the peak you were aiming for and looks back on miles and miles of forested valleys and hills, carpeted with pine and cedar.

The two of you run over to a small waterfall splashing down the rocks at the edge of the clearing and wash the sweat and grime off your faces with the crystal clear mountain water, smelling the freshness of the air.

After preparing the campsite, and with the setting sun casting velvet shadows over the valleys below, you eat your evening meal beside the crackling fire and waiting tent, miles from anywhere and anyone, nursing aching muscles and hands, calloused through your gloves by the winch cable. You look forward to the night's rest and to more challenges and more breathless views tomorrow, wondering what took you so long to get here.

chapter five

TREAD LIGHTLY!

NOT JUST FOR TREE HUGGERS

To learn 4-wheeling, you need a laboratory, otherwise known as the great outdoors. But if we all go out and tear up the ecostructure with our mud tires, pretty soon the great outdoors will only be available to hikers and bikers (pedal type, that is). So long as we follow a few common-sense ecological principles, we 4-wheelers can retain access to large amounts of off-highway real estate and head off trail closures that would restrict us from public lands.

Sure, learning to drive over challenging terrain is fun, but this book is aimed more at 4-wheeling as a means to the end. The skills of 4-wheeling are the tools used to achieve the goal of driving into secluded, breathtakingly beautiful country.

Off-highway recreation expanded rapidly in the 1980s, but so did damage to the environment as a result of careless or ignorant use by 20 million 4WD rigs, all-terrain vehicles (ATVs), dirt bikes, and snowmobiles. As a result, environmental groups lobbied vigorously to close the entire federal land system to motorized recreational off-highway use.

Fortunately, in 1986 a recreational specialist in the U.S. Forest Service named Cliff Blake, along with several of his Forest Service colleagues, developed an educational program to teach the responsible use of off-highway vehicles. They called this program Tread Lightly!, exclamation point included in the name! Like, "You better Tread Lightly! or pretty soon you Can't Tread At All!"

The program expanded and was endorsed by the BLM as well as the Forest Service. By 1990 it had become a national private nonprofit corporation and picked up a number of private sponsors, including most of the sport-utility and pickup truck manufacturers.

The organization reminds us of the ancient Native American proverb, "We did not inherit the earth from our parents, we are borrowing it from our children."

The "TREAD" of "Tread Lightly!" is an acronym for the principles of the program:

Travel and recreate with minimum impact.

Respect the environment and the rights of others.

Educate yourself, plan and prepare before you go.

Allow for future use of the outdoors, leave it better than you found it.

Discover the rewards of responsible recreation.

Tread Lightly!'s new tag line is, "Leaving a Good Impression."

SUPPORT THE TREAD LIGHTLY! PROGRAM

The Tread Lightly! principles serve our purpose. There are plenty of challenges for us on established trails. If you can do the Dusy or Rubicon Trails in California, you can do about anything a 4WD rig can do. The U.S. Department of Agriculture,

Figure 21. Tread Lightly! so you don't become the reason for closing a trail to motorized recreation.

through the U.S. Forest Service, manages 156 national forests, which have a total area equal to the three West Coast states combined—California, Washington, and Oregon—spread throughout the contiguous states, Alaska, and Puerto Rico. They contain about 100,000 miles of trails.

The U.S. Department of the Interior, through the Bureau of Land Management, manages 272 million acres of land spread throughout the western U.S. and Alaska, one-eighth of all the acreage in the United States. There are probably another 100,000 miles of trails in the BLM land. Fifty or so of these trails are included in BLM's Backcountry Byways program, especially designated for beauty and/or interest.

BLM TRAILS

BLM trails are classified into four types:

Type I: Very easy, paved, all-weather. Family car okay.

Type II: Not paved, but usually improved. May be rough or rutted. High-clearance 4WD vehicles desirable.

Type III: Unimproved dirt, often with rocks, steep hills, and mud. 4WD required.

Type IV: Trails for mountain bikes, dirt bikes, and ATVs. 2WD or 4WD rigs not authorized.

Maps of the national forests are available from U.S. Forest Service offices; maps of BLM lands can be obtained from BLM offices. (See the resource list in

Appendix C for the addresses.) Detailed topographical maps of specific areas can be obtained from the U.S. Geological Survey office in Denver or from a number of private dealers. The Forest Service maps are especially useful, because they show in detail the many numbered trails criss-crossing our national forests.

TRAIL RESTRICTIONS

To tell whether or not you can legally drive a 4x4 rig on a particular trail at a particular time of year, refer to the trail legend on your map. Some Forest Service offices publish an Access Guide, which details the trails and their restrictions. If available, it's very helpful. Trails can be restricted for any one of a dozen reasons, including the protection of wildlife, soils and vegetation, water quality, areas involved in research, and the general public from unsafe conditions such as fires, among others.

Specific restrictions apply to different classes of vehicles, including all vehicles greater than 50 inches wide (which includes sport-utes and pickups), vehicles with three or more wheels less than 50 inches wide (ATVs), motorcycles, snowmobiles, and mountain bikes. The restrictions vary according to the time of year. All this information is contained in the Access Guide for a particular forest. It's also contained on signs posted at the beginning of the restricted portions of the trails (Figures 22).

Figure 22. The regulations about trail restrictions vary from month to month in the national forests. As this U.S. Forest Service sign at the trailhead indicates (inset), you're out of luck if it's October.

ECOLOGICAL WHEELIN'

Follow ecological 4-wheeling principles when leaving the pavement. It is, after all, the responsible thing to do. When winching out a stuck rig, use a nylon strap to protect the anchoring tree. After using a ground anchor or accidentally spinning your wheels, fill in the divots. Avoid driving off designated trails, especially over meadows, streambeds, and other ecologically delicate areas. Be sure to close all gates you open.

A vehicle is "high-centered" if it is hanging up on a rock or log between the front and rear wheels. To get out of this situation, you need to jack up a wheel and build a ramp under it so you can drive off the obstacle. Use rocks for the ramp, if at all possible. If you have to use lengths of logs, cut them from fallen dead trees already lying around. Don't cut down a standing dead tree and take a chance of destroying the nesting place of one of your forest hosts. Even using fallen trees disturbs the habitat to some degree. That's why it's better to stick with rocks. (See Chapter 10 on winches and jacks for more details on getting unstuck.)

If you're having trouble traveling up a muddy slope, use your winch to help you. That's better than spinning your tires furiously and futilely, grinding deep ruts in the trail as you try to inch your way to the top.

Leaving the land undisturbed is the basic principle of sound ecology and the fundamental basis of the Tread Lightly! philosophy. This includes leaving dead logs and other ground cover undisturbed for the benefit of the ground dwellers among us. There just is not enough wood to go around for every camper to depend on local logs for their fires, and pretty soon the land will be stripped bare. Bring firewood from your personal home supply or buy it at the supermarket, either bundles of firewood or artificial logs of the Duraflame variety.

Pack out what you pack in. Don't make the next group using the area think you started a private landfill. There are few things as repulsively unecological as a bunch of empty beer bottles and cans littering an otherwise beautiful campsite. And remember why you're doing all this. You're doing these things because, number one, it's the responsible thing to do, and number two, by doing your part to protect the environment, you put the brakes on restrictive laws prohibiting recreational 4-wheeling.

LAND ETHICS

The whole subject of using the land intelligently comes under the heading of land ethics. The U.S. Forest Service and BLM are developing their land ethics programs with input from the private sector by interfacing with the private members and sponsors of Tread Lightly! and another program called Leave No Trace.

The various governmental agencies are working together to classify trails for recreational use. In Utah, for instance, the Forest Service and BLM now coordinate their regulations and maps so you won't find yourself 'wheeling along a BLM trail approved for motorized travel and suddenly come up against a NO ENTRY sign when the trail enters National Forest land.

There is a classification of land use, used by both the BLM and Forest Service, to help determine which trails to open and which to restrict. This classification divides land into six categories. You'll run across it when you get involved with the BlueRibbon Coalition and other groups networking with the federal agencies in regard to off-highway recreation. The categories are:

1. Urban
2. Rural
3. Natural roaded
4. Semiprimitive, motorized
5. Semiprimitive, nonmotorized
6. Primitive

PRESERVING ECOLOGICAL RECREATION

Large areas of the United States have been designated as Wilderness. These areas are inaccessible to everyone except hikers and horses. You can't even ride a bike across them. The idea is to preserve these regions in their natural state. The problem is that by authorizing only nonvehicular traffic, the regulations governing these areas deny their use to

large segments of the population. Anyone who can't hike long distances carrying a heavy pack can't enjoy these vast expanses of land. This eliminates families with young children, older individuals still vigorous enough to enjoy camping and day hiking but beyond the age at which they enjoy backpacking, and people with disabilities.

I've met and received letters from a number of individuals who participate actively in off-road driving, even though they're paraplegic. Their rigs are specially equipped with hand controls that allow them to operate their vehicles over rough terrain. They enjoy the outdoors. But they can't backpack.

I met an older couple who were members of an off-road 4-wheel drive club in the Southwest. Most members of the club were in their 70s; they themselves were in their 80s. Before a club trip to a remote area, one couple would scout the proposed route in their 4x4 to make sure it wasn't too easy! They could camp, and they sure could drive, but they couldn't have hiked 20 or 30 miles with 60 pound packs on their backs.

I know a number of couples who regularly take their young children on camping trips, using their 4x4 to access beautiful and remote backcountry. They believe in teaching their kids about ecology and the environment by immersing them in it for days at a time. But they couldn't do it if they had to hike in.

Some of the more active environmental groups feel they need to keep lobbying for Wilderness designation of more and more land to protect the environment. But is it really fair to shut off so much beautiful country from such large segments of our population? These are, after all, public lands. The risk the environmental groups run is a backlash from the public, when people suddenly realize just how much of the country is being shut off from their use and enjoyment.

On the other hand, if 4-wheelers go out and trash the countryside, ignoring Tread Lightly! principles, they're asking for trail closures and limited access to the outdoors. Fortunately, most participants in organized off-road recreation have gotten the message, and clubs sponsoring activities such as 4-wheel driving, snowmobiling, dirt biking, and ATV (all-terrain vehicle) events are educating their members in the importance of being friendly to the environment. Many of these clubs regularly perform ecologically oriented services such as maintaining and restoring trails, rebuilding bridges, cleaning up campgrounds, and replanting forests.

It's important that the recreational public monitor the classification of land so the restriction of trails is reasonable and not arbitrary. It's also important to join your local 4WD club to add another voice (and vote) to groups that are striving to keep trails open for ecological motorized recreational use and to have arbitrarily closed trails reopened.

If you're a 4-wheeler who's a member of an environmental activist organization, let the organization know that you're a member who supports ecologically oriented off-road recreation. Speak out on these issues. You might be surprised to learn how many of your fellow members drive 4x4s or have snowmobiles and even dirt bikes hidden in their garages. By the same token, you should also join your local 4WD club to let them know your concerns about the environment.

All off-road recreationists should join the BlueRibbon Coalition, a networking group interfacing with off-road recreational clubs and governmental agencies to encourage environmentally friendly motorized outdoor recreation. The coalition stresses the importance of following ecological principles of land use. Its Recreation Code of Ethics contains 11 points:

1. I will respect public and private property and respect the rights of all recreationists to enjoy the beauty of the outdoors.
2. I will park considerately without blocking access to trails.
3. I will keep to the right when meeting another recreationist and yield to traffic moving uphill.
4. I will slow down and use caution when approaching or overtaking another.
5. I will respect designated areas and trail-use signs.
6. I will avoid blocking the trail when stopping.
7. I will not disturb wildlife and will avoid areas posted for the protection of wildlife.
8. I will pack out everything I pack in.
9. I will adjust my travel speed to be in line with my equipment, my ability, the terrain, the weather, and other traffic. I will volunteer assistance to those in trouble.
10. I will not interfere with the rights of others. I recognize that people judge all trail users by my actions.
11. If I meet a horseback rider, I will pull off the trail if possible and shut down my engine. If I'm wearing a helmet, I will remove it and greet the rider.

The motto of the BlueRibbon Coalition is: "Preserving our natural resources FOR the public instead of FROM the public."

By encouraging networking among Congress, the governmental agencies, off-road recreational clubs, and the environmental activist organizations, we can restore balance between protecting the environment and preserving for recreational use the public lands we all own. Join Tread Lightly! It only costs 20 bucks a year. This organization will keep you informed about new trails opened up by the BLM. Find out where your closest 4WD club is by contacting the United 4WD Association in Shelbyville, Indiana (see Appendix C, Resources). Become acquainted with your local Forest Service and BLM personnel and let them know your concerns over proposed trail closings and your desires to have certain trails reopened. Join the BlueRibbon Coalition, network with your legislators through this group, and encourage continuing access to public lands. Write your senators and representatives about your concerns over the closure of public land.

With all of us supporting Tread Lightly! and the BlueRibbon Coalition, we're doing our best to encourage ecologically oriented off-road recreation and to ensure the continued availability of off-highway recreational land. These organizations depend on our dues and contributions for their operations. Join them.

chapter six

PACKING UP
THE BASIC TOOLBOX

Selecting and organizing all of your gear presents a challenge. It's not practical to prepare for every possible situation. Choices depend on circumstances and personal preferences. Are you just camping for two or three days near a populated area, or are you traveling for a month or two in desolate country? Are you taking a leisurely vacation, or are you escaping an urban disaster? Are you traveling in a large group, dividing up responsibility for food, camping supplies, and spare vehicle parts? Or are you and your family traveling alone or in a small group, where a higher level of self-sufficiency is required? Is it summer or winter?

The following lists are offered as guidelines. Pick and choose among the possibilities, depending on your own special circumstances and comfort level. Don't be intimidated if some of this gear seems pretty technical. Special equipment comes with detailed instructions, and we'll cover the use of most of it in upcoming chapters.

You don't have to modify your SUV at all to enjoy off-roading. Just carry a few basic items, such as a Hi-Lift jack and a heavy board to support it, a couple of heavy-duty tow straps, a Safety Seal tire kit to fix punctures without even taking the wheel off the rig, a good quality electric air compressor that plugs into the cigarette lighter, flashlights, fire-building material, a fire extinguisher, a sturdy shovel, a first aid kit, some simple tools, duct tape, and rope.

If you'll be going farther off the beaten path, add food and water and a CB radio. In the winter, carry tire chains for all four wheels and make sure that every person in the party has a heavy down sleeping bag or the equivalent. You can upgrade your gear gradually as you become more comfortable with off-road recreation.

BASIC CONSIDERATIONS

The basic needs are food, clothing, and shelter. Items to keep close by you in the driver's compartment include a flashlight, fire extinguisher, maps, sunglasses, CB radio, and first aid kit. Make sure the flashlight, fire extinguisher, and any other heavy items are tied down (Figure 23). Keep a hatchet, ice ax, or spring-loaded center punch nearby to break the windows for emergency exit.

Keep a few basic tools handy so you don't have to open up large storage boxes in the back of the rig just to make minor repairs. These include screwdrivers (regular and Phillips), pliers, vise grips, combination wrenches with open and box ends, Allen wrenches, a pocket knife, duct tape, twine, and a length of rope.

Tie down everything. Someone once suggested that if you can't decide whether or not to tie something down, just think about lying on your back and asking a friend to drop the item onto your face.

35

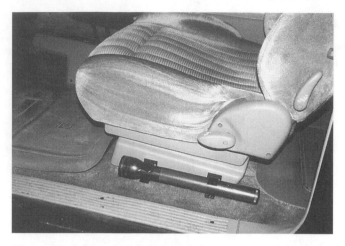

Figure 23. A large flashlight kept in easy reach in brackets screwed or bolted to the side of the front seat.

Figure 24. Tie down your load.

Since this is what would happen in a rollover, it should convince you to tie down everything. Use rope or a strong cargo net. Bungie cords aren't secure enough for heavy items (Figure 24).

THE LISTS

The following lists of items fall into four general categories:

1. Stuff for getting your rig unstuck and for keeping the tires functional, such as winch equipment, jacks, and tire equipment (Figure 25).
2. Stuff for keeping safe and for getting "unlost," such as a CB radio, maps, compass, Global Positioning System (GPS) device, medical supplies, hunting gear, and fishing equipment.
3. Food, shelter, and items for comfort and convenience.

4. Equipment to keep your rig running, such as vital fluids (engine oil, brake fluid, transmission fluid), tools, and spare parts.

(See also Chapters 7 and 10 for additional details about such items as winches, CB radios, and GPS devices.)

Gear for Getting Unstuck and for Keeping the Tires Functional

Winch and Towing Stuff

Winch, mounted to the frame in the front, and strong enough to pull one and a half times the gross vehicle weight rating (GVWR = the weight of your vehicle, passengers, and total payload) of your rig. Total winch coverage would include an additional rear-mounted electric winch or a portable electric winch that you can attach to the receiver hitch in the back. A portable hand winch (a "come-along") may get you by as the back-up winch.

Tow straps, which can double as tree protectors and safety lines. You need at least two, but three or four would be better. Each one should be rated for at least 20,000 pounds. They should have a loop sewn in each end. Avoid ones with metal hooks attached—if the hook breaks, it will act like a cannonball and can severely damage people and rigs.

Snatch blocks, also called pulley blocks or shackle blocks, so you can use the winch cable double-lined. One is better than none, but you need at least three when double-lining and turning a corner with the pull.

Tow hooks attached to the frame of your rig. You should have at least two in front, and it's best to have two in back as well.

Tree strap, to protect both the tree you use as an anchor and to protect your winch cable. A tow strap can be used instead of a specific short nylon tree strap.

Clevis pins, also known as D-shackles. You need at least two of these. Four is better, to give you more versatility.

Receiver shackle, which is attached to a short steel bar that fits in your receiver hitch (Figure 26). It's a good idea to carry one in case you need to get towed by someone who has a rear hitch but no rear tow hooks.

Chain, 20 feet, with a hook attached to each end, for anchoring to a large boulder if you don't have a tree handy. You can also use the chain as a "choker" to attach to a log that you have to winch out of the way.

Figure 25. Getting unstuck stuff. 1) Attached winch. 2) Tow hooks, front and back, attached to frame. 3) SureClaw wheel anchors and wheel straps. 4) Winch remote switch and instruction book. 5) Chainsaw. 6) Tow straps. 7) Portable winch (come-along). 8) Heavy gloves. 9) Wire mesh goggles for eye protection. 10) Small crowbar for handling winch cable and hook. 11) D-shackles. 12) Snatch blocks (pulleys). 13) Receiver shackle. 14) Max-Ax multipurpose tool. 15) Chain with attached hook on each end. 16) Tire chains. 17) Hi-Lift jack. 18) Heavy pry bar. 19) Ground anchor (Pul Pal). 20) Nylon rope. 21) Duct tape. 22) Tarp to put over winch cable.

Wheel chocks, to stabilize the rig when winching someone up a hill or out of a boggy spot. You also need chocks as you winch a rig up a hill to hold it in case the winch fails. SureClaws work well.

Gloves, always worn when handling winch cable to protect your hands from metal slivers at frayed spots.

Winch hook, to hold the hook attached to the winch cable when the cable hook gets close to the fairlead (the opening in the winch from which the cable emerges). A small crowbar works well and can be used for other jobs as well. Don't take a chance on winching your hand into the fairlead.

Tarps or blankets to put over the winch cable during winching, to hold it down in case it snaps.

Come-along portable hand winch, especially necessary if you don't have a rear-mounted winch or a portable winch that fits in the receiver (Figure 27). There are times when you need to winch a rig rearward instead of forward. This can be done by running the front winch cable under the rig, but damage to the cable may result, or you may tear up components on the bottom of the vehicle. It's better to winch directly against a rear tow hook or receiver shackle. (See Chapter 10 on winching for more details.)

Heavy bolt cutter, for cutting the winch cable in case it snaps and becomes tangled around the front bumper, brush guard, and winch housing.

Extra winch cable.

U-clamps, three, for repairing a broken winch cable. They need to be the proper size for your cable (e.g., 5/16", 3/8").

Jack Stuff
Hi-Lift jack, at least 48 inches.

Figure 26. A receiver shackle—basically a D-shackle fitting into the rear hitch receiver—in place.

Figure 27. A come-along portable winch.

Board to set the jack on, 2" x 10", 2 feet long.

Traction strips, to use under your wheels in sand, mud, or snow. Four boards, 2" x 10", 3 to 4 feet long, grooved. Four pieces of carpet, 2' x 4'.

Hydraulic jack, to lift your rig by the axle, which may be necessary in certain situations.

Tire Equipment

Full-size spare tire.

Air compressor, for airing up tires after driving in sand or mud or to air up after a flat. An under-the-hood compressor is probably best, but you can buy good ones that plug into your cigarette lighter. With both an under-the-hood one and an electric one, airing up goes twice as fast.

Air hose, for an under-the-hood compressor.

Tire gauges, regular and low pressure. Get a good low-pressure gauge to record pressures accurately when airing way down for mud or sand.

Quadra-Flate device. Four interconnected hoses attached to a valve and gauge, allowing you to deflate or reinflate all four tires simultaneously. Use it with an under-the-hood air compressor or an electric compressor plugged into the cigarette lighter. (See Chapter 12 for more information.)

Tire sealant spray. Watch out! It's flammable. If you are smoking a cigarette while letting air out of a tire in which sealant has been used, your face will be history.

Tire-sealing kit, for punctures and small holes. Safety Seal makes a heavy-duty professional kit with self-vulcanizing hole-plugging strips. (See

"Safety Seal" under the "Tires" section of the resource list in Appendix C.)

Super glue and gel, to use in a pinch on a match stick, nail, or sheet metal screw if you run out of plugging strips.

Valve cores and remover.

Valve caps.

Inner tubes and boots, for those bigger holes.

Heavy fishing line, to sew up sidewall rips before gluing in the boot and putting in the inner tube. Don't count on this repair at highway speeds, but it may last long enough to get you back to camp.

Tire chains, for snow, ice, or mud. With only one set, put them on the back wheels. If you put them on the front, your rear end comes around when you brake going downhill on a slippery surface, throwing you into a skid. Chains designed specifically for mud have bigger links than snow chains.

Tire wrench, a good heavy-duty one. An X-shaped one is probably best, but it's easier to store and just as effective if you cut off the limb opposite the one that fits your wheel lugs.

Tire irons, or small crowbars, for the happy occasion when you have to wrestle the bead of the tire off the wheel rim to make a major repair. Heavy screwdrivers work also. Pop the bead to get it started by laying the deflated tire flat on the ground and putting a board over the tire (avoiding the rim of the wheel), then driving over the board (again avoiding the rim of the wheel). You can also use the board on the tire as a base for the Hi-Lift jack and jack up the rig, using its weight to pop the bead.

Tie-down strap with a rachet. A tubeless tire

unseated from the beads for repair is difficult to reseat. The portable air compressors don't provide enough pressure to force the beads back on the rim. Put the tie-down strap circumferentially around the tire and tighten the rachet. This forces the beads against the wheel and creates enough seal so the smaller compressors can pop the beads back in place.

Unstuck Tools

Soft-headed hammer, to hammer out bent wheel rims.

Machete, to cut brush.

Max-ax, the multipurpose ax, pick, and shovel.

Saws, hand and chain. Use the chain saw to cut dead logs into ramps to get out of high-centered situations or to ramp on or off hills that are too steep for your approach and departure angles. Don't forget to pack extra saw chains, sharpening files, chain lube, and oil for the fuel mixture.

Pry bar, heavy and long, to move rocks, logs, etc.

Gear for Keeping Safe and for Getting Unlost

Finding Your Way Stuff

Maps, compasses, and global positioning system (GPS). Forest Service, BLM, and USGS topographic maps are recommended. How to use these items separately and together are basic survival skills that we won't cover in this book. Get some practice using them before your life depends on doing it right. Harry Lewellyn has published some good articles on these topics in his newsletters. Back issues are available. (See the resource list in Appendix C.)

Field glasses.

Clipboard, yellow legal pads, or other writing paper. Use for writing journals, menus, etc. Paper attached to a pad will be less likely to blow around in the outdoors.

Ballpoint pens and pencils.

CB radio and extra antennas. (See Chapter 7 for details about citizens band radio.)

Mirror. You can detach an outside rearview mirror from your rig and use it for signaling. In an emergency survival situation, you can attract attention by setting your spare tire on fire using gasoline or oil. This creates a long-burning, black, smudgy fire visible for miles.

Whistle.

Flares.

Firearms. For hunting and/or self-defense. Rifle (.30-06, .308, .300 Magnum, 7mm Magnum, AK47, or Ruger Mini-30 for larger game; Ruger Mini-14 or AR-15 for varmint hunting), 12-gauge shotgun, and/or handgun. (.45, .357, or .44 Magnum).

Ammunition. .223-caliber cartridges for an AR-15 or Mini-14 are easier to carry, but 7.62mm or .30-06 cartridges are less likely to be deflected when shooting in dense brush.

Gun-cleaning equipment.

Fishing equipment. Poles, line, hooks, lures, nets, etc.

Medical Supplies

What you carry as medical supplies depends on the level of medical training of your group. Knowing how to clean and close a wound and splint an injured extremity are basic survival skills we won't cover in this book. It is highly recommended that you take a good first aid course before you encounter a medical emergency, and don't count on having a physician, nurse, EMT, physician's assistant, nurse practitioner, or veternarian in your convoy. How much or how many of each item you carry depends on how long you anticipate being on your own. Paladin Press carries a number of good books on outback medicine. (See the resource list in Appendix C.)

You probably will not choose to put together such an extensive store of medical supplies as is listed below unless you're going into desolate country for extended periods of time. Remember, it's your responsibility to learn how to use properly and administer accurately any items and medications you choose to bring along.

Medicine chest or other containers.

Betadine antiseptic.

Alcohol 70%.

Alcohol sponges, in individual foil packages.

Gauze sponges, in sterile packages.

Plastic or paper tape.

Band-Aids.

Steristrips, for wound closure.

Snakebite kit.

Fine-tip tweezers and magnifying glass, for removing splinters.

Magnetic eye probe, for removing metal fragments from the eyes.

Scissors.

Suture sets, disposable.

Skin staples and remover.
Suture material, sterile.
• 4-0 nylon, with cutting skin needle.
• 3-0 Vicryl, with round needle.
Scalpels, disposable #12 blade, sterile.
Syringes, 5 and 10 ml, in sterile containers.
Needles, sterile.
• 27 gauge, 1 1/4" long, for local anesthesia and basic injections.
• 18 gauge, 1/2" or 1" long, for drawing up medications.
• 22 gauge spinal, 3 1/2" long, for deep injections.
Medications. The following medications are listed for the convenience of trained medical personnel in your party. You open yourself to severe legal problems if you administer any of these medications and something goes wrong. *Don't do it unless you're a health care professional licensed to prescribe or administer pharmaceuticals, such as a medical doctor, osteopath, physician's assistant, or nurse practitioner.*
• Antibiotics.
    Amoxicillin.
    Cipro.
    Flagyl, for *Giardia.*
• Antibiotic ointment.
• Anesthetics, analgesics, and anti-inflammatories.
    Xylocaine, 0.5% plain, for injection; multiple use vial.
    Aspirin.
    Darvocet-N-100.
    Ultram, 50 mg tablets.
    Kenalog-40, 5 ml vial.
    Ibuprofen.
• Antihistamines.
    Chlortrimeton.
    Benedryl.
• Sedatives.
    Ambian.
    Versed for intravenous injection. Very helpful to sedate someone who needs to have a laceration sutured, a fracture set, or a dislocation reduced. *Versed is dangerous!* A person who's had Versed can stop breathing. Like any of these medications, it should *only* be administered by medical personnel trained in its use.
• Epinephrine 1:1000, 1 ml ampules, for severe allergic reactions.
• Antidiarrheals.

Lomotil or Immodium.
• Antacids.
    Cimetidine (Tagamet), 300 mg tablets.
• Medications for any personal medical conditions, such as insulin for diabetes, thyroid medication, glaucoma medication, etc.
Skin stuff.
• Hand lotion. Corn Huskers' Lotion, by Warner-Lambert, is the best all-round hand restorer I've found.
• Hydrocortisone cream, 1%.
• Antifungal ointment.
• Calamine lotion.
• Sunblock.
• Insect repellant.
Breathing stuff.
• Endotracheal tubes.
• Laryngoscope.
• Ambu bag.
Intravenous supplies.
• Ringer's solution, 1,000 ml plastic bags.
• IV tubing.
• Tourniquet, venous.
• Butterfly needles, 22 gauge.
• Angiocaths, 18 gauge.
Tourniquet, arterial.
Ace bandages, 3".
Inflatable splints.
Plaster rolls, for casting.
Crutches, collapsible.
Lumbosacral back corsets.
Cervical collars.

Food, Shelter, and Items for Comfort and Convenience

Again, the following lists are merely suggestions. Follow your own preferences based on past hiking and camping experience.

Food and Food Preparation

Ice chests, two. One for food storage with ice, the other for extra ice, opened as little as possible. Chill the food and drinks in the refrigerator and chill the ice chest overnight with ice water before loading it. Buy fresh supplies cold, if possible.
Propane stove and bottles.
Bottled water.
Eating utensils.
Plastic cups.
Cooking utensils.

Can opener.

Aluminum foil.

Thermos bottle, stainless. Fill it at night with hot coffee to warm you up in the morning before you get the fire going. Don't leave any airspace or it'll develop an acidic taste.

Coffee and tea.

Dehydrated food. MREs (Meal, Ready to Eat) soup, fruit, etc.

Rice and pasta.

Canned food.

Shelter and Convenience Items

Tent.

Tarps, two, 10' x 20'. Use for ground cover if your tent doesn't have a floor. String one up as a windbreak or lean-to to shield you from the elements.

Tarps, several, 6' x 8'. Use under your sleeping bag as ground cover. Put over your sleeping bag to protect you from a light rain. If you need to make repairs on tires or engine parts, work on a tarp to keep dust or sand away from your work.

Space blankets, one per person.

Sleeping bags.

Sunglasses, with UVA and UVB protection.

Trash bags, large and small.

Toilet paper.

Paper towels.

Cloth towels.

Dishwashing detergent.

Personal soap, shampoo, and toiletries.

Water purifying tablets.

Water filter system. The Guardian Sweetwater filter system, with the ViralGuard attachment, filters out over 99.9% of pathogens at a reasonable rate.

Fire starters to get a blaze going. Cotton balls covered with petroleum jelly can be ignited to get your tinder and kindling going. Charred cloth works well, too. Duraflame logs can also be used as fire starter.

Firewood. Bring your own, especially if traveling in a high-use area.

Charcoal lighter.

Waterproof matches. Carry alternatives to matches, too, in case you lose them or run out. A magnesium/flint bar available at any sporting goods store is a good choice. You can also ignite cotton balls covered with petroleum jelly, char cloth, or a ball of steel wool by producing a shower of sparks with jumper cables connected to your rig's battery.

Butane lighters.

Clothes. Be sure not to use cotton as cold-weather clothing, especially next to your skin. It won't wick moisture away and leads to real danger of hypothermia if you get wet from perspiration, rain, or snow.

• Warm jacket, parka, sweater.

• Warm headgear.

• Foul-weather gear.

• Hip-high rubber boots.

• Extra clothes.

• Gloves.

• Long johns. Make sure they're made of polypropylene or similar wicking fabric. Use expedition-weight polypro in colder weather. Again, never use cotton long johns, even those made of that warm-looking waffle-print fabric. If they get damp, they'll drain your body heat in a hurry.

Hiking boots. Be sure they're really waterproof, containing a Gore-Tex or similar membrane. For cold weather, boots containing Thinsulate Thermal insulation work well.

Snowshoes, for walking on top of deep snow rather than in it.

Equipment to Keep Your Rig Running

Tools, Security, and Safety

Fire extinguishers, CO_2 type.

Flashlights and batteries.

Toolbox. Use plastic containers or heavy canvas pouches for tools and parts. Metal boxes are noisy and don't protect the items inside very well.

Pliers.

Channel locks.

Crescent wrenches, various sizes.

Combination wrenches, box and open, 3/16" to 1" in 1/16" steps (or metric equivalents).

Screwdrivers, Phillips and regular.

Vise grips, two large, one small.

Socket wrenches, 3/16" to 1" in 1/16" steps (or metric equivalents), 3/8" or 1/2" drive with swivel rachet handle, 9/16", 5/8", 11/16" deep sockets.

Spark plug socket, deep, rubber lined.

Short pipe for leverage. The handle on your Hi-Lift jack works in a pinch.

Torque wrench.

Pipe wrench.

Impact screwdriver, for loosening corroded screws.

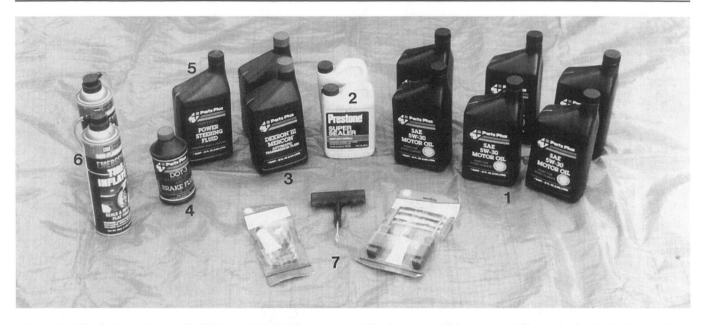

Figure 28. Vital fluids and tire stuff. 1) Motor oil (5-30W), 6 quarts. 2) Radiator stop leak, 2 pints. 3) Transmission fluid (Dexron III), 2 quarts. 4) Brake fluid (DOT 3), 1 pint. 5) Power steering fluid. 6) Tire inflation foam, 2 cans. 7) Tire-plugging strips and cement.

Cotter pins.

Lock nuts, assortment. Bring plenty. Don't use lock nuts twice. They lock by deforming when you screw them on. They won't lock properly again once you unscrew them.

Loc-Tite.

Washers, assortment.

Nuts and bolts, assortment.

"O" rings.

Lug nuts. At least five.

Allen wrenches.

Hammer.

Files, round and flat.

Scissors.

Hatchet.

Duct tape.

Swiss army knife.

Nylon rope, 200 feet.

Battery jumper cables.

Electrical tape.

Wire, galvanized steel, 18 gauge, malleable, 100-foot spool, for holding things together.

Silicone sealer.

Nails.

Tie-down straps.

Battery tie downs.

Rags.

Soft brush, for brushing away dust and dirt before working on an engine part or tires. A large paint brush works well.

Vital fluids. Check your owner's manual to find out exactly what kinds of fluids your vehicle drinks. I've listed the ones my '94 K-Blazer needs.

• Oil, 6 quarts, SAE 5-30.
• Brake fluid, DOT-3.
• Transmission and T-case fluids, Dexron III.
• Differential fluid, 80W90.
• Power steering fluid.
• Gasoline, in 5-gallon cans, at least two. Don't carry these full inside your rig at any time, and don't carry them full on a rear rack while on the highway. There's too much danger of fire if rear-ended. Carry these empty inside or outside your rig while you're on the highway. Fill them just before you go off-road, and carry them on a rear rack on the side away from your exhaust pipe (Figure 29). Empty them into your main gas tank as soon as you can. Before you store them empty in your rig again, air them out completely—recently "emptied" gas cans contain very explosive air/fuel vapors. If carrying metal gas cans on a rear rack or on your roof, touch them to the metal body of your rig before you open them to fill your tank. This gets rid of any static electrical charge that might have built up on them and lessens the chance of fire or explosion from that source.

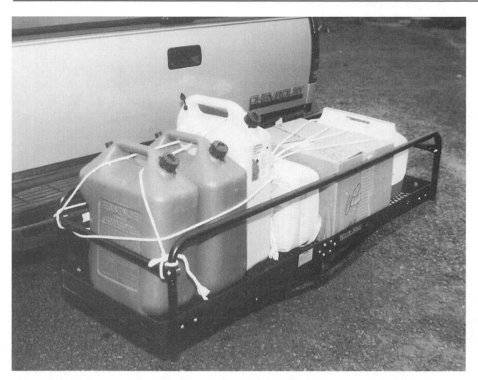

Figure 29. This receiver-mounted rack can carry up to 500 pounds of stuff. Note that the gas cans are carried on the side of the rack away from the exhaust pipe.

Funnel.
Oil filter.
Oil filter wrench.
Siphon hose.
Hand cleaner.

Spare Parts

According to Petersen's *4-Wheel & Off-Road* magazine, the 10 most likely on-the-trail failures are 1) failed tune-up parts that haven't been kept up to snuff—plugs, points, fan belts; 2) broken U-joints, especially front axle ones; 3) broken ring-and-pinion gears in a differential; 4) torn brake lines; 5) pulled-apart shocks and broken shock mounts; 6) broken leaf spring shackles and pivot bolts; 7) fluids contaminated by water; 8) rock damage to the oil pan, transmission, T-case, and differentials; 9) cut tires and aired-down tires knocked off the rim; 10) broken steering parts.

Be in tune with your vehicle. How does it feel as you make your way along the trail? Does a new noise need checking out? A clunck under the hood each time you brake or accelerate may mean a loose motor mount that needs tightening before a sudden stop sends the fan through the radiator. A new clunck in the drivetrain may mean a bad U-joint or ring-and-pinion gears on their last legs. If this sort of problem develops and can't be fixed trailside, you may decide to turn back or at least bypass the rougher parts of the trail if you can.

The following is an extensive list. What you decide to carry depends on the remoteness of your travel route, how long the trip will take, and your experience in dealing with broken rigs. Obviously, if no one in your party knows how to diagnose and remove a broken part, it's a waste of time bringing its replacement along.

Keys, two extra sets, kept in different locations. Keep one set in a hidden magnetic box attached to the underside of the vehicle. The extra set won't help you very much if it's in the pocket of a member of your party disappearing into a bed of quicksand or being dragged away by a grizzly.

Alternator.

Alternator bracket.

Bearings and seals, for front and rear axles.

Drive flange, for each axle.

Gasket material. A trick from the "Homegrown How-Tos" section of Petersen's *4-Wheel & Off-Road* magazine advises punching out neat round holes for the bolts by hammering on empty fired cartridge cases with the opening placed down on the gasket material. For a 1/4 inch hole, use a .22-caliber case. A 9mm case makes a 5/16 opening. A .38 case equals 3/8 inch, and a .45 equals 7/16. (Do not use reloading cases with the primers intact!)

Front axles, right and left.

Rear axles, right and left.

Front hubs.

Extra ignition parts. Points or spare ignition module, static protected.

Epoxy putty. Q-Weld works well. Use it to plug leaking holes poked in the undersurface of the rig, like the gas tank, oil pan, transmission, T-case, or differentials.

Radiator Stop-Leak. If you are caught in an emergency without Stop-Leak, uncooked egg whites dumped into the radiator will cook at the site of the leak and plug it. Uncooked rolled oats do the same thing. A raw potato, jammed into the leak on each side of the radiator from the outside, may also work.

Formula 12/34. Nonflammable spray for displacing water and drying off wet ignition and spark plug wires.

U-bolts, for axles.

U joints, two of each type.

Tie-rod ends.

Radiator hoses, 5' each of 3/4", 5/8", 1/2". If you are caught without spare hoses, you can repair a rip in a hose by drying it off, then wrapping it with duct tape. Wrap the duct tape with 18-gauge steel wire. Leave the radiator cap loosened so the pressure in the system won't blow open the repair. With a large rip, sew it closed first with heavy fishing line, then wrap it.

Extra radiator cap.

Carburetor repair kits, or spare electronic control module (ECM), static protected.

Fuel line hoses.

Fuel line filter.

Fuel pump.

Brake line hoses.

Fuses, assorted, heavy duty (30 amp).

Electrical wiring, insulated, 15' of gauges 10, 14, and 16.

Electrical connectors, crimp type and crimp tool.

Fan belts, three sets.

Spark plugs.

Spark plug wires.

Starter solenoid.

Shock absorber mounts for rear axle.

* * * * *

Again, pick and choose from all these things. Bringing everything would require a sizable trailer. These lists are to help plan your initial trips until you develop your own specific lists.

chapter seven

BEEFING UP YOUR RIG

WHAT'S YOUR CREDIT CARD LIMIT?

Beefing up your rig can mean cleaning out your bank account. Choices must be made. Let's assume you've got a stock 4x4 and are still interested in driving it to work, picking up the kids at school, and going to the supermarket without having your friends and neighbors staring and thinking you're about to enter the Baja 1000. You also probably don't want to carry a stepladder just to get in and out of the thing.

Even so, venturing very far off the beaten path requires a few modifications. Be careful about modifications that could void part or all of the factory warranty or extended warranty on your rig's drivetrain, however. Check with your dealer or extended policy insurance company before modifying the differentials, driveshafts, T-case, transmission, or engine.

ON-BOARD DIAGNOSTICS

Modifications are more difficult on newer rigs because of the on-board diagnostics (OBD) now required for emission control. Vehicles manufactured since 1996 have on-board computers that constantly monitor the state of the engine and store the data. The first generation of federal emission monitoring devices (OBD I) was introduced in 1988. The Society of Automotive Engineers (SAE) developed an expanded set of standards, which was adopted by the Environmental Protection Agency (EPA) and the California Air Resources Board (CARB) as OBD II, and this is the system currently being used in US vehicles. Full compliance with OBD II monitoring standards is required in all states by January 1, 2001.

OBD II standards require that the parts of a vehicle's emission control system be guaranteed for 100,000 miles. A red "CHECK ENGINE" light on the instrument panel signals emissions that aren't up to snuff or failure of a component in the emission monitoring system. This warning light is technically known as the MIL (malfunction indicator lamp).

OBD II data are analyzed by plugging a hand-held computer (called a scanner) into the computer terminal on the vehicle, which is located under the dash near the steering column. A larger computer console then plugs into the hand-held scanner and the mechanic reads data from the screens of the scanner and the larger console. For example, the diagnostic system that Chrysler uses calls the large console the MDS (Mopar Diagnostic System) and the hand-held scanner the DRB III. The MDS is connected to a satellite dish on the roof of each dealership, and every two weeks Chrysler updates each dealer's diagnostic software by satellite.

Independent repair shops can purchase a scanner (the OTC 4000 is one example) using a different interchangeable chip for each brand of car. This unit can be used by itself or can plug into a

45

Figure 30. Mechanic Todd DeBerg checks OBD II data from a '96 Grand Cherokee.

larger console containing a personal computer for more complex diagnostic tasks.

These systems read the history of the vehicle's emissions over a period of time, gathering data from a specified number of "global good trips" the rig has made. A global good trip occurs when a vehicle runs hot enough long enough to input meaningful emission data into the OBD II system. It's possible for a car to fail a smog inspection just because its owner only uses it for weekly trips to the post office and grocery store. In a year or two it hasn't made enough global good trips to generate the necessary OBD II data to get through the smog station.

Data concerning other aspects of the engine's performance and the vehicle's other computer systems are also available in the OBD II computers, but the main thrust of the system is for emission control. The consumer can still add winches, accessory lights, and stereo equipment to the vehicle, but any attempt to alter the engine components or other parts of the drivetrain will cause the "CHECK ENGINE" MIL light to display on the panel, and the vehicle won't pass smog inspection until the condition is returned to specs.

OBD II is one of those good news/bad news things. The good news is that emission control requirements have led to the development of incredibly sophisticated engine-performance monitoring systems, resulting in much more reliable engines. The sequential fuel-injected engine in a modern 4x4 is considerably more economical, more powerful, and far less likely to leave you stranded in the backcountry than the engines of even a few years ago.

There are several pieces of bad news. The first is the difficulty of fixing a modern engine that leaves you high and dry away from a DRB III, MDS, and satellite dish. Another drawback is that the owner of a rig won't be able to modify it much. The Jeep Wrangler, for instance, now has OBD II. The Wrangler and its forebears, the CJ-5 and CJ-7, have been major favorites among 'wheelers for off-road modification. How can they modify their new Wranglers (or any other new rig) when tweaking it even a little causes the CHECK ENGINE light to glare at them and jeopardizes their emission certification?

Other OBD II fallout may include the eventual collapse of the numerous independent auto repair shops in this country if they can't afford the computerized equipment and software necessary to diagnose and repair the various OBD II vehicles out there. The survival of large segments of the aftermarket equipment industry is also in question. The Specialty Equipment Market Association (SEMA) addresses this problem in a pamphlet called *How Government Regulations Threaten Automotive Hobbies*, which you can obtain by calling 800-514-SEMA.

The final implication of OBD II is the privacy issue. A vehicle's OBD II computers contain a lot of data about *where* the owner drives. Paranoid? Maybe. But that doesn't mean it won't happen. After all, you can purchase automobile security devices that feed the police GPS data from your stolen car, helping them locate it.

There have been rumblings about an OBD III

standard.that includes a GPS device and radio transmitter, broadcasting information about the status of the vehicle's exhaust emissions as well as its position.

MODIFICATIONS

Essential modifications for off-road use, listed by my idea of priority, include a substantial roll cage (for an open vehicle), light truck tires, skid plates, front winch, heavy-duty alternator or dual batteries, rear hitch, tow hooks front and rear, lockers, nerf bars or running boards, front brush guard, and rear winch, portable electric winch, or portable hand winch (come-along).

Optional modifications or convenience items include a CB radio, GPS device, extra lights front and rear, suspension lifters, body lifters, oversize tires, differential gear modifications, under-the-hood welder, heavy-duty seats with five-point harnesses, under-the-hood shower, and front tow hitch.

Essential Modifications

Roll cage. An open vehicle like a Jeep CJ-5, CJ-7, or Wrangler needs a heavy roll bar or roll cage (Figure 31) attached solidly to the frame. Even if you are driving an enclosed rig with a metal top, attaching a roll bar to the frame behind the driver's seat will keep you safer in case of a rollover, as the roof of the rig may not hold up under the shearing forces generated as a vehicle rolls over. It may not be realistic to expect most sport-ute owners to put a big piece of ugly black pipe inside their expensive rigs, but if you're going to be climbing a lot of hills, you'd better do it anyway.

Tires. A huge variety of tires are available, and each 'wheeler has his or her own favorite. The ones that came stock on a rig might or might not be fine.

The basic requirement is that they be light truck (LT) tires. Some 4x4s come with passenger car tires. These aren't as tough as LT tires and are more prone to flats and sidewall damage out in the rocks. Passenger car tires carry the P designation, such as "P195" or "P205." Light truck tires have an LT before the number.

You can buy different specialty tires for mud, snow, high performance, and so forth. Traveling across the backcountry means encountering a lot of different types of terrain—hills, dirt, rocks, mud, creeks, gravel roads, sand—so "all-terrain" tires are probably the best choice for an all-around tire.

The standard-size tires are radials. The larger ones may not be, but they're still plenty tough with

Figure 31. An open vehicle needs a roll cage. Ideally, supports should also be placed on each side of the windshield, extending from the cage down to the frame.

multiple plies. When traveling on snowy or icy highways, consider siping all-terrain tires or buy dedicated snow tires, with or without studs. (More about siping and studs when we talk about driving on snow and ice.) For traveling mainly in the swamps, buy mud tires. The Interco Company makes a very impressive one called the Super Swamper Bogger. For traveling in generally rough country containing a variety of challenges—mud, snow, rocky trails, and gravelly hills—think about the rugged Baja Belted Sidebiters made by Mickey Thompson Tires. Both the Super Swampers and Sidebiters are big tires with large ridges on the treads, called lugs, and a lot of empty space between the lugs to throw out mud as the wheels turn. To get the taller sizes of these tires to fit, you have to use special brackets to raise your rig above the springs. This process, called lifting, creates more room in the wheel wells. These tires are great in rough country but aren't as highway friendly, noise-wise or ride-wise, as all-terrain tires.

Some avid 'wheelers always put tubes in their tires, feeling they reinforce the tubeless tires and make them less susceptible to damage. However, tubes complicate the process of repairing punctures with the sealing kits available now for tubeless tires. My advice is to use LT tubeless tires without tubes, but carry tubes along in case you need to reinforce a particularly extensive gash to get back home.

If a sidewall gash can't be plugged with a bunch of sealer strips, take the tire off the rim and sew up the gash with heavy fishing line. Then reinforce the cut from inside the tire by gluing a boot

47

Figure 32. Left, a puncture is repaired without taking the tire off the rig using the Safety Seal professional tire repair kit with self-vulcanizing repair strips.

Figure 33. Below left, skid plates bolted to the undersurface of your rig keep vital parts—such as the steering mechanism, the front differential, the T-case, and the transmission—from being ripped up by rocks. On this '94 K-Blazer with tires 30 inches high, ground clearance under the front differential and skid plate is 9.75 inches (A), under the A-arms, 9.5 inches (B), and under the frame, 11.1 inches (C).

Figure 34. Below, ground clearance under the rear differential (A) and shock mounts (B) is 8.75 inches.

over it and putting a tube inside the tire. That should at least get you back to camp or maybe even home if you drive slowly.

Plug small holes with Safety Seal's self-vulcanizing tire repair strips. The professional-level kit they sell is the best on the market (Figures 32). (See "Tires" in the resource list in Appendix C for ordering information.)

Skid plates. Skid plates protect the underbelly of your rig. Install steel plates on the undersurface of the vehicle to protect the steering mechanism, transfer case and transmission, differentials, fuel tank, and other vital parts. Be sure they're bolted on, not welded, so they can be removed easily for maintenance, but be sure they aren't bolted to both the frame and parts of your drivetrain. Become familiar with the location of your skid plates so you know what's protected and what isn't, and become familiar with the ground clearance at various points under your rig (Figures 33, 34).

The engine and transmission are attached to the frame with hard rubber mounts to allow for some give between the drivetrain and the frame as you bounce along the road or trail. A skid plate bolted to the T-case and to the frame, for instance, will cause severe strain between the transmission and the T-case. The connection between the two will break down and leak fluid. Bolt the skid plates to the frame under the components they're protecting, but not to the components themselves . . . with one exception.

Using a skid plate to protect a differential, attach it to an axle truss, a set of steel bars bolted directly to the axle housing. A truss protects the axle housing from bending with the stress of off-road jolts, and the skid plate keeps the differential intact.

Front winch. There's nothing like a winch to pull you out of a stuck situation. It should be one of the first add-ons you buy. Which winch? Different authorities have various opinions. Colorado's Bill

Figure 35. An open 12,000-pound Warn winch.

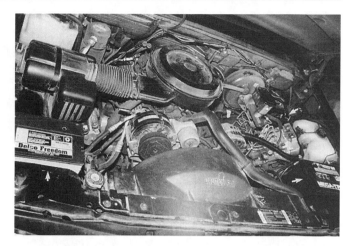

Figure 36. Heavy-duty winching requires dual batteries or a heavy-duty alternator or both. The arrows point to the dual batteries and the isolator. The second battery is dedicated to winching. It could also be used to power other accessories, such as driving lights or stereo equipment.

Burke of 4-Wheeling America, one of the chief gurus of off-highway driving, favors Superwinch. Mark Smith, the master of Jeep Jamboreeing, puts his faith in Ramsey. Mile Marker of Pompano Beach, Florida, makes a two-speed hydraulic winch that runs off the power steering pump. AM General installs a 12,000 pound Warn winch as a factory option on the Hummer, and Warn Industries sponsors an international 4-wheeling winching odyssey across some of the roughest country in the world. If your winch won't pull your rig almost straight up, don't bother to enter.

No matter which one you buy, make sure it fits your rig. Does it need a heavier bumper to hold it? If so, include that in your budget. How easy is it to get service? Does your local dealer have parts? If it breaks on the trail, will you or your buddies have spare parts?

Whatever winch you purchase, it's better to buy too much power rather than not enough. I put a 12,000-pound Warn winch on my full-size Chevy Blazer (Figure 35). Be sure the one you get pulls at least one and a half times the weight of your totally loaded rig (one and a half times the GVWR).

Heavy-duty alternator or dual batteries. Whatever winch you're using, it eats more amps than a stock alternator supplies. The original alternator that comes with a rig probably puts out about 70 to 105 amps. A winch can draw as much as 600 amps during winching. Warn says its 12,000-pound winch draws 400 amps at full 12,000-pound capacity and 302 amps with an 8,000-pound load. Its 9,000-pound model draws 400 at full capacity, its 8,000 pounder draws 423, and the 5,000-pound one draws 280 amps.

A heavy-duty alternator keeps up better with the winch. Buy one and keep the original as a spare. The Premier or Link-Arc under-the-hood welding systems come with an alternator that puts out 160 amps, or you can opt for either of their superheavy-duty 190 amp alternators.

Be safer still by installing a second battery under the hood along with a heavy-duty alternator. There are various ways to hook up the second battery—one choice uses an isolator, another uses a switch to change from one battery to the other. Still another uses a 200-amp continuous-duty relay. Wrangler Power Products sells a dual battery installation kit that uses a combination of switching and isolation. So does Custom Electrical Specialists (CES) with its Good Samaritan Dual Battery System.

I decided on dual batteries and an isolator for my rig (Figure 36). The main battery supplies juice to run the vehicle; the second battery supplies juice for winching. The isolator allows the alternator to charge both batteries but prevents the electrical system of the vehicle from drawing down the second battery. Only the winch can draw from the second battery. In my rig, the stereo and accessory backup lights draw from the main battery, but it makes sense to wire a bunch of accessory driving lights and a heavy-duty stereo system to the secondary battery to make sure the main battery can provide enough juice to get home.

Going with a switch either on the dash or under the hood lets you alternate back and forth between the batteries. For instance, you might draw from one battery one week and from the other battery the next week. With this arrangement, there's always a fully charged battery in reserve. If heavy winching depletes one of the batteries, just switch to the other one. The disadvantage of this system is that you have to remember to switch back and forth between the batteries every week or so.

Those who favor the continuous-relay option of hooking up the two batteries point out that the alternator runs cooler with this setup because both batteries supply cranking power to start the engine and both supply power for the accessories. The disadvantage is that the winch may draw down both batteries before you realize it, and you're stuck with two dead batteries and no way to get home.

Tough batteries are a must. Batteries are rated in CCAs (cold cranking amps), the number of amps a battery will put out for 30 seconds at 0° Fahrenheit. Some of the winch companies recommend a battery with a rating of at least 500 CCAs, but that's minimal. It's better to get one rated at 800 CCAs at least. The Optima battery provides this and has the additional advantage of being completely sealed and not containing liquid sulfuric acid, which can spill in a rollover. An Optima even mounts upside down!

When you install a second battery dedicated to winching, consider making it a deep cycle battery. Winching is very hard on batteries because it tends to draw them down to complete discharge. A standard high output "starter" battery will only withstand about 50 complete discharges, then it will be history and can't be recharged again. A "deep-cycle" battery, on the other hand, will withstand about 350 complete discharges. You'll stand a better chance of having your winching battery last for awhile if you use a deep-cycle battery for that purpose.

If you use a starter battery for your main battery and a deep-cycle battery for your secondary winching battery, it's important to keep them completely separated by using an isolator. That's to protect the main battery from getting trashed by discharging completely if your deep-cycle battery gets drawn down completely.

Generally speaking, you can't just use two deep-cycle batteries for your dual system because most don't have high enough output to start your engine reliably, especially in cold weather. But

Figure 37. The frame-mounted hitch comes in handy for towing or for mounting racks for carrying stuff.

there's an exception. The Optima company now makes a deep-cycle battery with a CCA rating of 750. This compares favorably with the CCA rating of their starter battery, which is 800, and makes their deep-cycle model entirely suitable to use as either a main battery, a secondary winching battery, or both. The deep-cycle model costs about 25 percent more than the standard model.

If you use two deep-cycle Optima batteries for your dual system, you wouldn't have to use an isolator. You could use some other power management system. If you used a standard Optima as your main battery and a deep-cycle Optima as your secondary battery, you *would* have to isolate them with an isolator or you'd run the risk of destroying your main standard battery with too many complete discharges.

Rear hitch and trailers. If your 4by came with a

tow package, you've already got a rear hitch, hopefully attached to the frame. Shy away from the ones attached to the bumper unless you want to leave your bumper bouncing around on the ground when towing a stuck vehicle out of the mud. If you don't have a rear hitch, put one on, securely attached to the frame. You need a hitch to pull a trailer, camper, or boat, or in case you need to attach a tow strap to your vehicle to pull someone out of a soft spot. A rear hitch is also handy for carrying other stuff (Figure 37).

Install as heavy a tow hitch as you can attach to the frame of your rig. It must be at least as heavy as the towing capacity of your rig. For instance, a Wrangler has a towing capacity of 2,000 pounds, so a Class I tow hitch is probably adequate, but to be on the safe side, install a Class II (3,500-pound capacity) hitch if you can. For midsize and full-size sport-utes, install a Class III hitch (5,000 pounds) if you can. However, it's best to limit off-road trailering to a weight of 2,000 pounds, even though your rig can handle more on the highway.

Before deciding how heavy a trailer your rig can tow, you need to know the the gross combination weight rating (GCWR) for your vehicle. This is the total weight of your loaded rig together with the loaded trailer. The GCWR for a particular rig is roughly the basic curb weight (no cargo) plus its towing capacity.

For example, a four-door Ford Explorer with a 4.0L V6 engine has a curb weight of 4,189 pounds and a maximum towing capacity of 5,100 pounds with differentials geared for power at 3.73:1. Ford lists 9,500 pounds as the GCWR for this particular model of Explorer.

The manufacturer's GCWR assumes the rig has mandatory options only, no cargo, and a driver weighing 150 pounds. In the example of the Explorer, curb weight (4,189) plus towing capacity (5,100) plus driver (150) equals 9,439 pounds, which is close to Ford's GCWR for this vehicle (9,500).

What does this mean? It means if you're planning to tow a trailer weighing the maximum towing capacity of your rig, you can't carry any passengers or any cargo. Every pound over this you carry in the 4x4 decreases the weight you can tow. You can increase the GCWR and the towing capacity by buying a vehicle with a more powerful engine.

Right now, the Ford 5.0L V8 engine is available in the 2WD and AWD Explorer, and it increases the GCWR from 9,500 pounds (for the V6 engine) to 11,000 pounds and the maximum towing

capacity from 5,300 to 6,700 pounds. This bottom line tells us that if you're planning to tow a heavy trailer, buy the most powerful engine available for your particular rig.

Trailers are divided into four weight classes: light-duty Class I, maximum loaded trailer weight 2,000 pounds; medium-duty Class II, loaded weight 2,001 to 3,500 pounds; heavy-duty Class III, loaded weight 3,501 to 5,000 pounds; and extra heavy-duty Class IV, loaded weight 5,001 to 10,000 pounds. Three-quarter and one-ton pickups equipped with a fifth wheel (a heavy-duty bed-mounted hitch) can haul up to 12,500 pounds. Different states have varying licensing requirements. Idaho, for instance, requires a license and title for all trailers 2,000 pounds and over, but all trailers 1,500 pounds and over require brakes that set automatically if the trailer becomes accidentally disconnected from the towing vehicle. Check with your local authorities before buying a trailer so you know what you're getting into.

Tow hooks front and rear. In addition to a hitch, you need tow hooks front and rear attached to the frame. They're helpful for double-lining a winch cable for maximum pull. (See Chapter 10 on winching for details on single-lining, double-lining, and triple-lining.) Hooks provide attachment points for the tow strap when pulling out a rig that's stuck, and they're also useful for attaching the strap to your vehicle in case you're the one who needs to be pulled out.

Lockers. We talked about differential locking devices in Chapter 3. To send maximum power to your wheels, you need to prevent the unloaded wheel from spinning, and the way to do this is to lock the open differential. Various locking devices exist. Some lock the differential absolutely and guarantee that the wheel with traction gets 100 percent of the power. These "lockers" are either manual or automatic.

Other devices limit the slip of a wheel without traction but don't provide full power to the wheel with traction. A limited-slip differential, or posi, falls into this category. So does Land Rover's Electronic Traction Control, or ETC.

Nerf bars or running boards. Nerf bars are long bars bolted to the bottom of the sides of the rig below the doors to protect the rocker panels. They also give you something to step onto when getting in and out of a rig. You can buy running boards instead, which offer a wider step and still protect the rocker panels. It's important that the nerf bars or running boards don't project below the level of the frame to avoid losing ground clearance.

51

Opponents of nerf bars feel they stiffen the frame and decrease a vehicle's maneuverability in the rocks. The more a vehicle can flex as it travels over rough ground, the better the grip the tires can maintain on the ground.

Front brush guard. A heavy frame bolted to the rig in front of the grille protects the grille from damage and the radiator from penetration if you end up headfirst against a rocky projection or tree limb. The brush guard needs to be heavily constructed and bolted to the frame. Some are lightweight and flimsy, designed for show rather than service. Avoid these. The brush guard should have extensions that project to each side to protect the headlights as well.

Rear winch, portable electric winch, or portable hand winch (come-along). Consider buying a rear winch. It's not always possible to winch yourself out in a forward direction when stuck. Sometimes you've got to go back the way you came. Since it's difficult to mount both a rear hitch and a permanent winch on the back of your rig, a reasonable compromise is to buy a winch that attaches to the rear hitch. A permanent electrical plug is installed beside the hitch. Just secure the winch to the hitch and plug it in. The disadvantage of a portable electric winch is its weight, which limits the size you can safely lift and attach to the rear hitch.

A portable hand winch, called a come-along, can be an effective spare. Use it when you need to be pulled out from the back. Using it double-lined, you can get 2,000 to 4,000 pounds of pull, depending on the size of the winch. (See Chapter 10 for more information on using a come-along.)

Optional Modifications and Convenience

CB radio. When you are wrecked, broken down, or hopelessly stuck, a Citizen's Band radio can be used to summon help and prevent disaster. If someone in your party is injured, being able to call for help may save his or her life. If you are traveling with another vehicle or in a convoy with a bunch of 4x4s, it's essential that the rigs be able to communicate with one another. ("Does anyone have some Dramamine?")

When driving on one-lane roads used by logging trucks, a CB is essential. A loaded truck heading downhill definitely has the right of way. Before using a logging road, find out from the locals what CB channel the truckers use. Sometimes the channel is posted informally on hand-painted signs at the entrance of the road. Tune in that channel and communicate as you drive. Notice the mileage markers, which on logging roads are usually hand-

painted on posts at the side of the road. At each marker, pick up your mike and announce, for instance, "Ford Explorer going up mile five." If you're at mile five and your CB suddenly says, "Downhill, loaded, mile eight," pull off the road at the first available turnout and wait 'til the loaded rig passes. When you're in a sport-ute or pickup, yield to all big trucks whether they're headed downhill or uphill, loaded or not.

At the current stage of radio communication technology, CB radio is the most practical way to accomplish these things, even though it has some drawbacks. It's limited in range. In flat, open territory you may be able to exchange chatter over five miles or so, but on hilly, winding trails, you may be lucky to reach out over 200 yards. Sometimes your radio waves skip around, bouncing off the sky, and you find yourself gabbing with someone in Borneo, Ireland, or Afghanistan. But don't count on being able to do this. CB transmission is basically line of sight.

CB clarity is often less than ideal, though single sideband (SSB) transmission on the more expensive units helps this problem a lot, once you learn the intricacies of tuning SSB. In spite of a CB radio's limitations, it's practical because it's relatively inexpensive, readily available, doesn't require an FCC license, and extremely simple to use. A good basic unit and antenna can be installed for less than $200. This is a wise investment for such a useful and potentially life-saving instrument.

Have someone who knows what they're doing install a full-size CB unit in your rig, matching the antenna and coaxial cable for standing wave ratio (SWR). If the SWR isn't right, transmission suffers severely, and the worst case can be severe damage to the radio (the transceiver). I have had poor luck trying to use portable hand-held units inside a rig, even powered from the cigarette lighter and attached to an outside magnet-mounted or window-mounted antenna.

GPS device. The Global Positioning System is the worldwide navigational system established by the United States and declared operational early in 1994. It cost approximately $10 billion and uses 24 satellites to tell exactly (within 300 feet) where you are on earth. The version of GPS available to the military is even more accurate. All that's needed is a battery-powered hand-held unit to receive the satellites' messages. Right now, GPS start under $100.

A GPS device establishes your position on a map. It tells you the exact location of your base camp. When; you go wandering in the forest around the camp, it always leads you back to family and friends.

GPS pinpoints search-and-rescue operations. There are computerized topographic map programs that let you input a GPS track you've traveled directly into your laptop computer. GPS is rapidly becoming an indispensable navigational tool. To use a GPS unit inside a vehicle, use an accessory antenna that attaches to the windshield with suction cups.

Extra lights. When off-road at night, it's helpful to have extra lights, especially directed to the side to pick up hazards not illuminated by the headlights. Bright lights directed rearward are also helpful, since the usual stock backup lights on 4bys and cars are too weak to do much off-road. Extra lights draw a lot of amps and can run your battery down fast if you're not careful.

Suspension lifters/body lifters. Lifting refers to elevating a vehicle higher above the ground. Some people do this for style, and there are a lot of chrome-covered superlifted show trucks that win prizes at the shows but won't ever taste the dust of a real trail. They're called "trailer queens" because they ride from show to show on flatbed trailers, rarely moving under their own power. Let's consider lifting for function, not show.

Lifting gives the advantage of allowing you to clear rough ground and rocks better than a stock vehicle. A rig gets on and off steep hills easier when it's lifted. The trade-off for better ground clearance is stability. A lifted vehicle is less stable, especially at highway speeds, and is more likely to end up shiny side down or door down than is an unlifted stock rig.

There are basically two types of lifting—suspension lifting and body lifting. Often a combination of the two is used. The goal is to get the drivetrain and the frame of the rig higher above the ground so they can clear rocks and logs easier and can travel over the top of a steep rise with adequate clearance. The basic way to get a rig higher is to put on bigger tires. With 29-inch tires on your vehicle and a current ground clearance of 8 inches, installing 33-inch tires gains additional clearance of half the difference between the old and new tire heights. The new tires are 4 inches larger in diameter than the old ones, so you have 2 new inches below the axle and your rig is now 10 inches above the ground.

However, 33-inch tires may not fit. They may bump the top of the wheel wells, and the front ones may scrape when turning the wheels. So the suspension has to be changed to elevate the frame higher above the axles. This gives your frame more clearance from the ground and may lift the body enough so the taller tires fit. If not, then the body needs to be blocked up from the frame to give your tires more clearance in the wheel wells.

There are advantages to using a combination of suspension lifts and body lifts. For instance, driving a full-size stock Chevy Blazer, your stock tires are probably about 30 inches in diameter. You can fit this rig with 36-inch tires using a 7-inch suspension lift. You'll have to make some minor modifications to the fenders, but 36-inch tires basically fit under 7 inches of lift.

However, 7 inches is a lot of lift, and your rig won't be very stable because the entire body and frame, including the engine, transmission, and T-case, are all riding up in the stratosphere. Four inches of suspension lift could be used along with 3 inches of body lift. This combination is more stable because it leaves the heavy drivetrain components lower to the ground and gives an overall lower center of gravity.

Unless you're dedicating your rig to off-roading, I'd advise against lifting, as you create other problems by doing so. The more you lift, the more strain you put on the driveshaft and universal joints. Lifting can also be a quick way to void the factory warranty on your rig's drivetrain. Check with your car dealer or your extended-warranty insurance company before you lift.

Putting on larger tires and changing the differential gear ratios also alters your speedometer—it will read slower than you're really going. This problem has broader implications than just feeling that icy hand in your stomach when you notice those flashing red lights in your rearview mirror. Chevy products, for example, use what's called a Vehicle Speed Sensor Buffer (VSSB) to feed computerized vehicle velocity information to the engine and powertrain control modules as well as to the antilock brake system. For the rig to perform optimally, it needs accurate speed information, so when changing the tires and/or gear ratios, you've got to reprogram or replace the VSSB. The bottom line is, when lifting, be sure to work with an experienced off-road mechanic who can help with all the necessary modifications.

Oversize tires. Big tires give better ground clearance. You might get away with an inch or two larger size without lifting, but usually you've got to lift to accommodate larger tires.

Differential gear modifications. Putting on larger tires decreases the power the drivetrain delivers to the ground, because the engine, T-case, transmission, and differentials have to work harder to turn the larger tire. To make up for this loss of power, the gear ratio of the differentials may need to be increased.

A stock transmission has been designed to deliver power to the wheels in a way that keeps the engine operating in its most efficient range of RPMs (revolutions per minute). Changing to a more powerful gear ratio in the differential increases the rate at which the engine must turn to move the rig at a particular speed. This increase in RPMs increases wear on the engine and takes the engine out of its most efficient power range.

If increasing the tire size or the power of your differential, you need to consider other modifications. For instance, installing an under/overdrive unit gives your transmission a greater range of gears. You can also modify the torque converter, which sits between the engine and the transmission. It acts like a hydraulic clutch to connect the power of the engine to the automatic transmission, except that it also increases the power delivered by the engine to the rest of the drivetrain.

These are major modifications that require careful consideration of the entire project before lifting your rig to the sky so you can install a set of 39-inch Super Swamper Boggers. Work with a mechanic who can help you do the gear/power calculations and determine just how much you have to do to deliver adequate power to your oversize tires. The trick is to reach a compromise between highway performance (with satisfactory gas mileage and engine wear) and off-road power to climb big rocks and steep hills. If you do decide to lift your vehicle, install big tires, and increase the power of the differential, consider adding the under/overdrive unit to help your drivetrain gear back down to highway conditions.

Under-the-hood welder. There are several arc welders available that operate with DC power and can be installed under the hood of a 4by. Some come with a heavy-duty alternator, which supplies power not only for the welder but for the winch, extra lights, and any other electrical accessories you've added on. A welding machine can certainly save the day when a crucial part breaks on the trail, provided you know how to weld. However, there are limits to the number of gadgets you can install under your hood. By the time you add dual batteries, ARB air compressor, alarm system, under-the-hood welder, and under-the-hood hot water shower with its heat exchanger and pump, you may find that you no longer have room for the engine!

Heavy-duty seats with five-point harnesses. The stock seats and seat belt/shoulder harness setups aren't very secure. In an off-center or lateral impact, it's very easy to be catapulted out from under the shoulder harness and even the seat belt. In a slow roll, a slack seat belt may not engage in time to protect you. With serious off-roading, consider installing heavy-duty seats with five-point aircraft-type safety harnesses.

Under-the-hood hot water shower. This is a nice convenience, if you've got room for it. It provides hot water for showers anywhere you can find a lake or stream. You can even draw the water for your shower from a 5-gallon container. It also gives you a way of pumping water from a stream into large containers for purification and storage.

Front tow hitch. If you will be needing to maneuver a trailer and boat down rough surfaces to the water's edge, consider adding a front trailer hitch to your rig. Pushing a boat trailer to the water is a lot easier when you can see what you're doing. Tow the boat trailer behind you as far as convenient, turn the rig and trailer around, then unhitch and rehitch the front of your rig to the trailer. Consider mounting the front hitch offset toward the right side of your rig so you can see beyond the trailer as you push it in front of you. The rule of turning the bottom of your steering wheel in the direction you want the trailer to go still works.

chapter eight

ROCKS AND RAVINES

BASIC CRAWLING

Rocky trails strewn with boulders mostly bigger than your ground clearance offer the greatest challenges and elicit the loudest expletives as you watch your rocker panels and doors gradually change shape and the rocks acquire the colors that used to be on your rig.

Last year, while hanging around a 4WD shop watching them put an ARB locker in my rear diff, we got to talking about backcountry travel. Paul, the mechanic I knew the best, told us about one of his trips from a couple of years ago.

It was early in September, and one of his buddies, a guy named Bert McJarvis, drew a moose tag in the state hunting lottery. This gave him a once-in-a-lifetime chance to bag a moose and was an occasion of great celebration among his friends.

To help make the most of his opportunity, Paul organized a hunting party to travel with him to First Light Butte, known as the home of several sizable moose herds. The rifle season for moose started on September 1, but so did bow season for deer and elk. So Bert took the new Mark II 7mm Magnum rifle he bought the spring before at a gun show in Spokane and put it on the rack in his F-250 pickup, right under the Browning semiauto .30-06 that always rode there. The rest of the group brought along their bows. Paul had a new Power Mag compound bow he was aching to unlimber.

The party ended up with about 15 guys, and the Thursday after Labor Day they loaded into seven 4x4

pickups and sport-utes, from Bert's F-250 lifted over 35-inch tires to a totally stock '89 Montero. They headed out to First Light Butte. These men had grown up with 4-wheeling, and the trip itself started off as no great challenge.

Once through Mancotta, they turned north off the highway, driving on the narrow gravel road 75 miles into the national forest. They wound along the forested banks of the Crystal River, its spring torrents tamed by the summer's heat. Just after crossing the bridge over Lost Fools Creek, and just before the gravel turned due east, they left the semi-improved road, turning left onto trail 4708B, finishing off the last 22 miles to the campsite at First Light. The Forest Service sign at the trailhead confirmed the legality of pickups and SUVs this time of year.

4708B was basically two shallow ruts in the ground, sprinkled liberally with potholes and piled with grapefruit-sized rocks, dipping frequently into muddy gullies that filled in the spring with impassable rushing water from the melting snow. The convoy stopped once to winch away a fallen tree, blocking the trail since the last Forest Service maintenance crew passed through. No big deal. The most difficult section was a half-mile stretch winding steeply uphill through a narrow rocky draw. The maintenance crew had cleared the trail of large boulders, and all the rigs made it up easily, some in 4WD Lo.

Once past the draw, the trail opened up and gradually lost altitude again, moving through broad green meadows alternating with dense forest. The land became wetter, and they passed by several large ponds filled with marsh grass. Great moose country! They entered the forest again and the shadow of the valley floor, shielded from the late afternoon sun by the mountains to the west. They drove to the base of First Light Butte, sternly rising 2,000 feet above them. In the morning the top of its face announces the rising sun with a pinkish glow. They made camp in a clearing next to a stream winding along its base.

They set out at dawn the next day, and by noon Bert had his moose. He was hoping for one with trophy-sized paddles but was afraid the mob of hunters would scare the animals off. If he didn't cash in on his moose tag this season, it would be another three years before he could enter the lottery again, with only a slim chance that he would draw a second tag. So he shot the first bull he saw, dropping it cleanly. It was on the small side but would still provide enough meat to fill his freezer and then some.

The bow hunters had good luck, dropping three elk and several deer. Paul got one of the elk with a clean 60-yard shot, his new bow living up to his expectations. They called it quits the middle of the second afternoon, under cloudy skies and cold drizzling rain. By the time they were cooking their evening meal, it was raining steadily and the wind had picked up. Wet gusts whipped across their tents, overturned their camp chairs, and scattered any belongings not secured inside their tents and rigs. They made the rounds of the tents and drove extra stakes into the ground. By the time they turned in it was pouring, and by midnight torrents of water crashed against their tents. The wind howled through the trees and whistled along the face of the butte.

By two in the morning the storm faded, and by dawn the clouds broke up, the sunlight filtering through, illuminating the face of the butte far above. They cooked and ate breakfast, packed their rigs with gear and fresh game, and started home.

It didn't take long to notice a severe change in the trail from three days before. The section running beside the series of ponds had several rushing streams flowing across it, and they forded these. The water was hub deep, but they all made it through except for one rig that stalled halfway across one particularly swift stream. They weren't sure if the engine was hydrolocked or not, so they winched it out, pulling the plugs to check for water in the cylinders. It was okay. The fan had sprayed water all over the engine compartment and drenched everything. The engine started again once they dried out the wiring, spraying it with Formula 12/34.

Some of the trail was a muddy mire, and the rigs, loaded with the game, struggled to make it. Most got through, but Bert's pickup, loaded with the moose, two elk, and one deer, bogged down and sunk to the hubs. One of the drivers already through turned around, chocked his

wheels, and double-lined his winch to one of Bert's front tow hooks. Bert double-lined his own winch to a tree and back to the other front hook. They dug down to the bottom of all four wheels to break the suction of the mud. With the two winches working, they eased his loaded rig through the 100-foot stretch of sticky stuff. Hitting the dry trail, they aired back up and continued on, gaining altitude as they climbed toward the ridge.

They got the bad news when they crested the ridge and looked down the steep, rocky draw they had come up three days before. The storm had washed out the stone-studded sides of the draw, unleashing an avalanche of rocks and boulders onto the trail and covering its length with rough, uneven piles of stone. The steepness of the trail multiplied the problems. They had to leave plenty of distance between each rig in case one of them lost control and rolled down the slope into the rig in front of it.

They inched their way over the rocks. Some of the lightly loaded rigs aired down to give their tires a better grip on the rocks, but the ones loaded with the game couldn't gain that advantage. Airing down would have decreased the load capacity of the tires too much. Unable to drive over the larger boulders, they moved most of them to the side of the trail with heavy pry bars they packed in their vehicles. They winched several of the largest ones out of the way, throwing chains around them and attaching the winch cable hooks to D-shackles attached to the chains. Bert got his lifted pickup over the 10 and 12 inchers, though he had trouble doing it because of his load. Most of the other rigs would have high-centered on these, so they ramped themselves over by putting smaller rocks on each side of the larger ones.

The main problem was the downhill slope. With gravity pushing the weight of the heavily loaded vehicles onto the front wheels, it was almost impossible to control the rigs and ease them gently down off the rocks on the far side. Time after time the rigs came crashing down off the rocks onto bruised front tires and suspension, even with drivers using their best left-foot braking techniques. Bruce Tunney had a lifted CJ-5, and he did the best of anyone by just using his starter motor to ease him over the larger ones in 4-wheel Lo. He idled over the rest, keeping his foot off the clutch, using maximum engine compression to ease him down the far side.

Besides producing a number of cosmetic insults to the rocker panels, fenders, and doors, the rocks took their toll mechanically. Ed Hadlock and Breck Matson in the Montero ripped a tire with a 3-inch gash in the sidewall. They put the spare on, and 20 yards farther along it happened again, ripping the sidewall of the spare. They finished the run to the bottom on that tire, shredding it completely. Then they repaired the first tire they'd ripped by popping the bead, sewing up the rip with heavy fishing line, reinforcing it with a boot, and throwing an inner tube inside. They put the tire back on the wheel and reinflated it. It held well enough to get them back home. If the rip had been smaller, they would have tried to repair it with several tire plugs in a row, which probably would have worked okay.

Austin Donnolley broke a front coil spring when a front wheel rolled hard off a rock. They removed the damaged spring and replaced it with a block of wood cut from a log. That got Aus' rig back in service, but every little bump on the trail from then on was a jolting, jarring reminder of his mistake. Misjudgments of clearance resulted in a hole in the fuel tank of one rig and a cracked rear differential in another. They plugged these with epoxy putty.

The rigs blew a couple of radiator hoses. They handled one of these leaks just by drying off the hose and wrapping it with duct tape, reinforced with malleable wire. The second hose had a larger split that had to be sewn with fishing line before the duct tape wrapping. They left the radiator caps loose so the normal pressure of the cooling system wouldn't blow the repairs out.

Soyt Martin lost control momentarily on the steep slope and fishtailed off the trail, ending up against a fallen tree with an inch-thick tree limb jammed through his radiator. They trimmed the fins away from the torn tubes in the core and rolled up the broken tubes, pinching them shut.

(No brake lines were torn on this trip, but that happened to a friend of mine once, without any spare lines or brake fluid. Plugging the broken line with a stick and replacing the lost fluid with water worked long enough to get him back to camp. It's amazing what you can get away with when you have to.)

It's amazing that no one broke any axles or U-joints, considering the torque the wheels of the loaded rigs were delivering to the rocks. Knocking off one shock mount gave a rougher ride home but wasn't a crucial problem.

Limping back, the battered convoy arrived in town well after dark. By the time they replaced the torn tires, repaired the broken springs, and did the body work needed to make the rigs presentable again, they had loaded their freezers with some of the most expensive venison to come out of the forest in several years.

USE LT TIRES

Make sure you're using light truck ("LT") tires, not passenger ("P") tires. (Review Chapter 7 for more details on tire choice.) If you will be crawling over rocks regularly, consider using one of the larger multiple-ply bias-belted nonradial tires. These have tougher sidewalls than radials. For instance, Mickey Thompson Baja Belted Sidebiters have two polyester plies running across the tire bead to bead, then two circumferential fiberglass plies running circumferentially around the tire, followed by two more bead-to-bead polyester plies. The treads run up on the sidewall, so in tight places you can climb up a rock with the side of the tire. Interco's Super Swamper Bogger is another large, tough, multiple-ply tire.

GO SLOW!

That's the bottom-line basic rule of rock crawling. And I mean like 3 miles an hour or less. That's why they call it rock *crawling*. The faster a rig goes, the more beating the tires take, especially the sidewalls, which are essentially unrepairable. A hole in the tread may be repairable with a plug or two or by removing the tire and booting it from the inside, using an inner tube for added strength. But a sidewall rip is usually the end of the tire, though the temporary measures we talked about in the last chapter may at least get you back to camp. With only one spare, a sidewall rip is an invitation to disaster.

Going slow also saves springs, shocks, axles, tie-rods, and U-bolts, none of which you want to break, especially if you haven't bothered to bring along spares. Sometimes fragged parts can be welded, assuming you have an under-the-hood welder and know how to use it.

The trick is to ease onto and off rocks gradually, staying in complete control the entire time (Figure 38). Approaching a rocky stretch of trail, get into 4WD Lo. Most rigs require at least a few feet of travel before 4WD Hi or Lo kicks in. Anticipate the need for low range and shift the T-case down before actually needing it.

With the transmission in lowest gear, look ahead and take in the pattern of the rocks, ledges, and gullies. Pick a line, meaning determine beforehand the best approach, route, and exit through the rocks. This gives you the best chance of reaching the other side of the rocks without high-centering, sliding sideways into a gully and rolling over, or getting stuck in a spot that's too narrow to pass through without ripping off the doors.

DON'T ROCK THE BOAT

Another reason to keep your speed down over any rough ground is to avoid rocking the rig from side to side. If you feel the vehicle getting set up in a series of side to side oscillations as you move from bump to bump, slow down immediately to break the cycle. Otherwise the oscillations can build up suddenly and actually tip the vehicle over, especially if you're driving a lifted rig or across the side of a slope.

Keep your speed down through tall grass, too. A variety of obstacles may be lurking under the ground cover, just waiting to smash whatever part of your rig they can get hold of—rocks, logs, pieces of old automobiles, discarded refrigerators. It's best to follow the rule of "walk it first if you can't see it from the driver's seat."

Another rough ground hint is to keep the side of your right foot firmly pressed against the transmission housing beside the accelerator. Otherwise, your foot may be bounced around erratically on the gas pedal just when you least want your speed or power to vary.

GET OFF THE CLUTCH

With a manual transmission, if you're stopped with a front wheel against a rock, start the engine with the clutch out and let the starter motor pull you over the rock. As your engine starts, it continues pulling you over the rocks at idle speed in 4WD Lo. Keep your foot entirely off the clutch. This gives much better control. It uses the power of 4WD Lo to pull you onto the rocks and the braking effect of engine compression to ease you down the other side. Use the brakes as necessary, but keep your foot off the clutch.

Some vehicles with manual transmissions won't start unless the clutch is pushed in. This is called clutch interlock. If you have such a rig, and if you're mechanically inclined, you could install a switch that allows you to disable the interlock when you're rock crawling. Then you can use the starter motor with the clutch out.

Starting out uphill or with a large rock in front of you, you may not be able to move with the starter alone. Use the clutch as necessary to keep the starter from burning out. With a relatively small engine or when heading uphill, you may need to use the clutch some, but riding it wears it out fast.

If you are not used to rock crawling, an automatic transmission is easier to use because there's less to think about. Use 4WD Lo in the T-case. Keep your right foot on the gas and your left on the brake. Use the gas lightly, easing your rig onto the rock. After climbing onto the top, gently apply left foot pressure to the brake and smoothly make the transition from climbing to dropping, easing the rig

Figure 38. Don't straddle rocks, logs, or stumps. Put your front wheel on the obstacle and slowly crawl over it. Make sure your frame can clear it once your front wheel is over it or you will end up high-centered. Use an observer whenever possible. (Photo by Irene Lamberti.)

down the other side, feathering the brake with your left foot. Avoid the wheels crashing down off the rock; that's asking for a broken spring or U-bolt.

Avoid wheel spin when climbing a boulder. Wheel spin leads to broken axles, driveshafts, U-joints, or differentials, because the drivetrain may not take the sudden shock when the tires abruptly grab again. This is especially true when multiplying the torque to a wheel using a locker or limited-slip differential.

How to Break an Axle in a Hummer

In a pre-1999 Hummer, you had to use brake/throttle modulation to get it moving if a wheel was spinning. After that, Hummers have electronic traction control, TT4. Brake/throttle modulation, which uses a combination of the brake and accelerator to stop wheel spin, is no longer necessary. If a wheel doesn't have traction, you prevent it from spinning by applying the brakes hard. Then, while still stepping on the brake, you press on the accelerator. Since the brakes are locking the axle that's tending to slip, torque is directed to the other axle that drives the wheel that does have traction. Then you gradually ease up on the brake, still applying the gas, and use the brake sort of like a clutch. The trick is to find the right balance between brake and gas to move the rig.

There's a catch. If you do this wrong, it's easy to break an axle. In fact the Hummer is designed so that the axles break more easily than the rest of the

Figure 39. The approach angle is the maximum angle a hill can have and still let the front end of the rig clear the ground when it starts up or comes down off the hill. The departure angle is the angle of clearance at the back of the rig. In this rig, the approach angle is 28°, the departure angle 38°.

Figure 40. The breakover angle is the angle your vehicle encounters at the top of a hill or rise. It determines how steep a hill you can go up and still get back to the level at the top without hanging up your frame, driveshaft, or muffler on the ground as you make the transition. Here it's 24°.

drivetrain, such as the differentials, the T-case, or the transmission. The axles are also designed to be easy to replace in the field. Hummer owners are well-advised to carry extra axles with them when they go off-road. When an axle in a Hummer breaks, that's good, because that means you didn't break something more expensive and more difficult to repair.

In case you ever want to break an axle in a Hummer, here's how to do it. First, you get a wheel spinning, maybe by getting the rig tipped up on some rocks so that one wheel's in the air. This wheel, with it's 37-inch tire and all the CTIS (central tire inflation system) fittings, weighs 165 pounds. Then you jam on the brakes. Hard. A Hummer has disc brakes, but they're inboard (that is, they're not on the wheel, like most brakes). Instead, a Hummer's brakes sit next to the differential and apply drag to the axle itself. So when you've got this 165 pound wheel spinning on the outer end of the axle, and then you suddenly apply a lot of braking to the inner end of the axle, something's gotta give, namely, the axle.

Obviously, the point is, when you get a wheel spinning in a Hummer, don't apply the brakes forcefully. Let up on the gas, let the wheel slow down, and then gently drag the brakes a little to bring the wheel to a stop. Once the wheel's stationary, then you can mash hard on the brake and go through the brake/throttle modulation thing to transfer torque to the wheels with traction.

CLIMB ROCKS—DON'T STRADDLE THEM

Don't try to get over a rock by straddling it. Put a front wheel on it and climb over it. Watch out for high centering when the wheel goes over it. Make sure there's enough clearance for the frame. If clearance is lacking, pick another line or build ramps out of rocks, logs, or dirt.

When traveling through rocks, look over your hood. Use any available observer (called a "spotter") outside your rig to guide you, but only one. Two or more will give you mixed messages. If you do not have an observer, get out of your rig frequently to judge the lay of the land yourself. One way or another, follow a precise line through the boulders.

PROTECT YOUR THUMBS AND WRISTS

Keep your thumbs out of the steering wheel. The front wheels twist when striking against bumps and dropping off rocks and logs, wrenching the steering wheel violently from side to side. Gripping the wheel hard with your thumbs anchored inside leads to sprains or even fractures of your thumbs and wrists.

AIRING DOWN—PROS AND CONS

Some 'wheelers prefer to air down when driving over rough trails, especially when traveling over rocks. My K-Blazer has a Tuff Country 4-inch

59

suspension lift and BF Goodrich Mud-Terrain T/A tires (LT285/75R16s) that are about 32 inches tall when aired up to street pressure of 35 pounds. I routinely air down to 15-18 pounds when driving off-road on rough trails or rocks. I've got an under-the-hood ARB compressor, which makes airing back up pretty easy.

Reducing tire pressure gives better traction over rocks and softens the ride, but sidewalls are more susceptible to damage and more vulnerable to penetration by jagged rocks when less rigid. The rims of the wheels are also prone to damage with the soft tires offering less protection. Coming down hard on a rock, the soft tire gives and the rim could bend or crack. The tire won't hold air with the bead not seating against the damaged rim. All in all, it's probably safer not to air down in the rocks until you've had considerable experience crawling. (See Chapter 12 for more about airing down for mud and sand.)

STEEL WHEELS

Cast-aluminum wheels look sharp, but if you damage one coming down hard off a rock, the rim may crack. The tire will no longer hold air. The rim on a steel wheel will bend, and you can pound it back out on the trail. When rock crawling, you're safer with steel wheels. Forged-aluminum wheels are even better because they're stronger and withstand damage well, though they're expensive. If damaged, they bend rather than crack and can be pounded out too. You can get forged aluminum wheels from the Mickey Thompson Company or from Alcoa Wheel Products International.

CROSSING GULLIES, RIDGES, AND LOGS

Cross gullies at an angle. The principle is to put only one wheel at a time into the gully so the other three can maintain traction and keep you moving. The angle at which you can take the gully depends on the approach and departure angles of your rig. The approach angle determines the clearance the rig has between the front bumper and the front wheels.

The departure angle determines the clearance at the rear of the rig (Figure 39).

The breakover angle is also important. It's the angle from the bottom of the frame between the front and back wheels to the bottoms of the wheels themselves (Figure 40). It determines how sharp a ridge your rig can go over. The smaller your breakover angle is, the more obliquely a gully must be entered.

Cross logs at an angle, too, putting one wheel at a time up and over the log. Avoid high centering. Build ramps on each side of the log if necessary.

Sometimes you have to travel along a narrow gully or ravine with steep sides. If you are unable to drive on one side or the other because of the steepness of the sides, you may be able to straddle the center and ride along the sides on the outside edges of the tires. You may even have to ride on the sidewalls for short distances.

DRIVING ON ROCK SLABS

When traveling on a smooth rock slab, examine the surface and decide how much traction it offers. Some slick slabs, like granite, can send you sliding and slamming sideways into a rock or tree at the side of the trail. Sandstone varies in the traction it offers, some types tending to crumble, others gripping your tires like sandpaper.

Large tree roots slanting across the trail also offer a slippery surface, especially when wet, throwing the rig sideways as you cross and slamming a rear panel into the tree if you let your guard down.

THE BOTTOM LINE

Pick your line carefully, move slowly, and keep your rig under complete control. Once committed, keep moving. Use an outside observer to guide you. Don't straddle a rock; drive directly onto it. Use the steady momentum of 4-wheel Lo to carry you up. Use engine compression with gentle left foot braking to ease you off.

chapter nine

HILLS

HOW TO STAY SHINY SIDE UP AND RUBBER SIDE DOWN

One of the basic rules of 4-wheeling says, "Know what's up front." This applies especially when traveling uphill or downhill. It's more than a little disconcerting to scratch and claw your way to the top of a steep hill, only to be teetering on the edge of a cliff on the other side. Avoid this by walking the hill first, even if it means a long, hot climb.

By the same token, when you are ready to head down a challenging slope, stop the engine, set the brake, chock your wheels, and walk the path you'll be taking to the bottom. You see things while walking that you won't notice sitting in your rig—things you don't want surprising you on the way down, like the deep gully across the trail that could spin you sideways, flipping you rubber side up, or the slippery granite slab in the middle of the hill, robbing you of what little traction you've got, or the sudden change in the fall line, pushing you into the canyon on your left, or the massive, unwinchable fallen tree blocking the trail just around the curve at the bottom of the hill.

A hill difficult to drive down is even more difficult to drive back up if the trail proves impassable. If it looks as if you will likely be unable to complete the downhill run, find out ahead of time and don't start down at all.

WHAT'S YOUR ANGLE?

Know your rig's angles of approach and departure as well as its breakover angle. (Review Chapter 8 about rocks and ravines for illustrations of these angles.) When a hill makes an angle with the flat ground greater than your approach angle, you will bury your nose in the hill as you start up (Figures 41, 42). If this happens, build a small ramp out of rocks or logs to make the approach more gradual. A somewhat more risky tactic is to approach the hill at a 45° angle. As soon as the uphill wheel bites the slope, swing the rig quickly around so it's heading straight up the hill. If you miss your timing on the turn uphill, though, a steep slope could throw your rig over onto its side.

The approach angle also determines if you can drive off a hill back onto level ground without getting buried in the flat dirt at the bottom of the hill (Figure 43). The greater these three angles, the more maneuverable the rig. Stuff hanging down below the bumpers, such as a hidden winch, accessory lights in the front, or a spare tire under the back overhang, decreases the approach and departure angles and makes the rig less maneuverable.

A Hummer with an approach angle of 72°, a departure angle of 37.5°, and a breakover angle of 29° can climb on and off steeper hills than a Land Cruiser with corresponding angles of 34°, 22°, and 23°. Putting a winch on the front of a Hummer drops the approach angle to 47°, since it hangs down a bit. You lose maneuverability but gain the capability of getting unstuck.

GOING UPHILL

If you have a manual transmission, pick the gear you use by judging the steepness of the hill and the traction it offers. The trick is to avoid wheel spin. Put the T-case in 4WD Lo. If the hill's not too steep and if the surface is loose or slippery, put the transmission in second or even third gear and see if that offers enough power to get you up the hill. If you start out in the lowest transmission gear, you may overpower the wheels and spin them. Once they start spinning, it's very hard to regain traction.

If the hill's steep and the surface offers good traction, you may need first gear. Start with the vehicle parked and the engine off. Let the clutch out and start the engine in gear. After activating the starter, let your foot off the brake and let the starter carry you forward. With the rig in first gear with the T-case in 4WD Lo, the starter moves you forward and the engine starts at the same time. Gently step on the gas, moving forward at about 2,000 RPM and drive straight up the hill without shifting. Shifting can cause a momentary loss of traction, causing the wheels to spin as you let the clutch back out. At the top, pause to break momentum before starting downhill on the other side.

With an automatic transmission, you don't have much choice. You automatically start out in the lowest gear (low range) unless your rig has one of the rare automatic transmissions that allows locking out low gear. Facing the hill, put the T-case in 4WD Lo and start the engine. If the hill is steep, put the transmission in the lowest range. If not too steep put it in the second lowest range. Keep the parking brake on until ready to move forward. Don't take the parking brake off with the transmission still in park or the transmission may lock in the park position as the car drifts backward a few inches down the hill. This is "torque lock" and can be impossible to get out of without pushing or winching the rig back up the hill to unlock the transmission. This can happen when taking off the parking brake with the transmission in park whether headed up- or downhill.

Put your left foot on the brake and your right on the gas. Let the parking brake off, accelerate, and ease your left foot off the brake. Drive steadily straight up the hill. Don't shift—stay in the lowest range all the way to the top. Stop momentarily at the top to break momentum before starting down the other side.

Before you start up the hill, pull the seat forward and make sure it's latched securely on the seat rails. You don't want to lose contact with the pedals as gravity forces you backward against the seatback. But don't forget to turn off the air bag if your rig's equipped with a switch to let you do that. Pulling the seat forward may put you in the zone of deployment of the air bag, injuring you seriously if the bag goes off.

Don't try to back up a steep hill, thinking it might be better to use reverse gear. That's too hard on your vehicle.

Rock Your Steering Wheel for More Traction

When losing traction on a soft surface in 4WD, such as loose dry dirt, gravel, or mud, rock the steering wheel quickly about half a turn back and forth. This helps the front wheels regain traction as they turn from side to side (Figure 44).

This maneuver can also help going uphill on snow. You can try it on ice or in deep snowy slush, but in those situations you're probably looking at putting chains on all four wheels or breaking out the winch.

Don't Spin the Wheels

Avoid wheel spin, which could bury your tires in deep ruts and make your next try up the hill much harder. Spinning can also explode a tire, possibly damaging the rig and injuring passengers. My friend, Keith Hanson, whose crew sells and fixes a lot of Jeep and Dodge products, tells me they see a lot of burned-out differentials in rigs whose wheels have been spun excessively. There are a lot of reasons not to spin your wheels.

A limited-slip differential (a posi) helps traction some, but on a steep hill, it may still allow a wheel to spin. Get by this by setting the emergency brake a little—not all the way; just a little. This preloads the posi and may fool it into locking the wheels together more than it would normally do. This won't work if your parking brake is attached to the driveshaft rather than to the rear wheels.

Bogging Down Before the Top

Starting up a hill that's too steep to finish puts you in one of the most dangerous situations of 4-wheeling. With your upward momentum stopped, in

Figure 41. It looks at first like the rig might have a good enough approach angle to just clear the hill.

Figure 42. But nope—the nose gets buried in the hill as the rig continues the approach. Not enough approach angle. To make it up this hill, build a ramp with rocks or logs to make the approach more gradual.

roughly two seconds you can slip around sideways and roll over and over down the hill.

Don't turn around! This is the first rule. DO NOT TRY TO TURN AROUND; DO NOT TRY TO COME DOWN FORWARD! If you lose uphill forward momentum, back down the hill. Trying to turn around creates a huge risk of rolling over as the rig comes crosswise on the hill.

Stomp on the brake and clutch and shift into reverse the instant the rig loses forward momentum. If you can't make it, secure the rig by pressing the brake down hard. Don't pump it. If the engine dies and you release the brake, you'll lose the power assist and you won't be able to reapply the brake hard enough to hold the vehicle. If you've got a manual transmission, get the clutch in fast to keep the engine running. It's easier to shift into reverse with the engine running. If you have trouble hitting reverse, run the gear shift through the forward gears (still keeping the clutch in, of course) and coax the lever into reverse. If the engine's dead, it sometimes helps to tweak the starter (clutch still in) as you coax the transmission into reverse.

It's important to do all this before you've lost upward momentum and your wheels start spinning or you risk losing control as the spinning rear wheels force the rear end to one side, resulting in a rollover.

If the surface holds you, stop and gather your wits. Slowly ease off the brakes and back down the hill, letting the engine compression and 4WD Lo control your speed. If you have to use the brakes, feather them very gently. With a steep hill, you're probably going faster than you like, but trying to brake down to your comfort zone runs the risk of skidding around sideways and rolling. Put up with some excess speed, focus on steering the rig straight backward, and ride it out. With an automatic transmission, you probably won't have enough braking effect from engine compression and will need to feather the brakes at least some.

The importance of getting into reverse the instant you lose forward momentum is that with a manual transmission, you may not have a "synchromesh" reverse gear. That means you will not be able to shift into reverse from a forward gear or neutral with the rig moving backward. Rocketing backward down the hill, you won't have engine compression to slow you down. Trying to control downhill speed with brakes alone is courting disaster.

Your engine is more likely to die if you head up a steep hill with a carbureted engine. A fuel-injected powerplant is much easier to live with if you're doing serious climbing. If your engine quits with your rig just a few feet short of the top, and you have a manual transmission, you may be able to crawl the rest of the way up by using your starter. Put the rig in 4WD Lo and use first gear in the transmission. If the hill's steep enough to cause your carburetor to quit, you'll probably need first gear. You can only run the the starter 10 to 20 seconds at a time before you have to let it cool. This maneuver drains your battery fast, so it only works if the distance you have to travel is really short. It also only works if your rig doesn't have a clutch interlock keeping the starter from working unless the clutch is in.

Another option is to winch the rig down the hill, if you can find an anchor point. Let the winch cable out slowly under power. Your battery won't last long with a dead engine, but maybe you can at least get down to a less steep area and get your engine started again. Another rig can winch you down, using a shackle block to change the direction of pull at the anchor point.

If you can't winch the rig down, can't get the engine started, and can't get the manual transmission into reverse, a desperation maneuver involves putting the transmission into first gear (forward), then gently pushing the clutch in to allow the vehicle to coast backward. Let the clutch out to slow it or stop it. You probably won't have much clutch left by the time you reach the bottom, but hopefully you and your rig will be otherwise intact.

If you can get your manual transmission into reverse, even if the engine doesn't start, it will still drive the power steering pump and the power brake booster, giving you at least a little steering and braking.

With an automatic transmission, you need to get into reverse instantly so the engine won't die as the rig starts to drift backward. With a dead engine, you're in serious trouble, because you can't restart the engine unless you put the automatic tranny in park, a maneuver almost guaranteed to skid you around sideways as you lock the wheels while sliding backward downhill. Some automatics let you start the engine with the transmission in neutral, but sliding backward down the hill is hardly the time to be figuring out how to get the engine running again.

Practice these things on small, easy hills first. Don't wait to try them out when you're at an abrupt halt on a hill so steep that all you can see through the windshield is sky.

GOING DOWNHILL

Know what's ahead and what's at the bottom by walking the route first.. Will you need to turn suddenly to avoid going over a cliff or stay off a rock or tree?

Stop at the top to interrupt momentum. Starting down, use 4WD Lo range and the lowest transmission gear that will slow you down without sliding. With poor traction or a particularly steep hill, gravity may pull the rig downhill faster than the lowest gear can keep up with. The wheels will slide rather than rotate, and you will lose control of the vehicle. In that case, use second or third gear of the manual transmission or shift your automatic into the

Figure 43. The author inches Bill Burke's Defender 90 down an unforgiving rock face in Moab, Utah. The generous approach and departure angles of the Defender let it negotiate steep terrain. (Photo by Bill Burke.)

Figure 44. If you start to get stuck while driving up a hill with poor traction, such as in loose dirt or gravel, turn the steering wheel quickly from side to side to move the front wheels back and forth. This increases the traction and gives you a good chance to get up the loose surface without having to air down.

range above low. If using the brakes is unavoidable, feather them very gently.

When traveling in 4WD Lo, slow down before downshifting. The low range of the T-case accentuates the speed difference between the higher gear and the lower gear of the transmission, and downshifting when traveling relatively fast results in a severe jolt and possible wheel lock and skidding.

In some rigs, you can switch on the air

conditioner to get more engine compression to slow you down. Switch the fan to high, making the compressor work harder. The effect is most noticeable with a manual transmission and the T-case in low range. It doesn't work on all rigs, though. For instance, the engine compression on my '94 K-Blazer doesn't change with the air conditioner on or off, but try it on your rig. When easing down a steep hill, you need all the help you can get. By the same token, shut the air conditioner off when traveling uphill so it won't rob needed power from the drivetrain.

If the rear end starts to slide, steer into the direction it's sliding and apply light gas as needed to straighten the rig. Don't hit the brakes or you risk making the rear end come around rapidly and sliding down the hill out of control or even rolling over.

Lean down the hill as you drive. That is, lean forward in the driver's seat toward the steering wheel and aggressively assume control of the rig and the hill. This is an essential principle well-known to downhill skiers, motorcycle riders, and rock climbers. Skiing with your body leaning up into the hill causes your skis to scoot out from under you, leaving you sprawled unattractively in the snow. Hugging the face of a cliff you're rappelling down, your boots lose their grip and you bob up and down on the static line like an oversize yo-yo. By leaning out on the rope, gravity pulls your feet against the rock, increasing your foothold. Putting all your weight on the back wheel of a motorcycle or mountain bike while going downhill gives you understeer and risks loss of control. Leaning forward aggressively or at least balancing your weight between the front and rear wheels gives both better control and the feeling you really are in control.

So don't be tentative driving your rig down a steep hill. Lean forward. Obviously, shifting your weight of 100 to 200 pounds isn't going to exert much effect on the weight and balance of a 6,000 pound rig, but it gives you the feeling of control. You're more alert and ready for whatever comes up. It's a matter of style. Go for it—with skill and caution, but with decision and purpose.

CONSIDER WINCHING

Using common sense, you may decide that a hill's just too steep to negotiate safely. Break out the winch and ease the rig up or down the hill gradually, securing it with wheel chocks and safety straps as you go. As you read in Chapter 5, it's more environmentally friendly to winch up a hill than to tear up the trail with spinning wheels.

SPREAD OUT

Going uphill or downhill, leave plenty of distance between rigs. Anticipate the driver above you losing control and hurtling down the trail much faster than intended. If that happens, are you far enough behind him (going uphill) or ahead of him (going downhill) so he won't hit you? If he rolls over, are you caught in his path? Go up or down dangerous hills one rig at a time.

DRIVING SIDEHILL

Driving "sidehill" means driving across a hill rather than straight up or down it. It's a dangerous path because of the risk of your rig's center of gravity shifting downhill and causing a rollover.

It's always good practice to load your equipment and supplies as low in the vehicle as possible. This is especially true when anticipating a sidehill drive. Load the heaviest items on the floor of the cargo section; load the lightest items on the roof rack.

Before you enter a sidehill stretch, shift the heavy items to the uphill side of the rig and move the heaviest passengers to the uphill seats. You can even put people out on the uphill running board, like ballast for a sailboat that's heeling over. Limit sidehill angles to a 25° grade (also called a 47-percent grade). You can buy a gauge that tells you how much the rig is tilting forward, backward, or sideways, or you can use a much cheaper simple protractor (Figure 45). (See Appendix A, the glossary, under "Grade" for more details about expressing a hill's slope in degrees or percent.)

Moving up from a 25° sideways tilt increases the danger. At high angles, if you drop the lower wheels into a rut or pothole or run the uphill wheels onto a rock or log, over you go. If you must drive at side angles greater than 25°, consider unloading the rig except for keeping the heaviest items on the uphill side of the floor. Unload the roof rack. Let the passengers walk ahead of you and scout the surface. Ask them to clear the path, moving rocks and logs out of the way and filling holes and ruts with rocks.

The width of the rig's track (the distance between the centers of the tires) helps determine the sidehill angle a vehicle can handle. A Hummer can usually handle 40°, an angle that would tip over most other rigs.

If you start to slide when crossing a hill, turn downhill immediately and apply light gas as needed. Continue on downhill, even if that's not where you

Figure 45. Use a protractor to judge your sidehill angle. This one is attached to the dash with Velcro. This rig is traveling 20° sidehill.

Figure 46. Grades are usually expressed in percent on advisory signs. This 14-percent grade is the same as a 9° grade.

were planning to go. If you slide, chances are you're going to end up at the bottom of the hill anyway. Better by far to drive down than roll down. You're more likely to slide in dust or mud. Damp dirt has the best traction.

If you have to drive across a steep sidehill in an emergency situation, use an anchor strap to secure the vehicle. Connect two or three tow straps together with D-shackles, securing one end to a tree, boulder, or ground anchor and attaching the other end to the frame between the front and rear wheels. Then drive around sidehill, following the arc of the tethering safety strap.

This arrangement won't protect you completely from a rollover, but it lessens the risk. You need several tow straps to pull this off, because you have to drive until you reach the end of the arc of the first set of straps. Then, keeping the first one connected for safety, connect a second set of straps to a tree or ground anchor farther ahead along your path. Once that's done, disconnect the first set and continue. A little tedious, but it beats rolling over and over down the hill.

ROLLOVER RECOVERY

You can get into a rollover situation without even realizing it. Suppose you're leisurely driving up a fairly steep trail, having no problem making it, and for some reason you decide you've gone far enough. It's time to go back to camp. If you don't think about how steep the trail is, you might casually try to turn the rig around at a wide place in the trail so you can head back home in a forward direction. Don't do it! You seriously risk rolling as you're turning around. Back down the steep part, using plenty of engine compression, until it's safe to turn around.

Ending up with the rig lying on its side with the door against the ground is called being "door down." Completely upside down with the roof against the ground is "shiny side down," or "rubber side up," with tires pointing toward the sky.

Before embarking on a serious 4-wheel drive trip, tie down everything. Everything. During a rollover, any loose items will fly around the inside of the rig and fall with a lot of force against passengers' heads. Use nylon tie-down straps, especially for heavy items such as jacks, chains, toolboxes, and ice chests. Bungee cords aren't secure enough to be safe.

Tie yourself and the passengers down, too, with seat belts. It's especially important during off-highway activities that all passengers, including those in the rear seat, have seat belts available and that they use them. A loose passenger bouncing around the cabin during a roll can injure the other passengers as well as himself. Unbelted occupants may also be thrown out of the vehicle during a roll, with the vehicle rolling over them on the way down the hill, turning a survivable low-speed roll into a fatal disaster.

It's difficult to secure dogs and other pets, and most people don't do it. However, dogs thrown around during a rollover injure not only themselves but the passengers as well. Loose restraining straps fastened to a harness on your four-legged buddy keeps it and you safer in the event of an accident.

Strap the battery or batteries down to lessen the chance of the connections loosening and causing a fire. Gel batteries are best because there's no battery acid to spill and they still work upside down, giving you a better chance to use your CB radio to call for help if necessary.

Keep a flashlight and fire extinguisher secured within reach of the driver's seat. Use a CO_2 fire extinguisher because dry chemical extinguishers corrode the engine and electrical connections. Following a rollover, watch out for signs of fire, smell for smoke or gasoline, and listen for sounds of sparking from loosened electrical connections.

As you're rolling, try to get your foot on the brakes so that landing on your wheels won't send you coasting rapidly down the hill. Keep your hands off the steering wheel. During a roll, it wrenches violently from side to side. Hanging on could give you a broken wrist or thumb.

Whether ending up shiny side down or door down, turn off the ignition at once. Determine how fast you have to get out. With gasoline leaking, sparks flying, or smoke visible, you have to get out as fast as you can any way you can—uphill, downhill, through the doors, through the windows. But if you have a little time, some ways of getting out are safer than others.

If you are being held upside down by the seat belt, support yourself before you unfasten it. Wrap your legs around the steering column, hold on to the steering wheel, or brace yourself with your hand against the roof below you and slowly unfasten the belt.

With the rig on its side, the lower side passenger should undo his or her seat belt first and get out of the way while the upper side passenger gets out of the belt. That way, if the upper passenger falls while undoing the belt, the lower passenger won't be injured.

Assess the other passengers for injuries, and assist any who need help extricating themselves from their seat belts. Get out of the rig on the uphill side; if you try to get out downhill, the rig could crush you if it rolls again. Get out through the windows if you can, or use the back door or hatch if you can crawl back there and get it open. Opening the uphill door can be difficult and dangerous, because gravity may slam it shut as you're getting out.

If your vehicle has electric windows, the danger of fire may make it risky to leave the ignition on to operate them. You may have to smash them out to exit if you can't get to the back hatch. Use a tool secured within reach—a hatchet, ice ax, or spring-loaded center punch, for instance (Figure 47). Don't try to smash out the windshield to exit—the plastic laminate of the safety glass makes it too hard to break.

Once everyone is safely out, avoid injury from exposed, sharp broken parts on the underside of the rig, and watch out for hot spots like the exhaust system. No one needs third-degree burns adding to his misery. Watch out for broken glass inside and outside the vehicle.

Mop up battery acid, gas, and oil. Check for broken parts on the underside. If the vehicle is on its side, it's easier to do this inspection before you turn it shiny side up again. Your goal is to make sure the rig is safe to drive. If it's not, you'll have to tow it home or haul it back on a trailer or flatbed truck.

Check for bent driveshafts, broken U-bolts or tie-rods, and broken or loose exhaust system parts (watch out—they're hot). Look for broken brake or fuel lines and leaks in the gas tank. Inspect the tires and the wheel rims for damage. Secure cracked and broken windows with duct tape to keep pieces of broken glass from working loose and falling on people.

Make whatever repairs you can, depending on your experience, skill, and what spare parts and tools you have with you. You can secure loose parts with wire if you're carrying a roll of 18 gauge. A broken brake line can be plugged with a stick secured with a hose clamp, cautiously using the brakes of the other three wheels to stop as you drive home. (If you've lost brake fluid, you'll have to bleed the brakes, if you know how, and replace the loss with more brake fluid. Water will work temporarily if you don't have extra fluid with you.)

You can pound out bent wheel rims, plug gas leaks with epoxy putty, and replace broken U-bolts if you've got spares. If someone in your party has an under-the-hood welder and appropriate expertise, you can repair broken parts such as tie-rods, suspension parts, or even the frame if it's cracked. (When performing arc welding on a vehicle, be sure to disconnect the battery and alternator to avoid damage to the rig's electrical system.)

You can right the vehicle with people or winches. Deciding how to get the rig back on its rubber feet depends on several things. How many people are available? With a bunch, it's probably easier to right the rig by physically turning it over with people power. Everybody should wear gloves and watch for broken glass and sharp parts. Rolling it back upright with people means rolling it toward the downhill side, because it's much harder to roll the rig uphill than downhill. It's dangerous anyway to stand on the downhill side to try to roll it uphill. The rig may be unstable and roll over on the whole team.

Before rolling a rig upright, secure it with a tow strap anchored to an uphill tree or boulder to keep it stable as it comes over on its wheels.

If there are not enough people, or if you can't roll the vehicle farther downhill (the hill's too steep or it came to rest beside a river or against a large boulder on the downhill side), then you've got to roll it uphill by winching it over with another rig. Make sure the vehicle with the winch is at least two vehicle lengths away from the rolled rig. The winching vehicle should be perpendicular to the rolled vehicle.

It's best to wrap a nylon tow strap around the rolled rig and attach the winch to that to protect the metal and paint. A winch cable wrapped around the downed rig does further damage. Wrap the strap all the way around the rolled 'ute to get better leverage for the roll back upright. Attach it to something solid, like the frame or the post between the front and rear doors. Don't use the roof rack, a rearview mirror, or body panels. Consider digging out part of the uphill ground to make it more level and to give the vehicle better stability when it lands upright.

After the vehicle is recovered, check it out further. Open the hood and check for broken items. Check the radiator and fan—make sure the radiator hasn't been pushed back into the fan. Make sure the hood latches securely—if it won't, tie it shut so it won't fly up on the drive home. Put oil back in the crankcase. Check the coolant level in the radiator. Check the tires further for damage. Check the wheels again to make sure the rims aren't bent.

Cautiously try to start the engine. If it doesn't crank easily, stop and pull the spark plugs. Check for oil in the cylinders. Crank the engine again with the plugs pulled to drive oil out of the cylinders.

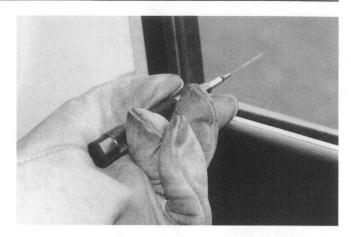

Figure 47. Use a spring-loaded center punch to break out a side window in an emergency.

Once started, check the oil pressure. Check the steering—turn the wheel and make sure that the power steering works all right without leaking. Make sure the front wheels clear any bent parts as you turn the steering wheel all the way from one side to the other. You can straighten bent parts with a jack or pry bar. You can also use a winch from another rig to pull bent parts straight. Make sure the brakes work and the pedal stays firm as you press on it hard. If it fades down to the floorboard, you may have lost too much brake fluid to drive safely, or you may even have an active brake fluid leak. Check it out before you start driving. Check the lights before you start out, too, especially if you'll be traveling after dark.

If lucky enough to roll over completely and land on the tires again, do all these checks anyway. You may have lost oil, coolant, or gas. Battery acid may have splattered all over the engine compartment. You may have broken a tie-rod, U-bolt, shock mount, or spring. You may have torn a tire or bent a wheel rim. A lot of damage may have occurred during the roll, and you need to find it before hitting the highway home.

After checking for damage and fixing what you can, tow or drive the vehicle back home or to some other spot where you can check it over and fix it in more detail.

AN OUNCE OF PREVENTION IS WORTH FOUR TONS OF WINCHING

The best treatment for a rollover is prevention. Use good technique when going uphill and downhill, and use common sense when deciding whether or not to try that sidehill run. Load gear to keep the center of gravity as low as possible.

chapter ten

WINCHES AND JACKS

UP AND OUT

There's nothing like a winch to get up a steep hill when traction's poor or to get down a hill that's too steep to drive safely. There's nothing like a winch to get out of bumper-deep mud, a stream when the ignition system's drowned, or a ditch beside a snowy road, or to drag a rock or log out of the way when it's blocking the path. There's nothing like a winch to rescue a buddy who's stuck and who never got around to putting a winch on his own rig.

By using common sense and scouting the trail ahead before committing, you won't get stuck in the first place most of the time. But if you do get stuck or if you are deliberately clawing your way over a particularly gnarly trail, then a winch, a Hi-Lift jack, a set of two or three tow straps, and a bunch of D-shackles and snatch blocks will get you over or through most obstacles.

WHICH WINCH?

See the discussion about winches in Chapter 7 to help decide which winch to buy. Be sure the winch has pulling power equal to one and a half times the fully loaded weight of the rig. With a loaded rig weighing 6,000 pounds, you need at least a 9,000 pound winch.

The fairlead is the plate on the front of the winch. The winch cable, also called wire rope, comes out through an opening in the fairlead. A roller fairlead has rollers on all four sides of the opening. The other type, a hawse fairlead, is just a bracket through which the winch cable passes, like the opening in the bow of a ship with a huge hawser coming out of it. A winch with a roller fairlead is best because it reduces friction on the cable during winching operations.

Some people prefer a hidden winch, tucked neatly under the front end of the rig or stowed inside a compartment in an oversize bumper. A hidden winch looks neat, but it has a major problem. When winching, you can't see how the cable goes on to the winch. Piling up at one end causes binding on the drum, and the winch will stop working (Figure 48). Binding or fraying the cable as it goes onto the drum weakens it, and it could break while winching, with disastrous results. I prefer an exposed winch to see how much cable is left on the drum while unspooling and to see what's happening to the cable while winching in.

A hidden winch is often installed behind and under the front bumper, limiting the approach angle and reducing front-end clearance. A low winch closer to the ground is more likely to be buried in the mud when getting stuck in a bog, so you slop around more pulling out the wire cable and plugging the remote control cable into a mud-filled socket—just when you need the winch most.

Figure 48. Make sure the cable doesn't pile up at one end like this while you're winching. An open winch lets you see if this is happening.

If you want your rig to look especially nice on the supermarket parking lot, get a hidden winch. If planning on really wheelin', put the winch out where you can see it.

WINCHES AND AIR BAGS

Installing a winch on your rig has gotten more complicated now that most 4x4s come equipped with air bags. It's easy to mess up the air bag sensors when trying to do so. The winch manufacturers are working with 4x4 manufacturers to develop winch mountings compatible with the air bag systems. If you're adding a winch, make sure the people who install it understand the potential air bag problem. If you'll be installing it yourself, check with the winch and rig manufacturers first. If you haven't had experience repairing air bag systems, it's probably wise to have the winch installation done professionally.

DUAL BATTERIES

Make sure you have enough amps to drive the winch. A large winch uses a lot of juice. With only a single battery, you can easily run it down to zero during a prolonged winching exercise. Install either a bigger alternator or a dual battery system or both. (See Chapter 7 for a detailed discussion of dual batteries.)

Use the winch with the engine on and running fast enough to feed the amps to the winch. If the winch motor seems to be pulling hard or slowing down (called *lugging*), it's a sign that the battery is running down and the winch isn't getting enough

juice. Let the battery charge back up before starting to winch again. Stop winding if the winch gets too hot to touch. Let it cool while the battery recharges. You can speed up the cooling process by pouring water over the winch.

WINCH CONTROLS

Most winches are operated by working switches on a small remote control box attached to a long cable plugged into an electric socket on the winch motor. The long remote cable lets you stand back as you operate the winch, well away from the dangerous steel winch cable.

Winch controls usually have a toggle switch that moves in two different directions. One direction pulls the winch wire rope cable in under power; the other lets the winch pay out the cable under power. You would use this second position when lowering a rig down a steep slope. Be sure you're familiar with which direction is which on the toggle switch before operating the winch.

Some winches now come equipped with radio-controlled remote switches, which allow you to stand even farther away from the cable. Just be sure that no one else nearby is winching with their radio remote switch on the same frequency as yours! If they are, you and they may be in for some nasty and dangerous surprises, with the winches stopping and starting in a seemingly random fashion.

Both the long remote cable and the radio remote switches let you operate the winch while sitting inside the rig. This lets you move your vehicle as you winch, if necessary, while keeping you protected in case the winch cable breaks and whips back toward the rig.

USE A TREE STRAP

When using a tree as an anchor to pull against, attach the winch cable to a nylon strap placed around the tree. Never wrap the wire rope directly around the tree. The tree strap does three things:

1. It lets people coming along the trail behind you use the same tree for their anchor point because it saves the tree. People who don't get a feeling of satisfaction from that need to do an attitude check. They may be among those giving the regulators excuses to close trails.
2. It helps you Tread Lightly! by not leaving a permanent mark around the tree.

Figure 49. Avoid a flat angle of straps or chains meeting at the D-shackle.

Figure 50. A sharp angle is stronger.

3. It saves your wire winch cable. Wrapping the cable around the tree and hooking it back onto itself kinks the cable and ruins it.

It's convenient to use a tow strap as a tree strap. There are two schools of thought on whether you should just pass the nylon strap around the back of the tree or whether you should wrap it around the tree once or twice. Both schools think their method is easier on the tree. The "back of the tree only" school thinks that you protect the bark on the front of the tree by keeping the strap only on the back. The "wrap once or twice" school thinks you protect the bark more by distributing the force circumferentially around the entire tree and that the friction of the nylon loops against each other prevents undue force from the pull from constricting the tree. I think it's probably easier on the tree to pass the strap around it entirely once or twice, but I don't know the correct answer. As you can see from the photos in this book, I do it both ways.

Both a tree strap and a tow strap should have a strong loop sewn into each end. Pass a D-shackle through these two loops so the nylon loops sit on the inside of the curved part of the shackle. Screw the threaded bolt across the open end of the shackle, backing it off one-half to one full turn after you reach the end. Backing off prevents the threads from binding after a heavy pull.

Straps around trees and choker chains around boulders or logs should be long enough to avoid a flat angle at the D-shackle. A sharp angle is much stronger. In other words, the farther from the tree the end loops are, the stronger the setup is (Figures 49, 50).

Figure 51. A double-line pull with the winch cable passed through a shackle block attached to the anchor. The cable is then brought back to the rig and hooked to a tow hook. A tarp's been wrapped around the cable to help control it if it breaks.

ATTACHING THE WINCH CABLE TO THE ANCHOR POINT

You can single-line or double-line the winch cable. Single-lining means simply running the winch cable from the winch to the anchor point and hooking it directly to the D-shackle. You have a single line going from the rig to the tree.

Double-lining doubles the power of your winch (Figure 51). It requires using a pulley block (also called a snatch block or shackle block), a heavy pulley with a large metal hook or other fitting that attaches it to a D-shackle. Attach the hook to the threaded bolt of the D-shackle on the tree strap. Run

71

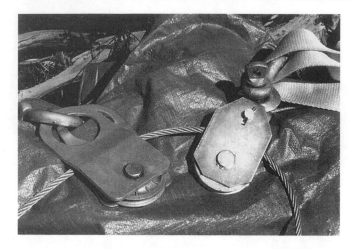

Figure 52. The shackle block opens to let you run the cable around the pulley. Here are two different types of shackle blocks.

Figure 53. Attach the winch cable hook to the tow hook with the opening facing up so that if the cable hook breaks or slips off, it's forced down into the ground.

Figure 54. Triple-lining for extra power. The cable runs from the winch on the rig to a shackle block attached to the anchor point, back to another shackle block attached to a tow hook on the rig, then back to a D-shackle attached to the anchor point.

Figure 55. Triple-lining with a come-along. The portable winch is hooked to a D-shackle attached to the anchor point. The cable goes from the come-along to a shackle block attached to a receiver shackle on the rig, back to another shackle block at the anchor point, then back to a tow hook on the rig.

the winch cable from the rig to the snatch block. The cover on the pulley opens up to let you run the cable around the pulley (Figure 52).

Pull the cable back to the rig and hook it to one of the front tow hooks attached to the frame. If you don't have tow hooks, hook the cable to some other part of the frame. Don't hook the cable to anything else, such as an axle, tie-rod, shock absorber, or bumper. These parts don't stand up to the heavy pull of winching and can bend or break. Attach the cable hook to the tow hook with the opening facing up. If it

breaks or slips off, it's driven into the ground rather than up into the air (Figure 53).

FOR MAXIMUM POWER

Use a single line for easy pulls, a double line through a snatch block for harder pulls. With a light-duty winch or for particularly heavy-duty winching, you can get even more power by triple-lining. Run the cable from your rig through a snatch block attached to the tree strap, then back to the rig and

Figure 56. When winching another rig, chock your wheels. These are SureClaw wheel anchors.

through another snatch block attached to a tow hook on the rig, then back again to the tree strap (Figures 54, 55). This is probably overkill in most winching situations, but keep it in mind for situations that seem to be overworking your winch.

With double-lining or triple-lining, you trade power for speed. Double-lining moves the rig forward one-half as fast as single-lining. Triple-lining moves it one-third as fast.

You get more power from double-lining or triple-lining for another reason besides the mechanical advantage of the multiple lines. Using multiple lines requires you to pull more winch cable off the drum, and this is good. The inside layers of cable on the drum have greater pulling power than the outer layers. The winch is rated according to the pull generated by wrapping the cable around the bare drum.

A 12,000-pound winch will generate 6 tons of pull on the inside wrap. Each layer of cable on the drum pulls about 1,000 pounds less. With cable wrapped on the drum four layers deep, the outside layer will generate about 9,000 pounds of pull. However, always leave at least five wraps of cable around the drum on the inside layer. Unreeling the cable out all the way risks breaking the cable loose from the drum under a heavy load.

The other problem that could occur when unreeling all the way involves the automatic brake some winches have. The brake may not function if the cable spools off the drum in the wrong direction. When winding the cable out all the way, you may

accidently rewind it back onto the cable the wrong way by forgetting to use the reverse switch before rewinding it. Winches have a decal on them indicating the direction the cable should come off the drum. My Warn winch cable comes off the bottom of the drum. Always pay attention to the decal. When replacing the cable, make sure you wind it back on the drum in the right direction.

While winching your rig out, you can sit inside it with the remote cable through the window. Sometimes it helps to crawl forward in 4WD low and low gear as you winch. Go slow and easy, and avoid creating slack in the winch line.

WINCHING OUT ANOTHER RIG

When winching another rig out of a stuck spot or using another rig as an anchor to move your own, attach your winch cable or snatch block to a tow hook or to some other point on the frame of the other rig. When winching another rig out of a stuck spot, anchor your vehicle with the parking brake set and the wheels chocked (Figure 56). Leave an automatic transmission in neutral. Avoid using park, which may break the transmission from the strain of pulling the other vehicle.

There are times when winching out another rig requires anchoring your rig to a tree or other anchor point. This might occur on frozen or snowy ground where the pull on your winch cable is moving your rig ahead rather than moving the other rig toward

Figure 57. Use a shackle block to create a double-line pull or to change the direction of a single-line pull. Here we move the log toward the tree with a double-line pull and three shackle blocks to change direction. When rescuing another rig, change the direction of pull when there's not enough room to get your vehicle directly in front of the stuck vehicle.

Figure 58. Changing the direction of a double-line pull with three shackle blocks: one on the object you're winching and two to handle the incoming and outgoing cable at the anchor point.

Figure 59. When using a front-mounted winch to winch a rig backward, run the cable under the rig and through a D-shackle attached to the rear hitch receiver.

Figure 60. Carry the winch cable under your rig with the hook attached to the receiver shackle.

you. The common way to do this is to run a chain or cable from a tree strap anchor to a receiver shackle attached to your rear hitch or to your rear tow hooks. However, if your rig is exerting a strong off-center pull with the front winch, its frame may be twisted between the front winching force and the rear anchoring force and can sustain permanent damage. It's safer to run the anchoring chain or cable all the way under the rig and attach it to an anchor point on the front of the frame of the rig, close to the winch.

CHANGING THE DIRECTION OF PULL

When winching without enough room for a straight pull, use the snatch block to change the direction of pull. To create a double-line pull with a change in direction, use two snatch blocks at the point the direction changes—one block for each line of the cable, and a third snatch block at the vehicle being winched (Figures 57, 58). Use this technique to winch out another rig when there is not enough room to get directly in line with it.

Figure 61. To keep the cable hook from catching under the rig as you winch it back forward, slit a plastic funnel and slip it over the cable near the hook.

WINCHING BACKWARDS

There are times when you have to winch a rig backward in the direction it came from. There are basically three ways you can do this: 1) run the winch cable from the front-mounted winch all the way under the rig and out the back to the anchor point; 2) put a portable electric winch in the rear-mounted hitch receiver, plug it into the electric harness wiring for the trailer, and winch from the rear of your rig; 3) use a portable hand winch (a come-along). There are pros and cons associated with each method.

Running the Cable Under Your Rig

The advantage of this method is that you use the front-mounted winch you already have. There are several disadvantages. When you pull the cable backward, it comes down off your winch at a sharp angle, binding hard against the lower roller of the fairlead. The pull isn't very efficient, and the cable can't travel back and forth smoothly across the winch drum. This tends to make the cable bunch up in one spot on the winch.

The cable running along the bottom of the rig can catch on various things and damage them, such as the shocks, muffler, steering gear, and so forth.

The rig tends to wobble as it's being pulled. When winching a rig forward from a front-mounted winch or backward from a portable rear-mounted winch, you're dragging the rig from a fixed point and

the pull tends to straighten the rig out as it moves. Running the cable all the way under the rig, the attachment is at the front but the pull is from the back. The rig sort of balances on the length of cable running under it. If the cable moves to one side or other under the rig, the torque acting on the front of the rig may twist it sideways. This can cause the cable to bind against one of the rear tires. It's hard to steer the rig to keep it straight. You can lessen this problem by running the winch cable through a D-shackle attached to a receiver-mounted shackle. This keeps the cable in the middle of the rear of the rig and lessens the torque tending to twist the rig as you're pulling it (Figure 59).

Another problem with this method is the difficulty of pulling the cable all the way under the rig from front to back when stuck in deep mud. Think about lying down full length in hub-deep, wet, slimy mud trying to work the cable all the way under your rig to the back. Ugh! Makes even the most avid 'wheeler consider some other brand of recreation.

Avoid this gooey situation by planning ahead. When you are about to go through mud and you think you might have to winch your vehicle out backward, run the cable under the rig before entering the muddy section while you're still on high, dry ground. Attach the cable hook to the rear D-shackle (Figure 60). Then it's ready if you need it. But now you have another potential problem.

75

If it turns out you need to winch your rig forward after all, you've got to bring the winch cable forward again. Just dragging it from back to front under the rig, the cable hook may hang up on something under the vehicle. Then you get covered with slime anyway freeing the hook to get it forward.

Petersen's *4-Wheel & Off-Road* magazine recently printed a tip from one of its readers to help out with this problem. Simply slit a plastic funnel (or an empty plastic bottle with the bottom cut out) and slip it over the cable near the hook with the opening facing the hook. Tape the slit closed with duct tape. When pulling the cable and hook forward under the vehicle, just slide the funnel down around the hook and it won't catch as it passes forward under the rig (Figure 61). Lacking a funnel, at least wrap the hook with duct tape to close the opening before dragging it forward.

Using a Portable Rear-Mounted Electric Winch

Pulling your rig backward with a winch mounted in your rear hitch receiver is efficient, but you're limited in the size of winch you can use because you have to wrestle it up into the receiver. You're probably limited to a 3,000- or 4,000-pound winch at the most. You're still risking a back injury if you try to attach even this small a winch by yourself because of the awkward angle involved as you try to fit it into the receiver. The other problem with a portable electric winch is that it takes up quite a bit of storage room inside your rig.

Using a Portable Hand Winch (a Come-along)

This is the easiest alternative for rearward vehicle retrieval, but you're limited in the weight you can drag because of a come-along's smaller size. A pull of 4,000 pounds is possible by double-lining one of the heavier come-alongs.

I had to recover my Blazer one day when a trail suddenly disappeared. Neglecting one of the basic rules of 4-wheeling, I didn't get out and walk the trail to see where it went (Figure 62). Another 2 feet and the vehicle would have slid headfirst down the steep bank. With the rig nose down over the edge and the weight off the rear wheels, there was no traction to back up.

With the parking brake set, wheels blocked, and transmission and T-case in neutral, I put a tow strap around the rear tow hooks and attached it to a shackle block with a D-shackle. Another tow strap went around a tree, with the hook of the come-along pulley attached to it. The come-along cable went around the shackle block pulley and back to hook to the come-along frame, creating a double-line pull (Figure 63).

Figure 62. Whoops! Where did the trail go? Two more feet and the rig would have been down the bank headfirst.

Figure 63. Vehicle retrieval.

Figure 64. Ground anchor (Pul Pal). This is one type of ground anchor available. It gives an attachment point for the winch cable when there's no tree or boulder handy.

Figure 65. Dig the vehicle partially out if the winch is straining too much in the wet, heavy snow.

Carefully winching the rig backward away from the bank, I released the parking brake when there was enough tension on the winch cable and yank straps to support it. Moving the blocks to keep them against the wheels, I hauled the rig toward the tree, safely reaching firm ground.

Another lesson learned—again. Even the most solid-appearing trail can suddenly disappear in a washed-out section. Walking a narrow trail includes inspecting the edge of the surface next to a drop-off. Heavy rains may have undermined it, preparing it to drop your rig on its side in a ditch (at best) or down a cliff (at worst). The margin of error between balancing your rig at the top edge of a cliff and having a search-and-rescue team recover you and the rig from the bottom of that same cliff may only be 2 feet. If you can't see it, walk it first.

OTHER ANCHORS

Without a tree for an anchor, pass a chain with a hook at each end around a large boulder and anchor to that. Attach the hook to the chain links; don't attach the two hooks together—they're too hard to separate after pulling on them. Don't use a tree strap or tow strap to anchor to a rock—the harsh stone surface frays it and ruins it. Make sure the boulder is heavy enough to anchor the weight of the rig. It's embarrassing to winch a large rock loose and have it come tumbling and bouncing downhill onto the hood of your 4by.

Another anchor can be your spare tire buried in the dirt or a buried log. You can also use a Danforth boat anchor in sand or loose soil. Pul-Pal makes a neat ground anchor to winch against. It

looks like a cross between a boat anchor and a plow—just bury its plow in the dirt instead of the ocean floor (Figure 64).

If there is no large tree to fasten a tree strap around, use several smaller trees. Pass the tow strap completely around the entire group of small trees so it's enclosing the front trees as well as the back trees. That way, the trees closest to the rig are providing strength for the anchor along with the ones in back.

In wet, heavy snow or in thick mud, there may be too much drag on the vehicle for the winch to handle. If the winch is straining to the point of breaking the cable, stop winching and dig the vehicle partially out before winching again (Figure 65).

CABLE PILEUP

With the winch cable not winding evenly back onto the drum, you may need to stop winching and chock the wheels or secure the rig with a tow strap attached to a tree. Pull out the cable and rewind it evenly before winching again.

You can also handle uneven distribution of the cable when it's piling up on one side of the drum by chocking the wheels, releasing the cable, and pulling out the cable that's been piling up plus some. Rewind the cable, piling it up on the opposite end of the drum. This creates more room on the end of the drum the cable wants to pile up on.

When setting up for a pull off to one side, anticipate cable pileup. Before you begin winching, pull out a bunch of cable and rewind it intentionally

Figure 66. Always hold the winch cable hook with a heavy wire hook or small crowbar. Always wear gloves and eye protection when working around the winch cable.

Figure 67. Attach a tow strap to a heavy-duty receiver shackle.

piled up on the side of the drum opposite the direction of pull. This leaves room for the pileup to occur as you winch the off-center load.

MORE SAFETY TIPS AND OTHER HINTS

On a trail where you're using your winch frequently, save power by not rewinding it between stuck spots. Carry the cable by wrapping it figure-eight fashion around your front bumper. Be careful, though, because it's exposed to damage in this position. Avoid scraping it against rocks.

Winching a rig up a hill, stop every few feet and rechock the wheels. If the winch or cable breaks, the chocks prevent the rig from rolling down the hill. With an especially steep hill, use a tow strap as a safety anchor. Secure one end to a tow hook on the rig and the other end to a strap around an uphill tree. Take up the slack in the safety strap as you winch.

Never plug the remote switch in until ready to start winching. There may be a short in the remote and the winch could start as soon as you plug in the remote cable rather than when you actually activate the toggle switch. Make sure you know which winching direction each position of the toggle switch controls.

Never go near the winch cable when it's under tension. Don't touch it and don't step on it. If a winch cable breaks, it can whip around with lethal force. Many off-road experts advise putting something over the winch cable to help control it if it should break, such as a blanket, tarp, heavy jacket, or sleeping bag (as shown in Figure 51). However, Tom Telford, one of the Warn Industries engineers, points out that as

the cable reels onto the winch drum during winching, you'll have to move the tarp to keep it from getting pulled into the fairlead and tangled in the cable on the drum. This violates the "don't go near a cable under tension" rule, which he feels is much more important than putting a tarp over the cable. Keep away from the cable yourself, and keep all bystanders and pets well out of the winching area.

When winching under a lot of tension, winch from inside your rig. Sit in the driver's seat and pass the remote cable in through the window. Don't pass it inside around an open door. The door might swing closed and damage the remote cable. For more protection, winch from inside the rig with the hood up. This protects you even more if the winch cable breaks.

Wrap the remote cable around the brush guard or the rearview mirror to take up the slack. Don't let it drag on the ground—your rig might run over it and damage it. Let the winch pull steadily. Don't use extremely short bursts, because a winch draws more amps as it's getting started. "Jiggling" the switch on and off rapidly draws down the battery faster and is hard on the solenoid. On the other hand, don't keep it on so long that it overheats.

After you use the winch, it's best to pull out the cable and rewind it smoothly back onto the drum under a light load. Just spooling the cable back onto the drum loosely causes the outer layers of the cable to work down into the inner layers the next time you winch under a heavy load. This can jam and fray the cable. However, rewinding under a load isn't always practical. At least rewind it onto the drum smoothly, exerting as much counterpull on the wire cable as you can.

Figure 68. When getting ready to tow a stuck rig out of the mud, sand, or snow, leave about 5 or 6 feet of slack.

Figure 69. Drive forward, letting the elasticity of the yank strap help snap the stuck vehicle forward.

When rewinding and putting tension on the cable by hand, stand at least 5 or 6 feet away from the winch to keep your hands away from the fairlead. Always wear heavy leather gloves. Handling the wire cable with your bare hands results in metal slivers working their way into your skin. The gloves should fit loosely so you can jerk your hands out of them if they get caught on the cable and start to disappear through the fairlead.

Activate the switch and walk in about 4 feet of cable. Release the switch and grab the cable back at 6 feet. Walk in another 4 feet of cable. Do not get closer than 2 or 3 feet to the winch. Always use a heavy wire hook or the curved end of a small crow bar to handle the winch cable hook (Figure 66). Don't take a chance on mashing your hand between the cable hook and fairlead with thousands of pounds of force. This a common winching accident! Take your winch and winching very seriously.

Spray the cable frequently but lightly with a moisture-displacing lubricant such as WD-40 or Teflon spray. Avoid covering it with a layer of goo that picks up gravel and dirt. At least once a year, pull the cable out and clean it with a wire brush and kerosene.

BOAT TRAILERS

When towing a boat on a trailer, if the shoreline's too rough to let you get your rig to the water, don't forget your winch. Turn your rig facing the boat trailer, chock the wheels, and carefully winch the trailer down the slope into the water. This also saves your differentials and wheel bearings because you don't get your rig near the water and you don't risk contaminating the lubricants in them with water as you maneuver the trailer into the water.

SECURITY

Your winch is vulnerable to theft, especially if you live in a high-crime area. Discourage this by spot welding one or two of the bolts attaching it to the bumper assembly.

Watch out for vandalism, too. One rotten trick is free-spooling the winch cable and hooking it to something solid. Unaware of this, the rig's owner returns, hops in, and drives off, inflicting considerable damage to winch, rig, passengers, and whatever the cable's attached to when the vehicle hits the end of the steel tether. Discourage this by wrapping the entire winch and drum with a lockable steel cable, running it through the eye securing the hook to the end of the cable. This at least keeps the hook attached to the rig so it can't easily be attached to any distant object.

TOW STRAPS

Use a tow strap (also called a yank strap) to pull another vehicle out of mud or icy conditions. The strap should be heavy nylon, 20 to 30 feet long and 2 or 3 inches wide, with a heavy loop sewn into each end. Don't use a strap with metal hooks attached to it. A hook that breaks or slips loose can rocket into a rig like a shotgun slug, easily going through the tailgate of a pickup or a windshield (and a driver's head). Use a nylon strap rated for at least 20,000 pounds.

Figure 70. We climbed the stump with our front wheel but misjudged the clearance we'd have after we got over and ended up high-centered.

Figure 71. To get out of being high-centered, jack up the wheel closest to the obstacle with your jack and build ramps under that wheel and in front of the other wheel on that side with logs, rocks, or whatever.

Never attach the tow strap to the trailer ball on your hitch receiver when pulling someone out of the mud. The ball isn't designed to withstand that kind of force, and it can break too, flying at you with the force of a cannonball. When yanking someone out, attach the yank strap to a heavy-duty receiver shackle designed for the purpose (Figure 67) or secure the strap to a rear frame-mounted tow hook.

A nylon tow strap stretches about 15 percent. When attaching the strap between the stuck vehicle and the towing rig, allow about 5 or 6 feet of slack. Drive the towing vehicle forward and use the elasticity of the strap to help tug the stuck rig free (Figures 68, 69). However, do this cautiously. Don't take a huge run at it. The driver of the stuck rig should be trying to drive the rig forward as the towing rig starts out. Once unstuck, he should be ready to brake immediately to avoid overrunning the towing vehicle. This is a particular risk if the stuck vehicle is a lot lighter than the towing rig, like a Geo Tracker being yanked by a 3/4-ton pickup. When yanked free, the Tracker can fly through the air and land in the bed of the pickup. Literally.

There was a disturbing picture recently in *Tri-Power*, the monthly newspaper of the Pacific Northwest Four Wheel Drive Association. It originally appeared in a Warn Industries publication in 1990. A Jeep driver had fastened two tow straps together with a heavy shackle to haul out another vehicle. He probably drove forward pretty fast because he pulled the frame-mounted tow hook off the other vehicle, and the shackle connecting the two straps had hurtled through the Jeep's back window, driver's

Figure 72. Lower the wheel onto the ramp you've constructed and drive off. We ended up with a slightly bent running board and a broken running board bracket. Oh, well; that's what running boards and nerf bars are for.

Figure 73. Using the Hi-Lift jack as a mini-winch. You can use tow straps for lightweight winching, but it's a lot safer to use chains.

Figure 74. Attach the chains to the Hi-Lift jack by turning the top bracket 90° or by bolting the chain to the jack. Be sure the jack is set up so its base doesn't crack a headlight or damage the grill or radiator as you crank back and forth on the handle.

seat back, and windshield with a velocity probably in excess of 300 mph. Fortunately, the driver was only knocked unconscious when the shackle grazed his neck. If it had hit him squarely, it would have certainly killed him.

You've got to be very careful when using this technique. There are several substantial risks. We've already talked about the potential for pulling off pieces of one rig or the other and hurling them through windows, tailgates, or people's heads with the force of a cannonball. Don't join two tow straps together with a metal fitting such as a D-shackle, which can act as a projectile if one of the straps pulls loose. Keep your speed down and limit the slack to only a few feet. Don't start off right in front of the bumper of the stuck vehicle, getting up to 40 mph as the nylon strap tightens. As it tightens, the energy the strap stores is tremendous, and its very easy to break whatever part of the vehicles the strap is attached to. Be very careful if the towing rig is a lot heavier than the stuck vehicle, as we also mentioned above.

If you can't free a rig with just one other vehicle towing it, you may have to use a second or even a third vehicle. It's safer and more efficient to attach each towing vehicle to the stuck rig with its own separate tow strap so that the towing vehicles pull on the stuck rig in parallel, rather than in series. Use different length tow straps so the towing vehicles are staggered. This keeps one from skidding sideways into its neighbor.

If you attach the towing vehicles in tandem, or series, you risk twisting the frame of one or more of the

towing vehicles. In other words, don't have a towing vehicle in front with a tow strap running back to the front of the second vehicle, which in turn has a tow strap running back to the front of the third vehicle, which has a tow strap running back to the stuck rig.

But sometimes the trail is too narrow to allow you a choice. If you have to tow in series, protect the frames of the towing vehicles by pulling on both tow hooks at once, using a long chain or an extra nylon strap. Put a D-shackle around the center of the chain and attach the towing strap to the D-shackle. That evens out the pull on the tow hooks. If you don't have chains or enough tow straps to do this, at least make sure that the each towing vehicle is pulling along a single frame rail. That is, don't hook the front tow strap to a front tow hook on the right frame rail and the rear tow strap to a rear tow hook on the left frame rail. This will tend to twist the frame.

Winching and towing are serious endeavors, requiring experience, knowledge, and common sense. The skills involved are challenging, satisfying, and fun. Learning them takes only a little practice, and knowing you can get your rig unstuck in seemingly impossible situations increases your off-road confidence a lot.

THE HI-LIFT JACK

When high-centered, use a Hi-Lift jack, at least 48 inches high, to get out. Jack up the wheel closest to the high-centered spot and build a ramp under that wheel. Then drive off (Figures 70, 71, 72).

A vehicle is not very stable when elevated on a tall bumper jack. Chock each of the other three

81

wheels to discourage the rig from rolling off the jack. Set the base of the jack on a heavy board to keep it from sinking into soft ground. After reaching the elevation you need, put the jack handle in the fully upright, vertical position and slip a half-inch bolt through the hole in the jack's beam just below the latching mechanism. Should the jack give way, the bolt prevents it from dropping the rig back to the ground suddenly. Even when you are using these safety measures, never work under a rig supported only by a jack.

When ready to lower the rig, flip the jack's reversing lever down with the handle in the fully upright position. Never flip the reversing lever down with the jack handle down. This could throw the handle upward violently, severely injuring anyone within range. Remove the bolt from the hole in the beam and lower the rig carefully, keeping your hands firmly on the handle to maintain control of it at all times. This prevents it from flying up and hitting you in the face.

To get out of sand, put the Hi-Lift jack on a heavy board and jack up a wheel. Then put a board, aluminum strip, or piece of carpeting under the wheel. Do the same with the other wheels. Drive out of the sand on the traction strips.

WINCHING WITH THE HI-LIFT JACK

You can also use the Hi-Lift jack as a mini-winch. Use a chain on each side, one looped around the top bracket of the jack and the other looped around the lifting arm. If your jack doesn't have a top bracket, use a heavy padlock or bolt to attach the chain to the jack (Figure 73). Then crank the jack handle back and forth and pull the rig free.

You can use tow straps if you don't have chains, but they're not nearly as safe. If a strap breaks, it will fling the jack and other hardware with a lot of force. If a chain breaks, it falls harmlessly to the ground because it doesn't store energy like a nylon tow strap or wire cable. (Figure 74).

A friend of mine recently spent a couple of years running an overhead crane in a sheet steel warehouse in Chicago. Some guys from West Virginia worked there too. After work they often hung around in a little park across the street, sipping moonshine from a Mason jar and trading stories. I guess these guys had an endless supply of uncles and cousins making runs between the West Virginia hills and Chicago to keep them in plenty of white lightnin'.

They were avid 'wheelers who would put rigs in places most people wouldn't even dream of going. One summer a year or two earlier, three of them had pooled their

resources and flown to Hawaii to check out the Big Island and take a look at the volcanoes. Hank, Robert, and Rip landed in Hilo, checked into a motel, and went right to a 4x4 shop one of their buddies had heard about. They rented an old CJ-7 Jeep with a swapped-in V8 and a Ramsey winch on the front. It was only lifted a little, and it had pretty old all-terrain tires. The spare was even worse. There was one tow strap and a couple of D-shackles. A very rusty Hi-Lift jack was bungeed to the front bumper.

They headed up route 11 from Hilo and circled Kilauea Caldera on Crater Rim Drive. They explored a narrow trail leading through the fields of black lava, reminding them of the coal their fathers used to drag out of the West Virginia mines. Pretty soon they yielded to the temptation to leave the trail and drive on the black rock.

There are several reasons not to do this, and they discovered all of them. To start with, one of their front wheels broke through the top of a lava tube and hung up the rig. They winched out, slinging the tow strap around an outcropping of the lava and anchoring to it. Not a good idea. By the time they got the rig out of the hole, the tow strap was frayed halfway through in two places by the sharp rock.

They couldn't go any farther anyway, because they were close to a ledge in the lava field, overlooking a 7- or 8-foot drop onto a flat rock below. They got in the Jeep to turn it around and head back to the trail. But the Hawaiian fire goddess, Pele, must have been pretty upset to see these three haoles *come in and tear up the lava she'd spent centuries so carefully sculpturing. She made sure these boys' troubles were just beginning.*

The black rock in most of this field was rough and spiny a'a lava, like a superabrasive version of one of those sanding blocks you use to refinish furniture. It offered great traction but was obviously chewing up the already marginal tires. As Robert was swinging the rig around to the left to head back toward the trail, the rear end hit a sloping patch of pa'hoehoe lava, smooth and slick. He skidded sideways into the edge of a lava shelf that looked like a machete. The sidewall of the right rear tire was sliced clean through.

They took the Hi-Lift jack off the front bumper and started to lift the back of the Jeep to put on the spare, but the jack was so rusty it wouldn't budge. They dripped some engine oil on it from the dipstick but couldn't get enough oil to do any good. Hank crawled under the rig and loosened the oil pan plug enough to fill a cup. Dripping that on the jack, they finally got it moving. They jacked up the Jeep and Rip removed the wheel and the shredded tire. He grabbed the spare, but as he was lifting it onto the hub, he slipped on the slick rock and the same edge that slashed the tire gashed his foot wide open, right through his canvas shoes.

"Damn!" he shouted. Trying to regain his footing,

he dropped the spare. Half bouncing, half sliding down the slope, it came to rest on its side, teetering on the edge of the ledge. Robert rushed forward, bending to grab it. The fragile edge of the drop-off crumbled, dumping both him and the spare tire onto the rock below.

A chorus of "damns," "goddamns," "sheeeeits," and so forth rang out. Hank and Rip, cautiously approaching the fresh new edge of the ledge, looked down at Robert, half-sitting, half-lying, rocking back and forth holding his ankle. "I broke my damn ankle!" he said. "Now what're we gonna do?"

"We're gonna haul you up, you dumb shit!" Rip said.

"Who's a dumb shit? I didn't drop the damn tire!" Robert said. "Rip's the dumb shit."

"Aw shut up!" Rip yelled. "My foot's bleeding all over my shoe!"

"Okay, dudes, let's just cool it," Hank said. "We've got work to do."

Hank and Rip put the frayed tire back on the Jeep and let down the jack. They started the engine, pulled the winch cable out, and ran it back under the Jeep, unwinding it until they could drop the hook down to Robert. They threw down the tow strap, which he wrapped securely around the spare tire and wheel, grimacing and swearing frequently from the pain in his ankle. Taking a seat cushion out of the Jeep and putting it under the cable to protect it from the sharp edge of the ledge, they winched the spare up. Lying flat on their bellies with as little weight as possible on the ledge, they gradually worked the spare back over the edge.

Then they fed the cable and tow strap back down to Robert. Wrapping it around himself like a harness, he hooked the cable through the nylon loops. Rip and Hank winched him up, rolling him over the ledge and back onto solid rock. The red evening sun slipped beyond the horizon at the far edge of the ocean lying in front of them, but they weren't in the mood to enjoy or even notice their first Hawaiian sunset. It began to get dark.

Hank and Rip helped Robert hobble back to the rig, laying him on a flat rock. After putting on the spare tire, they loaded Robert into the Jeep, his ankle the size of a football. Carefully picking their way through the lava, they strained to see as the black rock absorbed most of the feeble yellow glow of the headlights.

Pele looked down and admired her handiwork, her consort at her side. "You know, dear," he said, "there's a lot more you could've done. You could've had the tow strap they frayed break when Robert was halfway up the drop-off. You could've had the spare tire blow when it hit the rock below the ledge. You could've had the ledge crumble some more from the weight of the winch cable over it. They should learn you're not supposed to use a winch for hauling people. You could've had the battery go dead because they've got such a lousy alternator in that old CJ. You could've had the . . ."

"Hold on there, my love," Pele broke in. "We don't want to discourage tourism any more than we have to. I think they've had quite enough for now—except for one more little thing."

"What's that, dear?"

"Well, you know all that moonshine they brought with them in the Mason jars in their checked luggage? When they finally get back to the motel, they're going to discover that all those jars broke."

"That's wonderful, dear!" her consort chuckled admiringly. "So if those boys want any moonshine tonight, they're going to have to wring out their extra underwear."

chapter eleven

SNOW AND ICE
ARTFUL SKIDDING

Different kinds of surfaces make a rig slip and slide—snow, ice, mud, loose dirt, wet roads, rock slabs, oily asphalt, or a combination of the above, like wet oily asphalt or packed snow at 32°, which at the melting point develops a superslick coating of water on its surface. The principles of this chapter apply to all these surfaces.

Anticipate the need for 4WD and shift the T-case before the situation gets critical. With a 4WD system that gives a choice between part-time and full-time, use full-time when hitting occasional patches of snow or ice on generally dry pavement. Switch to part-time, with the T-case locked, when you're on long stretches of wet pavement, ice, snow, dirt, gravel, mud, or sand.

Drive slowly and smoothly. When accelerating, if the wheels spin, back off the gas slightly, then gently reapply power and work the vehicle into forward motion. Brake smoothly and carefully. The main way to stay safe on snow and ice is to cut your speed way down. No amount of money spent on snow tires, studding, siping, chains, or 4WD rigs can make up for driving too fast on a slippery surface.

SNOW TIRES—STUDDED OR NOT?

If you will be driving mainly on snow and ice, buy a set of dedicated snow tires. Get a separate set of wheels with the snow tires mounted on them, and when winter comes, put them on for the duration of the season.

Many winter drivers swear by studded tires. Studs are little pieces of steel, about the thickness of a wooden matchstick, placed in the tread of a tire. They project out about an eighth of an inch and grip an icy road surface. Advocates of studded tires feel they give more control on icy curves and hills, but don't get overconfident with them. They may not help much when stopping on ice. On solid ice, consider using chains to improve stopping ability. Cable-type chains aren't nearly as effective as regular chains and may actually increase stopping distance, especially when used on dedicated snow and ice tires.

Studded tires aren't legal in all states, and those allowing them usually limit their use to the winter months. Check the regulations in your particular state before investing in studded tires.

As the engineering of snow tires improves, there is debate on whether or not studs are necessary. A state-of-the-art snow tire, like Bridgestone's Blizzak, probably grips and stops as well without studs as other snow tires do with studs. So why not get the best of both worlds and stud a Blizzak? Because the studs rob you of the qualities that make the Blizzak such a good tire. The composition of the Blizzak has been engineered to grip an icy surface. Studs lift the tire off the ice and prevent the tire from adhering to the surface.

Studs have other disadvantages. With a quick stop on dry pavement, they slide and prevent the tire from gripping the surface, thereby increasing stopping distance. Studs may not grip ice very well, either, after they get rounded off with a few weeks of wear. Some experts feel that studs don't hold well on curves and may actually encourage skidding because they don't withstand the sideways force of a turn. Studded tires are also noisy on dry pavement. So pay attention to the "studs versus no studs" debate as it develops. They probably improve the performance of mediocre snow tires, but you may be better off investing in top-of-the-line snow tires and staying away from studs altogether.

SIPING THE TIRES

If your rig is driven on snow often, you should have your tires siped, with or without studs. Siping is the process of creating a number of small cuts across the treads of the tires. These small cuts open up on packed snow or ice and increase the traction. With wide studded tires, have the center part of the tread siped. The studs improve the traction on the inside and outside of the tread, and the siping improves the traction in the center (Figure 76). Many snow tires come already siped.

Siping seems to have no major ill effect on the tires, though some truck fleets that sipe their tires feel it decreases tread wear by as much as 10 percent. There is also a disadvantage when driving on gravel roads without snow. Small bits of gravel become stuck in the small cuts and generate noise and wear.

THE FOOTPRINT OF THE TIRE

Obviously, only a small patch at the bottom of each tire is in contact with the ground at any instant. This patch is called the footprint of the tire. On dry surfaces, a larger footprint increases the grip of the tire. On slippery surfaces, particularly snow and ice, the grip of the tire is determined not only by the size of the footprint but also by its shape. A longer, narrower footprint grips better on snow and ice than a wider one covering the same area. As traction decreases, tire design and construction contribute more to grip than footprint size alone.

The size of the footprint is determined by several things. Proper tire inflation increases the size of the footprint. With overinflation, only the center of the tread sits on the road; the outside and inside of the tire float above the surface. With underinflation, the center of the tread doesn't grip the road firmly when traveling on a hard surface. It's important to keep the tires at their proper pressure for the surface you're traveling. See Chapter 12 about airing down for sand and mud for more information about the size and shape of the footprint with different tire pressures.

PROS AND CONS OF WIDE TIRES

Some people advocate using tires that are especially wide in proportion to their height for traveling on slippery surfaces, but wide tires don't provide as much as directional stability as narrower tires. Wide tires are advantageous for traveling on soft surfaces like sand or deep mud because they let the rig float on top of the soft stuff, especially when aired down to enlarge the footprint even more.

But on firm slippery surfaces like packed snow, trails covered with a layer of silty dirt, or wet rock, the footprint of the wider tires tends to be more rounded. The footprints of narrower tires act somewhat like skis, pointing the rig along the track of the ski-like footprint. However, the footprint of a wider tire is more like a saucer, like the metal ones you or your kids ride down snowy hills. Wider tires let the rig slide off the road when a sideways slope forces the vehicle one way or the other. A narrower tire resists that force. Think twice before you invest in wide tires unless you'll be traveling in deep mud or sand.

THE ART OF BRAKING

There is an art to applying the brakes properly on slippery surfaces. Brake while traveling in a straight line; braking during a curve can lead to skidding. When steering around an obstacle, brake first in a straight line, then let up on the brakes and steer around the object. Don't lock the brakes. Without ABS, an emergency stop requires pumping the brakes. Apply the brakes until they just lock, let up for an instant, then quickly reapply fast and hard. Alternate rapidly—press hard, release, press hard, etc.

With ABS, it's important *not* to pump the brakes because the computer in the system does that for you. To get the computer to work, apply steady, hard pressure on the pedal. It's very important to be familiar with the rig you're driving and to know if it has ABS or not. Applying the brakes the wrong way could cost your life. Again, *without* ABS, pump the brakes in an emergency situation; *with* ABS, apply the brakes steadily and hard—don't pump them. And remember, for ABS to work best, you should have tires with the same tread and pressure on all four wheels. Putting tires on the front wheels that are different from those on the rear wheels confuses the ABS computer.

A rig can't be braked hard and steered at the same time. When approaching the locking point, you lose steering. Brake in a straight line, then release pressure and steer. With ABS, there is some limited capability of steering while braking, but it's better not to count on it.

THE STEERING WHEEL

How do you hold the steering wheel? The high-performance driving courses I've taken all advocate holding the wheel on opposite sides, at the 3 o'clock and the 9 o'clock positions. The vehicle is turned by sliding the hands between the 12 o'clock and 6 o'clock positions, never crossing center with either hand. The hand on the side to which the rig is turning pulls down. The hand on the other side pushes up.

To visualize this technique, pretend you're gripping a steering wheel, right hand at 3 o'clock, left at 9. Go through these motions: to turn right, the left hand grips the wheel and pushes up, from 9 o'clock to 12. The right hand slides along the wheel from 3 o'clock to 12, meeting the left hand. Then the right hand grips and pulls the wheel down, turning it from 12 o'clock to 6 while the left hand slides from 12 to 6 on the other side to meet it. Then the left hand grips and pushes the wheel up from 6 to 12 while the right hand slides from 6 to 12 on the right side, meeting the left. Straighten out the wheel at the end of a turn, simply reversing these maneuvers.

The rig turns faster using this method than when reaching your arms across each other to opposite sides of the wheel. This method also gives a better feel of the road. You can tell how the rig responds to the surface.

WEIGHT TRANSFER

Acceleration or deceleration changes the grip of the tires on the surface. Stepping on the accelerator, the car surges ahead with the weight thrown backward onto the rear wheels. The footprints of the rear tires get bigger and the rear wheels have more driving force.

When you lift your foot off the accelerator or apply the brakes, the weight of the rig continues forward and is thrown onto the front wheels. The footprints of the front tires enlarge and develop more driving force and more steering ability.

In a curve, centrifugal force throws weight to the outside, and the outside tires are loaded, thereby developing larger footprints.

UNDERSTEER AND OVERSTEER

When a vehicle enters a curve, inertia makes it want to keep going straight. Early in the curve, it doesn't respond well to efforts to steer it. This condition is called understeer, because the vehicle is turning less than you're steering it.

Later on in the curve, the rig tends to keep turning even when you apply less steering pressure on the steering wheel. This is called oversteer, because the vehicle is turning more than you're steering it. Oversteer can develop from several factors. The steering geometry can lead to a tendency to oversteer, though most vehicles are designed with a little bit of understeer, which gives more steering stability and helps straighten the front wheels out after a turn.

A rear wheel drive vehicle tends to oversteer, while front wheel drive tends to understeer. This is because the driving axle on a rig in a curve has a tendency to keep going straight rather than turn. If the rear wheels are driving the rig, accelerating pushes the rear of the vehicle toward the outside of the curve, pivoting it around into oversteer (turning more than the driver intends). Accelerating a front wheel drive rig pushes the front toward the outside of the curve, keeping it from turning as the driver intends. This is understeer. A vehicle in full-time 4WD tends to be more balanced in a curve than a 2 WD vehicle with either front wheel or rear wheel drive. The oversteer tendency of the driven rear wheels balances the understeer effect of the driven front wheels.

Oversteer also comes from weight shift to the outside of the turn. Centrifugal force loads the outside of the rig and presses its weight down onto the outside tires, enlarging their footprints. This gives the outside wheels more driving force to pull and push the rig around the curve.

The tendency to understeer or oversteer is different for every rig. Some rigs with a strong tendency to understeer take a lot of pressure on the steering wheel to turn them. Others tend to take off around a turn and turn tighter and tighter as the curve progresses—they tend to oversteer, and you have to actively turn the wheel back straight to pull the vehicle out of the turn. Know your vehicle. Practice with it so you know if it has a basic tendency to under- or oversteer.

87

Figure 75. Off the road and into the trees. A classic front-wheel skid—the front wheels didn't bite and the car wouldn't turn.

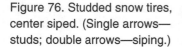

Figure 76. Studded snow tires, center siped. (Single arrows— studs; double arrows—siping.)

In the middle of the turn, a vehicle reaches a point where it changes between understeering early in the turn and oversteering later in the turn. This point is called the vehicle behavior point. Knowing where this point is for your rig will help you maximize its performance in turns. On dry pavement, this change is subtle. You can detect it more easily driving around a slippery curve.

The tendency to under- or oversteer is also affected by front-to-back weight distribution of the rig. For instance, as the vehicle heads into a curve going downhill, the weight of the car is thrown forward toward the front downhill wheels. In addition to transferring weight as a result of gravity, braking throws even more weight forward onto the front wheels. By turning the steering wheel with the front wheels loaded, you cause the rig to oversteer. It wants to turn more than you're actually steering it because the turning front wheels are gripping the road more tightly than the unloaded rear wheels.

When you are going uphill, the weight is thrown backward onto the rear wheels. When you are accelerating at the same time, even more weight is thrown onto the rear wheels. Heading into a turn under these conditions, the turning front wheels are unloaded compared to the rear wheels. What happens? Understeer—the car wants to keep going straight, because the unloaded front wheels don't turn the car well, and it takes more pressure on the steering wheel for the vehicle to turn.

You learn the characteristics of a vehicle by paying attention to these principles as you drive along a dry highway and by playing with the rig's steering dynamics going into curves uphill and downhill. Then, when you get on slippery surfaces where applying these principles makes the difference between a safe trip and disaster, you're ahead of the game.

Be aware that when you are driving in 4WD on a loose or slippery surface, the rig may alternate between oversteer and understeer as trail conditions vary and traction changes from wheel to wheel. Stay alert and pay attention to the feel of the rig and road. Let your rig and its wheels become an extension of your senses.

SKIDS

There are two types of skids—understeer and oversteer. Remember, understeer occurs when the front tires lose their grip and the rig refuses to respond to turning. Oversteer occurs when the rear tires lose their grip and the car turns too much because the rear wheels spin out. Front-wheel drive cars tend to develop understeer skids if you make the mistake of accelerating on a slippery curve; rear-wheel drives tend to oversteer from the rear wheels spinning out. Use weight-shifting to control skids, learning when to accelerate lightly and when to brake gently.

When you enter an understeer skid, the front wheels slide, refusing to turn, and the rig keeps going straight. The front wheels have lost grip and don't turn the car. This can happen from overaccelerating into a curve, causing weight to shift backward onto the rear wheels. Immediately straighten the front wheels and let off the accelerator or apply the brakes very gently, then gradually turn the front wheels again to guide the vehicle back on track. You have to straighten the front wheels before you can regain control. This takes courage, but it's essential (Figure 77).

The most common mistake in a front-wheel understeer skid is to keep turning the front wheels into the curve, frantically trying to get the car to turn. It won't work. The turned front wheels just keep skidding without turning the rig. Decelerate and straighten the front wheels simultaneously, then turn back gradually into the curve.

In an oversteer skid, the rear wheels slip to the outside of the curve and the vehicle starts to slide around into a 360. The instant you feel the rear wheels losing their grip, turn the front wheels quickly but only slightly toward the direction the rear wheels are sliding and gently accelerate to load the rear wheels. This gives them more grip as the weight shifts rearward (Figure 78).

Three mistakes commonly occur in a rear-wheel oversteer skid. The driver turns the front wheels even more into the curve, frantically trying to get the rig to go around the curve. This simply throws the car into a spectacular 360 and often ends with the vehicle sideways against oncoming traffic, rubber side up in a ditch, or rolling down a steep hill

beside the road. Don't turn more into the curve if starting a rear wheel skid.

The second mistake in a rear-wheel skid is hitting the brakes. This unloads the rear wheels even more and gives them even less traction, making the skid worse and more violent. Don't touch the brakes in a rear-wheel skid.

The third mistake is overcorrecting the front wheels in the direction of the rear-wheel slide. Overcorrecting throws the front end violently toward the outside of the curve, and the rear wheels rebound back toward the inside of the curve, causing a counterskid in the opposite direction. When you overcorrect in the opposite direction, the rig swings back again. This back-and-forth effect can go on for several cycles, finally ending with a 360 as the driver eventually loses control. Make corrections quickly as soon as you feel a skid occurring, but keep the corrections small.

SKID RECOVERY IN FRONT-WHEEL OR 4-WHEEL DRIVE

With a front-wheel drive vehicle or in 4WD, you can be much more aggressive when accelerating out of an oversteer skid. With rear-wheel drive only, it's hard to get the powered rear wheels to push the rig out of the skid. You must react very quickly as soon as the rear wheels start to come around. If they shift more than a few degrees to the outside of the curve before you turn toward the skid and accelerate, it's too late. You've lost it.

With front-wheel drive, the powered front wheels readily pull the rig out of the skid, and you can be much more aggressive with the acceleration you use as you turn toward the skid. You can still recover, even if the rear wheels have come around to almost 90°.

4WD also helps you recover from an oversteer skid more effectively than rear-wheel drive only. Accelerating aggressively uses the powered front wheels to pull the rig out of the skid, though not as effectively as with front-wheel drive only.

BE CAREFUL WHEN DOWNSHIFTING

When you are heading downhill on a loose or slippery surface, it's helpful to shift into a lower gear with a manual transmission or a lower range with an automatic. This allows the compression of the engine to slow you down so you don't have to use the brakes so much. Do this gradually! A sudden downshift can be like jamming on the brakes and can throw you into a skid. The sudden slowing of the wheels causes them to break free, and they lose traction. This can happen especially in 2WD, where downshifting can break the rear tires free and send them around in a violent oversteer skid. Slow down by gently tapping the brakes before you downshift in either 4WD or 2WD.

Weird things can happen when downshifting, even going uphill. A friend of mine was driving his family in their all-wheel drive van, using cruise control on a freeway. They came to a fairly steep upgrade and hit an icy patch just as the transmission downshifted to maintain the cruise-control speed. The sudden surge of power to the wheels broke their traction, and the van spun around in an all-wheel skid, making two complete revolutions. Fortunately, the van stayed on the highway and no other vehicles were nearby, so their frightening experience had a happy ending. The lessons, of course, are be careful when downshifting, even going uphill, and don't use cruise control on anything but a clean, dry highway in light traffic.

SLOW DOWN BEFORE THE CURVE!

Avoid being overconfident just because you've got 4-wheel drive or front-wheel drive. When approaching curves, slow down in plenty of time. Stay as far as you safely can to the outside of the curve as you approach so that you can make the turn as wide as possible. Turn more sharply in the beginning half of the turn so you can gradually straighten out as you pull around the turn. This keeps you from having to overcorrect halfway through, when a sharp increase in the rate of turning may throw you into a skid.

When heading into a curve going downhill on a slippery surface, the rig will tend to enter a rear-wheel oversteer skid because the rear wheels are relatively unloaded.

CURVES—ON-CAMBER AND OFF-CAMBER

Be aware of the slope of the curve as you go into it. A road sloped with the outside of the curve higher than the inside is said to be on-camber, and your rig will be relatively stable rounding the curve. Gravity pulls the rig down the slope toward the inside of the curve, counteracting the centrifugal force that tends to pull the rig toward the outside of the curve.

A flat curve isn't as stable, because gravity isn't offsetting centrifugal force. An off-camber curve is even worse, with the outside of the curve lower than the inside. This is a dangerous curve, very unstable, because both gravity and centrifugal force pull the rig out of the curve. Watch out for off-camber curves. When you see one come up, slow down before entering it. By entering the curve too fast and hitting the brakes to slow down, you unload the rear wheels, and gravity and centrifugal force can easily spin you out in a violent oversteer skid.

There's a trick to taking flat and off-camber curves at higher speeds. The 6 inches or so of pavement next to the shoulder usually slope down to meet the shoulder. The "inside" of the curve is the side on the direction of the curve. For instance, in a right curve, the road is curving to the right and the inside of the curve is the right side of the road. Putting the right wheels (the "inside" wheels) on the edge of the pavement where it slopes down, or on the shoulder itself, lowers that side of the rig and partially compensates for the loss of proper camber. In the United States, this works well for a right-hand curve, since we drive on the right side of the road. Using this trick on a left curve means crossing over into the oncoming lane, obviously not a good idea, especially on a blind curve.

DRIVING ON SNOW

How you drive in snow depends on how deep it is, what its consistency is, and what the surface underneath is like. With solid ground or hard-packed snow under a soft surface layer that's up to 8 or 9 inches deep, you can probably drive through it, getting traction from the solid surface underneath. A surface crust might be thick and firm enough to support you, but be careful. Breaking through it into a layer of powdery fluff that's several feet deep may get you hopelessly stuck.

Remember that a layer of crusted snow that supports a rig early in the morning may thaw enough during the day so it doesn't support you on the way home. Without an alternate route back, you're stranded.

With snow deep but thick in consistency, you may be able to float on top by airing down the tires on a relatively lightweight rig. Driving in thick mud is similar. Don't use chains while aired-down; the tires won't stand up to them when underinflated.

Don't air down when driving on packed snow. This actually decreases the adhesion of the tire to the road because it interferes with a process called

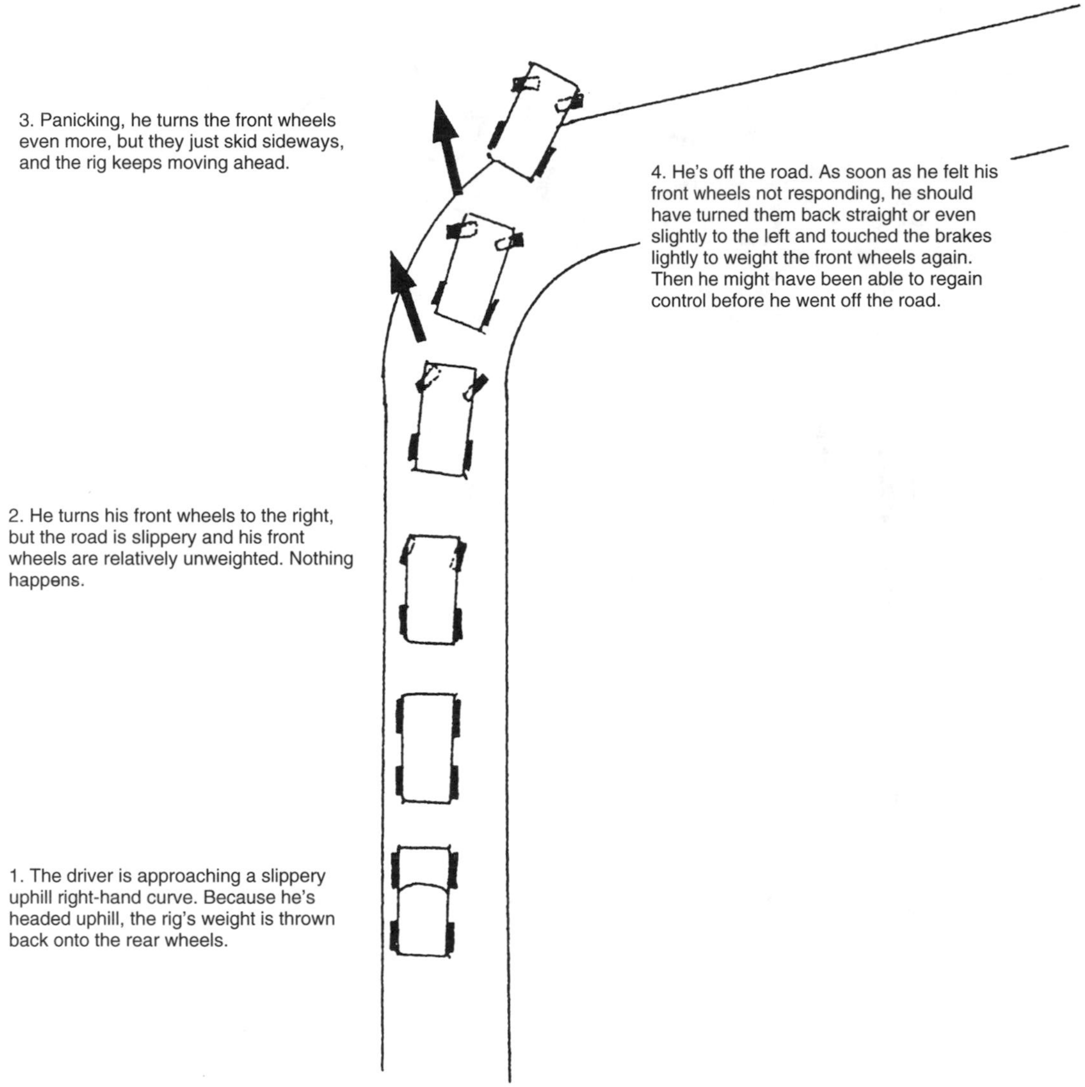

3. Panicking, he turns the front wheels even more, but they just skid sideways, and the rig keeps moving ahead.

4. He's off the road. As soon as he felt his front wheels not responding, he should have turned them back straight or even slightly to the left and touched the brakes lightly to weight the front wheels again. Then he might have been able to regain control before he went off the road.

2. He turns his front wheels to the right, but the road is slippery and his front wheels are relatively unweighted. Nothing happens.

1. The driver is approaching a slippery uphill right-hand curve. Because he's headed uphill, the rig's weight is thrown back onto the rear wheels.

Figure 77. The understeer skid.

differential compaction. It turns out that different clumps of snow crystals stick to each other better if one clump is compacted firmly and the other less firmly. Packed snow on a road is compacted firmly. The snow forced into the empty spaces in the tread of a snow tire is compacted less firmly. A tire's adhesion to a packed snowy road comes from the looser snow in its tread sticking to the firmer snow on the road. If you air down a tire, you lift the center portion of the tread off the road and interfere with adhesion of the snow in the treads to the road. You also change the angle of the grooves in the treads and interfere with the snow-to-snow adhesion. On deep loose snow or deep slush, do whatever works— airing down, chains, or the winch.

Traveling with other rigs is especially important when driving off-highway in snow country so help is right there if you get bogged down. Getting stuck by yourself miles from nowhere in cold, snowy weather is not a safe way to get experience in survival skills. And don't forget a CB radio when venturing out in the winter wilderness,

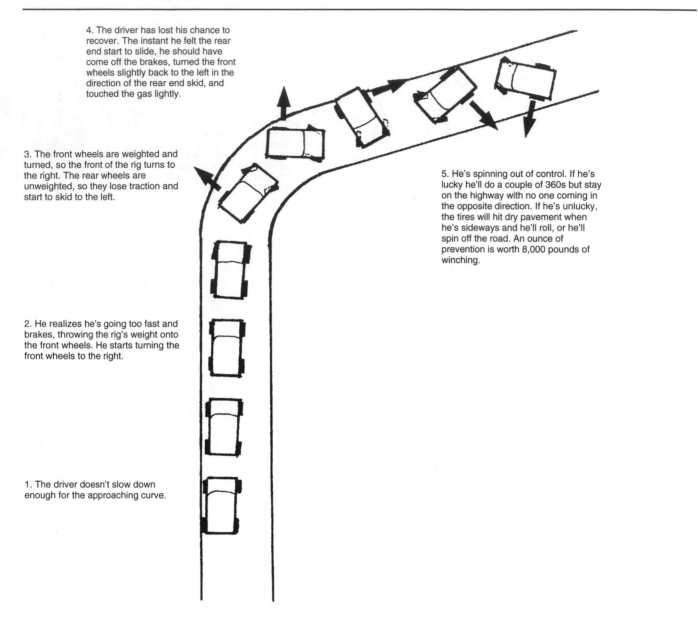

4. The driver has lost his chance to recover. The instant he felt the rear end start to slide, he should have come off the brakes, turned the front wheels slightly back to the left in the direction of the rear end skid, and touched the gas lightly.

3. The front wheels are weighted and turned, so the front of the rig turns to the right. The rear wheels are unweighted, so they lose traction and start to skid to the left.

5. He's spinning out of control. If he's lucky he'll do a couple of 360s but stay on the highway with no one coming in the opposite direction. If he's unlucky, the tires will hit dry pavement when he's sideways and he'll roll, or he'll spin off the road. An ounce of prevention is worth 8,000 pounds of winching.

2. He realizes he's going too fast and brakes, throwing the rig's weight onto the front wheels. He starts turning the front wheels to the right.

1. The driver doesn't slow down enough for the approaching curve.

Figure 78. The oversteer skid.

along with plenty of warm clothes, a cold-weather sleeping bag for each person, gas in the tank, and fire-building equipment.

GET HANDS-ON TRAINING

Driving safely on snow and ice is tricky. If you have the time, money, and motivation, it's safest to learn these skills with the help of qualified and experienced instructors. The Bridgestone Winter Driving School in Steamboat Springs, Colorado, offers courses in the art of keeping your rig on track when roads get slick. (See the Resources section, Appendix C, for more information.)

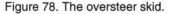

One of the main reasons many 4by families buy such a rig is to be safer in the snow. As a 4x4 owner, you'll certainly want to master the skills in this chapter, even if you never intend to drive your vehicle into rough off-road country. The unexpected blizzards the East Coast experienced during the winter of 1995–1996 taught us all that it pays to be prepared.

chapter twelve

SOFT STUFF
AIRING DOWN FOR MUD AND SAND

Though driving on snow, mud, or sand requires similar skills, each surface presents unique challenges. In this chapter, we'll delve into the fine points of negotiating muddy roads, swamps, beaches, and sand dunes.

SLOGGING THROUGH MUD

There are basically three ways to get across a stretch of mud: 1) let the rig sink down into it until your tires grab solid ground at the bottom; 2) air down and float on top as much as possible; 3) winch your rig across it. The problem is, different kinds of mud require entirely different techniques, and it's not possible to prepare for all the possibilities when planning a trip. Mud can be super sticky, wet and slippery, bottomless, or it can just form a thin layer over solid ground underneath.

When encountering a stretch of mud, stop, get out, and take a close look at the stuff. Poke a stick in it. How deep is it? If you don't feel solid ground 7 or 8 inches down, consider airing way down and floating on top. But before doing so, determine the following: Is it thick enough to support you? Are your tires wide enough to let you float on top? Is your rig too heavily loaded to float on top? With normal-size tires, a heavily loaded rig, or thin, bottomless mud, turn around! Don't try it, even with a winch. Unless the bog is in the middle of a forest,

you won't be able to find a decent anchor point to winch against, and if you sink up to the door handles, winching out may be impossible anyway.

You can get an idea whether the mud is thick enough to support your rig by walking through it a short distance and noticing what happens to your footprints. Do they keep their shape, indicating mud thick enough to have some body to it, or do their sides ooze in and fill them up, indicating thin mud that will suck your rig down to its roof?

Figure 79. With a few inches of mud over firm ground, let your wheels sink down and grip the solid surface without airing down. Never air down if you're using chains.

Figure 80. Before airing down. Street pressure: 35 pounds. The tires are LT265/75R16, total height 30 inches. Tire height, wheel rim to ground 5.63 inches.

Figure 81. After airing down. Sand/mud pressure: 10 pounds. Tire height: 4.0 inches: 71 percent of the original height.

If it's thick, it may support your vehicle, but do you have the right kind of tires to handle it? Thick mud tends to fill up your tire treads, obliterating their gripping effect.

To make it through thick mud, you need tires with an open tread. The ridges on the tread of a mud or snow tire are called lugs. A mud tire needs wide spaces between the lugs. This lets the tire clean itself as it revolves, throwing out chunks of mud and

preserving the grip. Tires like Interco's Super Swamper Boggers or Mickey Thompson's Baja Belted Sidebiters are designed to be self-cleaning in mud. If running on regular all-terrain tires or mud and snow tires, your rig may not be able to handle thick mud. If the mud's heavy enough to support you, your tires are up to the job, and your rig is not too heavily loaded, air down and go for it.

With thin mud overlying firm ground a few

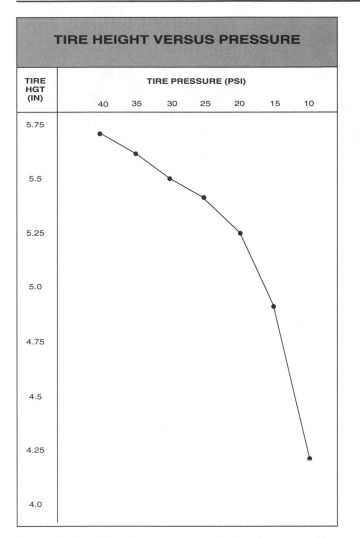

TIRE HEIGHT VERSUS PRESSURE

TIRE HGT (IN)	TIRE PRESSURE (PSI)						
	40	35	30	25	20	15	10

Figure 82. The height/pressure curve for the tires on my '94 K-Blazer. The height doesn't fall rapidly until the low end of the curve.

inches down, you're better off with narrower tires, inflated normally or even overinflated, allowing the wheels to sink down through the mud to the firm surface, where they can get a good bite (Figure 79). You still need tires with space between the lugs so the mud gets thrown off as the tire goes around.

If you do not have dedicated mud tires, use chains to get across a muddy stretch, provided there's a reasonably firm bottom to the stuff. You can buy dedicated mud chains with broader, heavier links, but snow chains work fine. Put them on all four wheels, as shown in the photograph on the front cover of this book. Be sure they're tight, and don't use them on aired-down tires. You should always avoid spinning the wheels, and this is especially true

when using chains. A spinning wheel with chains on it tears up the ground even more than a spinning unchained wheel. Additionally, chains on a spinning wheel are likely to break, tearing up your rig as well as the ground. But used carefully, chains can be a good friend on a muddy, rutted road.

There's an exception to the "no wheel spinning" rule. On mud or snow, the spaces between the lugs can fill up, turning the tread of the tire into the equivalent of a racing slick and causing it to lose grip. Judiciously spinning the wheel may be necessary to throw the mud or snow out of the tread to restore traction. The trick is to limit the aggressiveness of the spin so the wheel doesn't dig down into the soft stuff.

You can winch your way across a narrow patch of muddy ground, provided it's not too deep and you find a good anchor point on the other side. If another rig more lightly loaded and with tires better suited for the task can get across to firm ground, you can anchor to that vehicle. Chock the wheels of the anchoring rig firmly. SureClaw anchors are especially good in this situation. You may have to anchor the other rig to a tree or boulder to stabilize it. If each vehicle has a winch, use them both. Winching through mud taxes your equipment to the max, and you need all the help you can get.

When you're back up to speed after negotiating a stretch of thick mud, be aware that the stuff can dry and cake unevenly to your driveshafts and wheels. This throws the moving parts severely out of balance and can cause a wheel, tire, or driveshaft to give way if you don't stop and correct the problem. This situation is more likely to develop when you haven't been able to move fast enough to throw the mud off the moving parts while it's still wet, such as when you stop to camp overnight soon after crossing the bog.

After getting out of mud, stop after a few miles and check the driveshafts and wheels to make sure you aren't carrying potentially dangerous chunks of dried stuff on these parts. If you are, scrape them off while they're still wet, before you have to break them off with a hammer or crowbar.

RUNNING ON SAND

Driving on sand or deep, silty soil requires staying on top. There's rarely a firm undersurface within reach. This is best done with wide tires, aired down, and a lightweight rig. Just airing down regular all-terrain tires helps a lot, but if you're planning to make beach driving a frequent event, consider investing in a set of extra-wide tires such as the

95

Figure 83. Airing down gives your tires a much bigger footprint. Before airing down the footprint is 6.56 inches long at a street pressure of 35 pounds.

Figure 84. After airing down to 10 pounds, the footprint lengthens to 13.25 inches. It also becomes correspondingly wider.

Mickey Thompson Sportsman Pro. You can buy specialized sand tires with large paddle-like lugs on them, but they aren't legal to drive on the street.

Sportsman Pro tires are marketed mainly for drag racing, but they're street legal. They're good for sand because they're so wide. You can buy a set that's 31 inches tall and up to 18 inches wide. Aired down, you get a huge footprint keeping you on top. They don't work for general trail use, though, because the width and the tread design don't give you enough contact pressure with the ground to get you up steep hills or over large rocks. They aren't good for snow, either, because their width doesn't let them dig down to firmer ground underneath. Their narrow tread pattern fills up with snow, and the tire surface gets slick. Good snow tires have empty space between the lugs to let the treads throw the snow out and clean themselves as they rotate, similar to mud tires.

Beach sand can be treacherous when it's wet. Usually, wet sand just below the high-tide line is firmer because it's packed and supports a rig better than the loose stuff. Sometimes, though,

the layers of sand under the packed surface contain a lot of water and act like quicksand if the vehicle sinks through the upper layer. The surface won't support a jack, and there's no good anchor point to winch against. Another rig can't approach you to tow you out. You're really stuck if you get caught in sand like this, and if the tide's coming in at the time, you may say "sayonara" to your 4by. Before you play in the sand in a particular area, it's a good idea to check with the locals first. Ask them if there are any sandtraps around so you can avoid those spots.

You can encounter a similar condition driving on dried lake beds. Breaking through the seemingly solid crust drops the rig into a sea of bottomless mud. This is a dangerous situation because if the mud is thin, it will swallow the rig rapidly. Thicker mud may support it till help comes, but what help? With the rig in the middle of a lake bed, no winch can reach it. No other rig can risk driving out to help. If the consistency of the mud permits, try the usual rescue efforts with the Hi-Lift jack and traction strips,

TIRE FOOTPRINT VERSUS PRESSURE

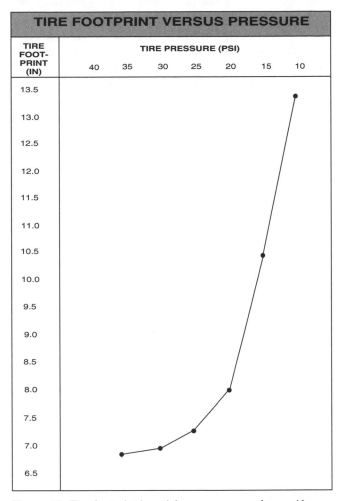

Figure 85. The footprint length/pressure curve for my K-Blazer's tires.

trying to back up onto more solid crust. If this fails, you're probably looking at professional rescue from a salvage company specializing in moving heavy equipment off the beaten path. This gets very expensive. The best plan is to travel with other rigs and never get beyond winching range as you explore new territory.

TRAVEL ON TOP

The key to traveling on top of deep mud or sand is airing down. Let the air out of the tires before entering the stuff. This does several things. It flattens the bottom of the tire and increases the footprint by two to three times. This makes the wheels more resistant to sinking into the sand or mud and gives the tires better grip to move the vehicle.

Airing down also gives the wheels and tires a smaller diameter. It's easier for the engine, working

through the drivetrain, to move the rig, because the smaller tire is like a smaller driving gear, which has a better mechanical advantage than a large one. Pumping uphill on your 21-speed bicycle, it's easier when downshifting the front gear to the smallest sprocket. This gives your legs more leverage on the chain. In your rig, the smaller wheels increase what's called the "net moving force" of the tires against the ground.

LET OUT A LOT

How much air do you let out of your tires? An amazing amount. Depending on the particular rig, load, tires, etc., there are times when you carry as few as 3 (yes—three) pounds, and pressures of 7 to 10 pounds are not uncommon. How do you know the best pressure for your particular rig? Experiment before going out on the beach or in the swamp. Measure how much air you need to let out to reduce the height of the load-bearing portion of your tires by 25 percent, down to 75 percent of the original height.

THE HEIGHT VS. PRESSURE CURVE

With your rig loaded like it will be in the sand or mud, and with your tires inflated at highway pressure (probably 25 to 35 pounds, depending on the vehicle and tires), measure the distance from the ground to the bottom of the wheel rim (Figure 80). Write these numbers down in a little table or on a sheet of graph paper. Then let out 5 pounds of air. Measure the height again, and write down the height and pressure on the graph or table. Repeat this—5 more pounds out, measure, write it down. Keep going. Remember, starting with a height of 5 1/2 inches, for example, you're aiming for 75 percent of that, or about 4 inches (Figure 81). You'll notice a surprising thing. The tire doesn't lose height rapidly until the air pressure reaches the lower end of the curve (Figure 82).

Airing down from 35 pounds, the first 20 pounds out reduces the tire height by about 15 percent of the original height, and the tire goes from 5 1/2 inches to slightly over 4 1/2 inches. But by letting out only another 5 pounds, to go from 15 to 10 pounds, the tire height drops another 10 percent of the initial height to about 4 inches. Writing the pressure and height down in graph form gives an appreciation of how much is gained from the loss of those last few pounds.

Many times, airing down to 15 pounds or so is sufficient and will give you enough increased traction to negotiate a soft patch just fine. But other times, like when you're up to the hubs in mud or sand, you need to push the envelope to keep moving. These are the times you're glad you took the trouble to learn how much air to let out of your own tires to reach that 75-percent level. These are the times you want as fat a profile and footprint as possible (Figures 83, 84, 85).

Airing down to this degree takes courage but pays off big dividends because you rarely get stuck in the soft stuff. It always helps to have a pioneer leading the way. In this case, it's Southern California's Harry Lewellyn, otherwise known as the Silver Coyote, one of the major gurus of 4-wheeling. When most other 4-wheelers were nudging their tires down to 16 or 18 pounds and wondering why they still had to dig and winch themselves out of sand and mud, Harry was measuring and experimenting and learning that the 75-percent figure was the magic number. He learned it often took airing down to the 10 pound level or below to accomplish that.

You need an accurate low-pressure gauge. Don't count on reading low pressures accurately with a standard gauge. Even if they register below 10 pounds, they often aren't accurate at the low end.

All four tires need to be at the same pressure for best performance. Airing down and back up is tedious because you've got to squat or kneel beside each tire for several minutes, checking the pressure frequently while the air's going out or back in. A company called Quadra-Flate helps the process by selling a gadget with hoses going to all four tires at the same time. This lets you air down or reinflate all four tires simultaneously and equalizes the pressure in all the tires as well. Equal pressure in all tires has fringe benefits. The ABS system works better, as do differential lockers. If you will be airing down frequently, the Quadra-Flate is definitely a valuable investment. (See Appendix C, Resources, for the company's address.)

Airing down sometimes helps in snow, but never air down and use chains at the same time. The chains can tear up the soft tires.

The trade off for airing down is loss of an inch or two of ground clearance. Take this into consideration when deciding whether or not to air down over a particular stretch of rough or muddy ground.

LIGHTEN UP

Aired down to this degree, the rig will tend to ride on top of the soft surface, provided you're not loaded to the max. If your goal is to have fun surfing the sand at the beach, use a Jeep or even a mini-ute. They ride a lot higher than the heavier midsize and full-size sport-utes. But when in the rough country and having to cross a patch of mud, sand, or loose silty dirt, then you've got to use what you're driving. Driving a fully loaded full-size sport-ute with the patch of mud or sand short, you may be better off partially unloading the vehicle and carrying your equipment across in several trips to keep the rig as light as possible.

WATCH OUT FOR THE WHEEL RIMS

Aired-down tires climb over obstacles better than fully inflated tires, with the tires conforming to the obstacle and gripping it better. You can use aired-down tires to rock-climb, but watch out for a couple of things. The super-soft tires don't protect the wheel rims, and you risk bending the rims while lurching and jolting over rocks. The sidewalls of the aired-down tires are more susceptible to damage, too. By the same token, if your aired-down tires hit a buried rock or log under the surface of mud or sand, the rims may be damaged. (See Chapter 8 on rock crawling for more information about airing down in the rocks.)

This is one of the major risks of airing down—damaging the wheel rims. The other is twisting the tire off the wheel. An underinflated tire tends to come off the rim, even with bead locks on the wheel. So the principle is to go slow and avoid sudden turns or skids. The larger the wheel, the easier it is for the aired-down tire to twist off the rim. Fifteen-inch wheels are more secure than 16-inch wheels.

AIRING BACK UP

When out of the soft stuff, air back up right away. Underinflated tires generate a lot of heat, and heading out at highway speed, soft tires won't last long. Obviously before you air down, you've got to have the means to air back up. The Quadra-Flate device helps here, too. Carry an efficient air compressor that you've tested before you're out in the country. If you're driving a Hummer, you've got an on-board air compressor and a switch on the dashboard that lets you air down and back up from the driver's seat.

Ideal tire pressure for highway travel lets your tires wear evenly. If overinflated, the central part of the tread bulges out against the road and wears out faster than the edges of the tread. Underinflation does the opposite—the inside and outside of the tread wear faster. See what's happening to your tires by drawing a line across the tread from side to side with chalk. Drive a ways and check the chalk lines. If the chalk lines are rubbed off in the center, your tires are overinflated. If they are thin on the edges, it indicates underinflation. With proper pressure, the chalk wears evenly all the way across.

KEEP MOVING, DON'T BRAKE, STEER GRADUALLY

Other principles of mud and sand driving are to keep moving and avoid using the brakes to stop. Once you've established momentum, keep going, smoothly and steadily. When you stop, let the vehicle coast to a stop. It won't take long with the soft surface slowing you down. Using the brakes, especially in sand, throws up mounds of sand in front of each wheel. When starting again, you will have to climb over these.

In sand or other soft surfaces, don't stop when heading uphill. It's much harder to get it rolling again. Try to turn your vehicle so it's headed downhill before you come to a stop. That makes it easier to get it moving when you start out again.

Once moving, go as straight as possible and steer as gradually as possible. Turning the front wheels increases the drag on the vehicle and may cause enough loss of traction to hang you up.

When in sand, don't drive directly in the tracks from another rig. The leading rig breaks whatever crust the surface of the sand may offer, and you will sink even deeper if you follow them exactly.

Get a feel for the surface on which you're driving. Use enough power to get moving, but not so much that you spin the wheels. Spinning wheels dig you right down in a big hurry, whether you're in mud or sand. With a manual transmission, put the T-case in 4-wheel Hi and the transmission in second or third gear to avoid overtorquing the wheels and spinning them. Staying in 4-wheel Hi lets you establish momentum once you get moving, and momentum does the most to keep you up on top.

With most automatic transmissions, you don't have the option of starting in anything but the lowest gear, though a few allow locking out the lowest range, such as the Mercedes G-wagen. Stay in 4WD Hi in your T-case. Low range may give too much power and cause the wheels to spin.

If your wheels are spinning no matter how carefully you apply the throttle, it sometimes helps to apply the brake gently with your left foot at the same time. This may retard the spinning wheels, trans-

ferring enough torque to the wheels with traction to get you out of there. You can also try setting the emergency brake a little; this may help, especially with a limited-slip differential.

If you're mechanically inclined, crawl under the rear of your rig and disconnect the emergency brake cable to the wheel with traction. Then, applying gentle throttle again, brake the spinning wheel with the emergency brake, transferring increasing torque to the wheel with traction.

PROTECT YOUR ENGINE AND WINCH

In the next chapter we talk about driving through water. One of the tips is to tie a tarp or piece of heavy canvas over the front of the rig to discourage water from entering the engine compartment. This trick helps in mud, too. If the mud is deep enough in spots to come up over your front bumper, the tarp will keep the winch free of mud and keep mud out of the radiator. With a layer of water on the bog you're in, the tarp helps keep the muddy water out of the winch and engine compartment. Use this trick only for short periods and watch the temperature gauge carefully. The engine overheats rapidly when the radiator is covered for very long, especially when working hard through deep, thick mud.

GETTING UNSTUCK IN SAND

With your wheels digging in and getting stuck, don't spin the wheels more. Just stop. Figure out if you want to back out the way you came or if you've got a better chance to reach firm ground going forward. Get all the passengers out to lighten up as much as possible. They'll need to push, too, but you don't have to tell them this yet.

Some people advise trying to rock the rig out, but rocking doesn't work well in sand unless there's a firm, packed surface a few inches down.

If stuck in dry sand, try soaking it if there's water around. Wet sand packs down and gives more traction than the loose, dry stuff. Wet the sand around all four wheels and in tracks in the direction you'll be heading as you drive out. Once you get moving, keep moving.

If no water is available, get out the Hi-Lift jack. The jack will sink into bare sand, so put its base on a board carried for this purpose. Jack up a wheel and put traction material under it. Boards or aluminum strips work well. Strips of heavy carpet may work, too. British 4-wheeler Jack Jackson, a veteran of many trips through the Sahara Desert, recommends using sand ladders. These are steel ladderlike devices made expressly for getting unstuck from the sand. Lighter weight fiberglass strips, called Waffles, are being developed for this purpose as well.

Whatever type of traction strip you choose, lower the wheel onto it and go on to the next wheel. If really stuck, put strips under all four wheels.

Now's the time to get your passengers to push hard as you drive out of the hole. They need to keep clear of the area right behind the traction boards, though, in case one or more kick backward if a wheel spins. If you get stuck again, repeat the jacking up process as many times as it takes to move onto firm ground. Once you get moving, don't stop to retrieve the traction strips until out of the soft section that trapped you. Go back and get the strips after reaching a more solid surface. Before you drive out of the hole, put a jacket or T-shirt on the ground next to the traction strips. This marks their position in the sand so you can find them again. The weight of your rig tends to bury them.

GETTING UNSTUCK IN MUD

If you are stuck in mud, you might try rocking the rig out. Do this by shifting quickly from a forward gear to reverse, gradually building momentum in each direction as you develop a rhythm forward and backward. Rocking is easier with an automatic transmission or at least a manual with a synchromesh reverse.

If rocking doesn't work, suction may be holding you in. Dig out the mud at the side of each wheel to break the suction. Air down if the mud doesn't have a solid underlayer. You may have to spin the wheels a little to throw mud out of the treads. If you can't get moving even aired down, it's time to unwind the winch. Anticipate using your winch before entering a mud bog and cover it and its housing with a piece of canvas or tarp first to keep the mud out of the mechanism and to make it easier to find the cable and controls in case your front bumper gets submerged in the slime.

DON'T GET STUCK WITH A TRAILER ATTACHED

If you are hauling a trailer, take even greater precautions to avoid getting stuck. Trying to break your vehicle free when it's got a trailer attached is a real test. You'd probably have to disconnect the trailer, get the rig unstuck, then winch the trailer out. Often the challenge is getting the trailer disconnected from the rig. Put a board under the trailer tongue jack and try to lift the tongue off the ball hitch of the rig. You run into trouble here if the rig and the trailer are at two different, weird angles, preventing you from lifting the tongue off. Your ingenuity and patience may be tested, eventually ending in unloading the trailer to lighten it and jacking up one side of the rig or trailer to realign the ball and the trailer tongue.

If you're taking your trailer off-road as a steady diet, you'll probably want to replace your ball hitch with a more forgiving pintle hitch. This latch-type hitch accepts a ring on the end of the trailer tongue and is used a lot by the military. In off-road situations, it doesn't bind like a ball hitch. The trade-off is more slack action and less stability on the highway.

FROZEN MUD

If the weather's cold, don't forget that a frozen swamp may support a rig in the morning, but in the warmer afternoon, heading back home through that same swamp, the rig may sink up to its door handles. Plan ahead. Frozen, crusted snow is the same: firm in the morning, soft in the afternoon.

After a day of wheeling on the beach or in the mud, clean your rig thoroughly. The damp mud and sand are everywhere, trapping moisture, holding it against the sheet metal under the rig and in the wheel wells, and encouraging corrosion. Hose down the undersurface of the vehicle as well as the engine compartment. Sand from an ocean beach contains salt and is especially corrosive. Get it off as soon as you can.

Unfortunately, protecting your expensive engine and drivetrain requires more than just a quick hosing down, especially when the rig's been exposed to saltwater or sand. For maximum protection, you should pull the wheels and clean the brakes. Otherwise, the sand and mud can score the drums or rotors. Change the oil and the lubricating fluids in the T-case, transmission, and differentials. Change the filters. You may have to repack the wheel bearings if they're wet and you don't have the sealed variety.

Driving in the sand and mud is fun and challenging, but your rig won't last long without paying close attention to maintenance. Washing corrosive salt and sand off quickly and keeping the oil and lubricating fluids clean are the keys.

chapter thirteen

CROSSING STREAMS

RIG SURFING

If you need to cross a stream, pond, or flooded area, make sure you know what you're getting into. If you can't tell how deep it is, walk it first. Without a pair of hip boots, just grit your teeth and wade across, unless you can talk your passengers into doing it for you. It's better to get wet checking the depth than to get wet climbing out of a hopelessly stalled, waterlogged rig in the middle of a stream you didn't test. A stream too swift to safely wade across is probably too swift to safely drive across. Rushing water can push even a heavy vehicle downstream into deeper water, where it can stall or overturn.

Make sure the stream bottom is firm enough to support your vehicle, and be sure there aren't any drop-offs or holes halfway across. Explore the bottom enough so you know there aren't any large boulders sitting there to bring you to a jolting, soggy stop. The bottom of a faster moving stream will tend to be more solid, because the swift current carries away mud. A slower-moving stream tends to deposit squishy stuff on the bottom, especially at the point where a faster, shallower stream widens and deepens to move at a more leisurely pace. If you can cross at a point where the water's moving faster, there's a better chance that the stream's shallower and that the bottom's more solid.

Don't forget that when driving across a deep stream or river with water up past the bottom of the doors, you'll lose traction because the body of your rig will be buoyed up by the water. You'll have less effective weight providing traction against the stream bottom. This can be a big problem if you've got to get up a slippery bank on the far side. Have your winch set up and ready to go if it looks like you'll have trouble getting out the other side.

HOW DEEP CAN YOUR RIG GO?

Be aware of the depth capability of your rig. Know the answers to these questions: how high off the ground are the air intake and vent openings of the differentials, T-cases, and transmission? How high is the distributor or other ignition components? Some rigs have a computer under the front seat; how will it fare when the water's deeper than the bottom of the doors? How well sealed are the spark plugs, wiring, and other parts of the ignition system?

The air intake should be at least 12 inches above the water level. Consider attaching a snorkel. ARB makes one for Jeeps, or you can fashion your own from PVC pipe. Turn the air intake to the rear to lessen the chance of water getting in. Extend the vent tubes from the differentials, the T-case, and the transmission. Relocate the computer to as high a level as possible. (You should probably ask an experienced mechanic to do this.)

PROTECT YOUR IGNITION SYSTEM

You can spray silicone coating on your ignition and spark plug wires to help protect them from

Figure 86. Know the depth of the water before committing yourself. Our boots are soggy inside the rig, but we know the bottom's safe.

Figure 87. With water above the bumper, tie a tarp or piece of canvas over the front of your rig before entering. As you move steadily ahead, the tarp keeps water out of the engine compartment and off the winch.

moisture. If the electrical system gets wet when driving across a stream, dry it out by spraying on a moisture-displacing substance such as CRC 5-56 or Formula 12/34, available at auto parts stores. Formula 12/34 is probably better because it's nonflammable.

KEEP MOVING, BUT NOT TOO FAST

Once committing the vehicle to the water, keep moving. Keep your speed steady, but not too fast. Create a small wave in front of your rig like the wave around the bow of a boat as it moves through the water. This helps keep water out of the engine compartment. However, going too fast can push the radiator back into the fan and damage both components. Too high a speed also forces water back against the fan, which sprays it all over the engine compartment. If you are anticipating water at bumper level or higher, it's best to disconnect the fan before entering to avoid spraying water over the engine.

You can discourage water from entering the engine compartment by draping a tarp or long piece of canvas over the front of the rig before entering the water (Figure 87). Open the hood and tuck the edge of the tarp into the opening in front of the windshield. Close the hood to trap the edge. Or tie the corners of the tarp to the outside rearview mirrors. Then drape the tarp over the hood, down over the grill and winch, and back under the vehicle about 5 or 6 feet. Tie each lower corner loosely to something under the rig so the material won't get dragged under one of the front wheels. As you move steadily through the water, the tarp will keep water away from the engine.

DRIVE AT AN ANGLE TO THE CURRENT

If possible, plan your course through the water so you drive at an angle to the current. This presents less surface area to the force of the current, with less chance of being pushed downstream. If the current is not too swift, drive angled upstream against it. This creates a bow wave and compensates for the tendency of the current to push you downstream off course. In faster currents, you may need to angle downstream to lessen the chance of the current itself pushing water into your engine compartment.

WINCH ACROSS RAPID WATER

Rushing water often creates an unstable streambed. Inspect the bed as you wade across a swift stream. If the bottom appears to be moving with the current, your rig may move with it right downstream. Don't take a chance—winch across.

Carry the winch cable hook across the stream and secure it to an anchor point on the other side. If the cable is too short for the width of the stream, you can extend the distance by stringing two or three tow straps together with D-shackles and anchoring to them.

It's also safer to use a heavy rope or cable to tether the rear of the vehicle to an anchor point on the near shore. This keeps the rig from being swung downstream, dangling on the end of the winch cable, where it could hang up on rocks or fall into a hole in the stream bottom. Maintaining control of the rear of the rig keeps you in the path you've chosen. Someone stays behind and gradually plays out the tethering line as you winch across.

Remember, if you get stuck in the middle of a stream with your winch underwater, the winch probably won't work and you won't be able to pull yourself out. With water over your front bumper, don't count on the winch. When leaving a bumper-deep stream, run your winch motor as soon as possible, heating up the winch housing and driving moisture out.

If you are thinking about fording a torrential stream high in the mountains, consider delaying your crossing until early the following morning. Freezing temperatures may have quelled the water from melting snow at higher altitudes, turning the torrent into a trickle.

If your rig bogs down in the middle of a fast-moving river or stream, it's more dangerous for you and your passengers to get out on the upstream side of the rig. The swift current may knock you off your feet and sweep you under the vehicle, trapping you there if there's not enough clearance for you to sweep on through or if you get hung up on part of the vehicle. Get out on the downstream side.

HOW TO RUIN YOUR ENGINE IN A HURRY

If the engine stops in midstream, resist the urge to try to restart it. If water has entered the cylinders, the engine is hydrolocked (sometimes called hydraulic'd), and you will ruin it by cranking it over. The pistons and connecting rods are forced against the unyielding water trapped in the cylinder. These and other parts can't stand up under the stress and will bend or break. I heard of a Jeep driving into a hole in a stream bottom on the Rubicon Trail. Water suddenly entered the cylinders with the engine still running, and the block cracked in two. That's an expensive swimming lesson.

If you are stranded in the middle of a river, pond, or stream, you may be able to haul the rig out using your own winch with battery power alone. Otherwise, you need to get another rig to winch or tow you out. Once on dry land, take out the spark plugs (or the injectors if you have a diesel engine) and check to see if there's water in the cylinders before trying to restart it. If there is, cranking the engine with the starter will force it out. Watch out, though. The water comes out with a great deal of pressure. Have everyone stand back before you turn the starter to avoid serious eye injuries or lacerations of exposed skin.

If you must cross water, use designated fording sites. Protect the delicate ecostructure of the streambed, and don't use it as a road to travel upstream or downstream. A great way to get a trail closed to 4x4s is for a bunch of 'wheelers to drive off-trail and rip up streambeds, meadows, hillsides, and the forest floor, leaving open gates and startled wildlife behind them.

TWO TRICKS FOR DEEP WATER

My friend Ragnar Benson recounts many adventures making his way around rough country. He told me about a trick he's used to get a rig through deep water in emergency situations: driving backward. The engine compartment rides in the wake created by the moving vehicle and stays dry. Floor the accelerator and drive as fast as you can, creating enough exhaust pressure to keep water out of the tailpipe. Don't stop or even slow down or water will pour into the engine compartment and the party's over. Also, be sure you have good enough departure and approach angles to let you make it up the bank on the far side. It doesn't do much good to make it across successfully and then drown the engine trying to get out the other side. I haven't had personal experience with this method, but Ragnar says he's here today because of it.

Another trick Ragnar uses to get across jungle rivers is hitching a ride in the wake of the big trucks used by the traders as they travel from village to village. These trucks are high and can cross a lot deeper water than an ordinary 4x4 can. Wait for one to come along the trail, and when he enters the river, tag along about 8 feet behind the rear of his rig. Your engine compartment rides in the dry depression created by his large wake. Taking advantage of this means staying close and making sure he's not going to stop before he's well out the far side. Again, be sure you've got enough clearance, both front and back, to make it out the other side.

BRIDGES AND FERRIES

Inspect backcountry bridges carefully before committing your vehicle to them. Rusted beams or rotted pillars may be waiting to turn your expedition into a nightmare. Ragnar follows the local tire tracks, pointing out that if locals avoid a bridge and ford the river instead, you're pretty stupid if you try to use that bridge.

Ragnar also emphasizes the importance of being sure you're engaged in 4WD before you drive onto a bridge that appears rickety. In 2WD, with your nondriving front wheels hanging up on the uneven surface of the bridge, you may push it away from its moorings and end up straddling an impassable gap,

front wheels on the bridge, rear wheels on the road, with nothing in between.

By the same token, driving onto a poorly secured ferry in 2WD may push it away from the shore and you'll wind up in deep water. Use 4WD so the front wheels pull you onto the ferry under power.

WHEN YOU'RE OUT OF THE WATER

Soon after the rig is out of the water, check the fluids in the differentials, the T-case, and transmission. If milky looking, they're contaminated and need to be changed to prevent severe damage to the drivetrain. If you don't have sealed wheel bearings, the grease in the hubs and bearings also needs to be changed. How important is this? It's like the dentist telling us we only need to floss the teeth we want to keep. You only need to replace contaminated fluids in the drivetrain if you don't want to buy new differentials, a new T-case, or a new transmission down the line. Seriously, it's important.

If you're only in shallow water occasionally, you can probably wait till the next lube and oil change before having the fluids checked. Unless you know what to look for yourself, you might want to have this done at the dealer because you need to have an experienced mechanic doing the check. The other alternative is just to have all the drivetrain fluids drained and replaced at the nearest Jiffy Lube-type facility.

Once again, after driving in the surf at the beach, clean the rig off thoroughly as soon as possible. The saltwater will quickly corrode the body metal and engine parts. Hose down the entire undersurface of the vehicle as well as the engine compartment. Get rid of all traces of the saltwater. Don't forget to get rid of the sand, too, because sand damp with saltwater corrodes your vehicle fast.

chapter fourteen

SUMMING UP
WHAT YOU'VE LEARNED

You've come a long way and learned a lot. If you're among the millions of individuals and families who are joining the ranks of 4x4 owners every year, then you've received a good, solid foundation in the art of off-road recreation and adventure.

If you're an experienced wheeler, I hope that you've gotten at least a few new ideas to include in your off-road repertoire and that you're encouraged to join Tread Lightly!, the BlueRibbon Coalition, and your local 4-wheel drive club to make your voice heard in issues of land use and off-highway recreation.

Let's summarize some of the points we've covered.

WHO NEEDS THIS BOOK?

Bob and Pat Collins decided on a used Jeep Cherokee because it was a reasonably priced sport-utility vehicle, giving them safety and mobility with plenty of space for passengers and cargo. As it turned out, the capability of the vehicle saved their lives. By now you have an idea of what 4-wheel drive vehicles can do and a taste of the challenge and adventure that go with off-roading.

BASIC 4-WHEEL DRIVE—GETTING STARTED

We looked at 4-wheel drive vehicles—4x4s, 4bys, sport-utes, and rigs in general. We talked about

both 4WD and 2WD. We talked about T-cases and differentials, 4WD Hi and 4WD Lo.

MORE ABOUT 4-WHEEL DRIVE— EXPLORE THE OPTIONS

We looked more at 4WD, both full-time and part-time. We talked about viscous coupling, gerotors, and gerodiscs, as well as differential lockers, posi's, and locking hubs.

CHOOSING A RIG—ARE YOU HAULING PEOPLE OR STUFF?

We talked about choices when choosing a rig, from Wranglers to Rovers, from Trackers to Hummers. Are you carrying people or stuff? Do you want a highway-friendly rig or a rock climber? When going sport-ute shopping, you can now help the salesperson familiarize you with the available options.

TREAD LIGHTLY!—NOT JUST FOR TREE HUGGERS

We noted that the establishment of Tread Lightly! slowed up the rush to restrict recreational use of federal land. Following the Tread Lightly! principles helps keep trails open for responsible ecological motorized off-road recreation.

105

We talked about services available from the Forest Service and the Bureau of Land Management (BLM) and about the importance of joining Tread Lightly!, the BlueRibbon Coalition, and your local 4WD club to network with others dedicated to responsible off-road motorized recreation.

PACKING UP—THE BASIC TOOL BOX

What do you need to take with you? It depends on your particular plans. When going on trails, travel with one or more other vehicles, with each vehicle striving to be as self-sufficient as possible. You may become separated and unable to depend upon someone else for spare parts, food, and other supplies.

But remember, you don't have to equip your rig fully or modify it at all to get started with off-road recreation. Choose what works for your comfort level, but carry the basic items mentioned in Chapter 6 at the least.

BEEFING UP A RIG—WHAT'S YOUR CREDIT CARD LIMIT?

We discussed the various ways you can beef up your rig for comfort and function. We're assuming you want to keep your rig more or less stock so people won't stare at you too much when you drop your kids off at nursery school. But using your vehicle to its full potential means adding a few things.

Essential modifications for off-road use include a roll cage (for an open vehicle), light truck tires, skid plates, front winch, heavy-duty alternator or dual batteries, rear hitch, tow hooks front and rear, lockers, nerf bars or running boards, front brush guard, and rear winch, portable electric winch, or portable hand winch (come-along).

Optional modifications or convenience items include CB (citizens band) radio, GPS (global positioning system) device, extra lights front and rear, suspension lifters, body lifters, oversize tires, differential gear modifications, under-the-hood welder, heavy-duty seats with five-point harnesses, under-the-hood shower, and a front tow hitch.

We also discussed the implications of the OBD II regulations.

ROCKS AND RAVINES—BASIC CRAWLING

We reminded you that rocky trails strewn with boulders higher than your ground clearance offer you some of your greatest challenges and loudest expletives.

The basic rule of rock crawling is *go slow*. The faster you try to go, the more you tear up your tires, especially the sidewalls, which are marginally repairable at best. Going slower and in control means less likelihood of wheel and tire damage. Make sure you're using light truck (LT) tires, not passenger (P) tires.

HILLS—HOW TO STAY SHINY SIDE UP AND RUBBER SIDE DOWN

Remember the 4-wheeling rule that says, "Know what's up front." This applies especially when going uphill or downhill.

Going uphill. Use momentum to carry you up. Avoid wheel spin, which just digs you into deep ruts and could cause a tire to explode, resulting in serious damage to folks or 4bys. If you lose traction on the way up, quickly rock your steering wheel a half turn back and forth. Know your rig's angles of approach and departure as well as the breakover angle. If forward uphill motion stops, *do not* try to turn around. Back down, getting into reverse instantly to maintain control.

Going downhill. Know what's ahead. Walk it first. Know what's at the bottom. Will you need to turn suddenly to avoid going over a cliff or to stay off a rock or tree?

Stop at the top to interrupt momentum. Shift into 4-wheel Lo in the T-case and use the lowest transmission gears. If engine compression makes your wheels slide, you may have to shift into a higher transmission gear. Stay off the brakes if possible. Use very gentle feathering if you must use them. With the rear end sliding, steer into the direction it's skidding and apply light gas as needed.

Sidehill. Avoid steep sidehill angles. The maximum is probably 25° (47 percent). Beyond that, there's no room for error. If the lower wheels drop into a rut or the uphill wheels run up on a rock or log, you can easily flip over. Keep heavy loads on the floor to lower the center of gravity, especially when anticipating having to drive sidehill.

Rollover recovery. Either shiny side down/rubber side up or door down. Tie down everything. Use seat belts for yourself and passengers. Loose passengers or pets bouncing around the cabin during a roll results in injuries to them as well as others. Unbelted occupants may also be thrown out of the vehicle during a roll, with the vehicle rolling over them on the way down the hill, turning an entirely survivable roll into a fatal disaster. People ejected from a vehicle during an accident are 25 times more likely to be killed than those who stay within the vehicle.

WINCHES AND JACKS—UP AND OUT

There's nothing like a winch for getting you up or down steep hills or through muddy bogs, getting you out of a stream when stalled, dragging you out of a ditch, or moving a log or rock out of your path. Make sure you have enough amps to drive the winch. Use either a bigger alternator or a dual battery system or both.

Always use a tree strap. It saves the tree and the winch cable. Wrapping a cable around a tree and hooking it back to itself kinks the cable and ruins it. Use a single line for easy pulls, a double line through a snatch block for harder pulls. If your rig is the one being unstuck, put the T-case in 4WD Lo and the transmission in low gear so you can crawl forward while winching or being winched out.

Use a Hi-Lift jack at least 48 inches high to get out of being high-centered. Jack up the wheel closest to the high-centered spot and build a ramp under that wheel and in front of the other wheel on the same side. Then drive off the high-centering spot.

Using common sense and scouting the trail ahead before committing keep you from getting stuck in the first place most of the time. But if you do get stuck or when clawing your way over a particularly gnarly trail, then a winch, a Hi-Lift jack, a set of two or three tow straps, and a bunch of shackle blocks (snatch blocks) and D-shackles will get you over or through most obstacles.

SNOW AND ICE—ARTFUL SKIDDING

Your rig can slip and slide on several different kinds of surface—snow, ice, mud, loose dirt, wet roads or rock slabs, oily asphalt, or a combination of these. The principles of handling curves and skids apply to all these surfaces.

Drive slowly and smoothly, especially when accelerating or decelerating. Don't let the wheels spin. If driving mainly on snow and ice, buy a set of dedicated snow tires and consider siping and studs. If planning to drive on ice, put on chains.

We discussed the footprint of a tire as well as weight distribution. We talked about the mechanics of understeer and oversteer skids and the response to them. We covered on-camber and off-camber curves.

SOFT STUFF—AIRING DOWN FOR MUD AND SAND

We discussed techniques for driving through mud and sand. The key to driving on top of mud or sand is airing down, i.e., reducing the air pressure in your tires to enlarge their footprints. Airing down also makes your tires smaller in diameter and increases the force your drivetrain can deliver to move your rig across the terrain.

For maximum traction, you need to air down a surprising amount. Reducing tire pressure to as low as 7 to 10 pounds may be necessary. This means letting out enough air to reduce the height of a tire (the distance from the lowest point on the wheel rim to the ground) to 75 percent of its normal value.

Once out of the sand or mud, air back up to highway pressure immediately to avoid damage to the tires or wheel rims.

CROSSING STREAMS—RIG SURFING

When crossing a stream, pond, or flooded area, make sure you know what you're getting into. If you are unable to tell how deep it is, walk it first.

Once you commit your vehicle to the water, keep moving. Keep your speed steady but not too fast to avoid pushing the radiator back into the fan. Drive at an angle to the current. Keep the engine running. If you get stuck with your winch under water, it probably won't work.

If the engine stops in midstream, resist the urge to restart it. With water in the cylinders, the engine is hydrolocked, and trying to start it will ruin it. Get on dry land, pull the spark plugs or injectors, and crank the starter to force water out of the cylinders. Make sure everyone's standing clear to avoid eye or skin injuries from the pressurized water squirting out of the cylinders.

SUMMING UP

Off-highway recreation is growing rapidly. Owners of all types of off-road vehicles are joining each other on the dirt roads and trails all over the country. The Tread Lightly! program has helped keep federal land open for recreational purposes. The BlueRibbon Coalition also networks to protect responsible motorized off-road recreation. Those of us interested in off-road recreation need to join Tread Lightly! and the BlueRibbon Coalition. Join your local 4-wheel drive club, too.

107

This book has acquainted you with principles and skills that will increase your enjoyment of off-road recreation. Now you know what's possible. You know what skills to develop so you can explore those out-of-the-way campsites, nestled in cedar groves beside crystal-clear streams, with no one else in sight or within earshot. You know how to go hunting and fishing in areas no one else has ever seen, and how to experience the adventure of challenging yourself on trails winding through some of the most beautiful real estate in the world.

This book has probably also expanded your ideas about preserving our freedom to use the great outdoors for the enjoyment and enrichment of all citizens. That includes those of us who want to use our versatile sport-utility vehicles as a means of bringing our families together and instilling traditional American values of freedom and self-reliance in our children.

Some sport-utility distributors are setting up courses to acquaint the public with 4-wheeling principles. You can visit Europa International in Santa Fe, New Mexico, and demo a Mercedes Gelaendewagen on their off-road course. If you're shopping for one of the Land Rover or Range Rover models, you can go to one of the many Land Rover Centres scattered around the United States. Each one has an off-road circuit where you can actually demo the vehicles in their element (Figure 88). The centres also run guided day-long 4-wheeling trips to acquaint their customers with off-road recreation. The Land Rover Company sponsors 4-wheeling training courses at various centers in the United States. Visit the Land Rover website for details. (If you live in England and own a Land Rover product, you can visit the factory in Solihull, where they'll train you on its 4-wheeling course.)

The Japanese have gone a step further: Toyota runs the $3.5 million Sanage Adventure Field outside

Figure 88. Dan Muggli, the director of the Land Rover Portland Centre, guides the author around their off-road demo track in a Land Rover Discovery.

Tokyo. It's an off-road park, where would-be 'wheelers can take their rigs on eight-minute laps up and down 30° hills, through 3-foot-deep simulated streams, and over boulder-strewn trails, all for $26 an hour. You can even belt yourself into a rig on a rotating frame to get a feeling of what it's like to be in a rollover. That's probably a wise move, because Sanage had more than five dozen rollovers in the first year of operation, though there were no fatalities or even serious injuries. Many similar courses are either planned or being built in Japan, including one by Honda.

You can get plenty of good experience in this country by signing up for courses and trips with Harry Lewellyn, Bill Burke, Rick Russell, Harold Pietschmann, or one of the other gurus of 4-wheeling. Take courses in executive protection from Tony Scotti's school near Boston, Massachusetts, to develop your high-performance driving skills and to acquire an understanding of vehicle dynamics in general. Perfect your winter driving skills at the Bridgestone Winter Driving School in Steamboat Springs, Colorado, under the direction of Mark Cox. If you live in England, you can train at David Bowyer's Off-Road Centre in Devon, one of the oldest established 4-wheeling schools around.

You can also join your local 4-wheeling club

and learn directly from your peers. Ask if the club conducts formal training courses in off-roading. Such a 4-wheeling course is offered twice a year by the Esprit de Four 4-Wheel Drive Club of Hollister, California, near San Jose. Under the direction of club president David Schmitt and safety chairman Bill Farley, the club takes 30 to 40 vehicles through the 4-wheeling course at Hollister Hills, one of the five California SVRAs (state vehicle recreational areas). The training includes running a 4-wheeling obstacle course, a permanent fixture at the park.

You can also visit the Hollister Hills SVRA by yourself, taking your rig through the course on your own, or you can go to the other Northern California SVRA at Prairie City, near Sacramento. Both these SVRAs are set up to accommodate sport-utes. Some of the other SVRAs only handle dirt bikes and ATVs.

However you choose to do it, it's a good idea to get hands-on training to develop these skills. It's time to subscribe to Harry Lewellyn's *Ecological 4-Wheeling* newsletter. Subscribe to the 4-wheeling and off-road magazines too. All these things and many more are listed in Appendix C.

This book is your manual and guide. Have fun. And Tread Lightly!

GLOSSARY

Aftermarket: This refers to equipment manufactured and distributed by a variety of manufacturers other than the original automobile manufacturer. (See also *OEM*, original equipment manufacturer.)

Autotrac: The full-time 4WD system used by General Motors. The Auto 4WD setting uses an electronic clutch to transfer torque from slipping rear wheels to the front wheels. It has a 2WD setting, 4WD Hi mode for driving off-road or in generally slippery conditions, and 4WD Lo mode.

Beater: A beat-up 4WD rig that just keeps going, sort of like the Energizer bunny.

Beefed up: A 4x4 rig with added accessories or modifications to make it better or at least stronger than stock.

Belly up: A rig or part of a rig that's broken is "belly up"; also "fragged."

Binder: Slang for rigs made by International Harvester (Scouts, for instance), since that company also makes farm machinery such as cornbinders.

Bog: An area of deep mud is a "mud bog." Rigs or tires designed to drive in deep mud are "boggers." You can also "bog" an engine by running it too slowly for the load.

Camber: The sideways slope of a road in a curve. With the inside of the curve lower than the outside, the camber is positive and gravity pulls the rig toward the inside of the curve to counteract centrifugal force. With the outside of the curve lower than the inside, the camber is negative, which is dangerous because both gravity and centrifugal force pull the rig to the outside of the curve and off the road. Camber also applies to a measurement of the steering apparatus and tells how much the top of the front wheels tilt away from (positive camber) or toward (negative camber) the center of the rig. Properly adjusted camber contributes to even tire wear. Too much positive camber in one front wheel causes the rig to pull to that side.

Caster: A steering measurement of a rig that tells how much the bottom of the front wheel steering axis is in front of the tire's contact patch (footprint). Positive caster is when the bottom of the axis is in front of the contact patch and contributes to good steering stability and self-centering of the steering wheel. (See also *camber*.) The adjustment of caster and camber determines the stability of a vehicle in forward travel and its characteristics when cornering.

Center disconnect: A method of connecting or disconnecting the front wheels to the drivetrain by means of a coupling at the front differential or front axle. Without a center disconnect, rigs engage 4WD by locking the hubs on the front wheels, either manually or automatically.

Centrifugal force: The apparent force acting to throw an object out of the circle when it's traveling in a curve. When you're driving a vehicle around a curve to the right, you'll feel like you're being pushed against the left driver's door. "Centrifugal force" is a useful concept, but it doesn't really exist. What is actually happening is that inertia is acting on you. According to the laws of physics, once a body starts moving it tends to keep moving in a straight line. A force must act on it to get it to turn in a different direction. In this case, the car door is pushing you out of a straight line path because inertia is making you want to go straight ahead, not turn in a circle. It's the force of the door pushing on you that you're feeling, not some mysterious force pushing you against the door. The vehicle itself must overcome the inertia making it want to keep going straight by the force of the friction of its turning wheels against the road. If you try to go around a curve too fast, inertia wins because you don't have enough friction to hold the tires on the road and the vehicle keeps going in a straight line off the road instead of following the curve of the highway. I have used the term "centrifugal force" in this book because it's such a common way to describe in plain language the way a vehicle behaves when going around a curve. My apologies to the engineers reading this book who wanted me to get rid of it in the interests of greater precision.

Chunk: Slang for the gears inside a differential, specifically, the ring and pinion gears; also "pumpkin."

ci: The abbreviation for "cubic inches," the displacement of an engine. Displacement is also expressed in liters. An engine with a displacement of 4.0 liters (4.0L) will also have a displacement of 244 cubic inches (244 ci). 1 liter = 61.0 cubic inches. 1 ci = .0164 L. (See also *displacement*.)

CJ-5, CJ-7: Model numbers of popular Jeep models, made before the current Wrangler model. CJ stands for "civilian jeep." The CJ-7 replaced the CJ-5 and was a little longer. The CJ-7 came with an automatic transmission. The CJ series was replaced by the current Jeep Wrangler, the YJ series. The '97 Wrangler begins the TJ series.

Closed differential: See *differential*.

Command-Trac: Jeep's name for one of its 4WD systems. It uses part-time 4WD with the front and rear driveshafts locked together. The system should only be used on slippery surfaces. It uses a chain-drive NVG 231 transfer case and allows shifting-on-the-fly. It's been available on the Wrangler and certain Cherokee and Grand Cherokee models, though Jeep is in the process of phasing it out in favor of Selec-Trac and Quadra-Trac II.

Control-Trac: The Ford Explorer's 4WD system. It uses full-time 4WD, which it calls 4WD Auto, and has an electronic clutch in the T-case to transfer torque between the rear and front wheels to increase traction with wheel slippage. In 4WD low range, the T-case is locked. There is a 2WD setting. The options are selected with a switch mounted on the dash. The T-case is a Borg-Warner 44-05.

Crawl ratio: The low-gear ratio available for high-power, low-speed travel, used for crawling over a rough trail filled with large rocks. It's calculated by multiplying the ratio of the lowest gear of the transmission times the ratio of the low range of the T-case times the gear ratio of the differentials. For example: transmission low gear 3.06:1 x T-case low range 2.72:1 x differential gear ratio 3.73:1 = 31.05, which are the gear ratio specs of the '95 Chevy Tahoe. A dedicated rock-crawler has crawl ratios around 70:1 or 80:1 or even more. The higher the numbers, the lower and more powerful the gears. 100:1 is more powerful than 30:1. The actual force delivered to the ground by the wheel and tire depends also on the tire size as well as the crawl ratio of the gears. In a Hummer, geared hubs reduce the ratio another 1.92:1. (See also *net moving force*.)

CTIS: AM General Hummer's central tire inflation system, which allows airing the tires up or down from the driver's seat while moving.

Curb weight: The basic unloaded weight of a vehicle.

Differential: A case between the two rear or two front wheels that contains a system of gears allowing the two wheels to turn at different speeds when going around a corner or curve. It also allows a wheel without traction to spin helplessly, which decreases the torque going to the wheel that still has traction. In this form, it's called an open differential. (See also *locker* and *posi*.)

Displacement: The volume of fuel-air mixture that an engine sucks in, compresses, and explodes. It depends on the diameter of each cylinder in the engine (the bore), the distance a piston travels from the top to the bottom of its stroke, and the number of cylinders in the engine. The formula for calculating displacement is: $\pi r^2 LN$, which is the cross-sectional area of the cylinder times the length of the stroke times the number of cylinders in the engine. The area of a circle is "πr^2" where π is the Greek letter "pi" which stands for the constant number 3.14. The letter "r" stands for the radius of the circle, which in this case equals 1/2 the bore, and in this formula the radius is squared (multiplied by itself). The L stands for the distance the piston moves, or the stroke. The N equals the number of cylinders in the engine. If the bore and stroke are measured in inches, the answer (displacement) is given in cubic inches (ci). If the bore and stroke are measured in metric units (meters or centimeters), the displacement is given in liters (L) or cubic centimeters (cc). For example, the bore of a Chevy 350/5.7 engine is 4.00 inches, or 10.16 cm, and the stroke is 3.48 inches, or 8.84 cm. It has eight cylinders. Displacement in cubic inches is: 3.14 x 2.00 x 2.00 x 3.48 x 8 = 349.67, which is almost 350 ci. Displacement in liters is 3.14 x 5.08 x 5.08 x 8.84 x 8 = 5730.59 cc (cubic centimeters). Since there are 1,000 cc in 1 liter, 5730.59 cc = 5.73 L, which is about the 5.7L Chevy advertises.

Door down: Slang for the position of a rig that has tipped or rolled over and is lying on its side with the door down.

Double-line: A winching term, which means pulling with your winch by attaching a pulley to the object pulled against, then running a winch cable through that pulley and hooking it back to your rig. This doubles the force a winch can exert compared to single-line pulling with the winch cable attached directly to the object pulled against. The winch can develop even more force when triple-lining.

EAS: Electronic air suspension, the system used by the Range Rover models (the 4.0 SE, 4.6 HSE, and County Classic) to adjust the height of the vehicle above the ground, either automatically or manually. It uses telescoping shock absorbers and air-cushioned springs to raise or lower the frame. When your vehicle is high-centered, you may be able to raise the rig with EAS and drive off without breaking out the Hi-Lift jack and building a ramp off the obstacle.

ETC: Electronic traction control. The system used by a number of vehicles to increase torque to a wheel with traction when the other wheel is slipping. When ETC senses a wheel spinning, it uses the ABS to brake the spinning tire. This is the opposite of what the ABS usually does – taking the brake off a locked wheel. With the spinning wheel braked, ETC increases torque to the wheel that has traction. The system goes by different names on various vehicles. Land Rover calls it "ETC" on their Range Rover models, Lexus calls it TRAC on their LX 470, Mercedes calls it ETS (electronic traction system), and the Hummer calls it TT4 (TorqTrac4).

Fairlead: The opening in front of a winch through which the winch cable emerges. A roller fairlead has rollers on the top, bottom, and sides. A hawse fairlead is a bracket without rollers. A roller fairlead is best because it lets the winch cable slide more easily.

Fragged: A part that's broken is fragged, like a fragged U-joint or a fragged differential. (See also *belly up*.)

Full-floating: A type of rear axle design that uses multiple bearings to carry the weight of the vehicle. If the axle breaks, the vehicle can still roll. With the differential locked, the opposite rear wheel and the front wheels still power the vehicle, assuming the vehicle is in 4WD.

Full-time 4WD: A 4-wheel drive system allowing a vehicle to be in 4WD all the time. It allows the front and rear wheels to rotate at different rates and uses a differential-type of device in the transfer case, or viscous coupling. Some systems have full-time 4WD in effect all the time, with no option for shifting into 2WD; other systems allow shifting between 2WD and full-time 4WD. Some full-time 4WD systems have only high range in the transfer case; others allow the driver to put the T-case into either high or low range.

Gnarly: Especially difficult, such as a trail.

Grade: The slope of a hill. The steepness of the grade is expressed in either degrees or percent. Highway signs advising truckers of an upcoming steep hill are usually in percent. A 7-percent grade means that for every 100 feet the road moves forward horizontally, it rises or falls 7 feet. A 7-percent grade would be the same as a 4° grade and is actually fairly steep for 18-wheelers. It's important to get a feeling for the steepness of a grade your rig can negotiate uphill,

113

downhill, and sidehill. Some manufacturers tell you in their specs what a rig can do. For example, they might say a rig can drive sidehill on a 30° grade or a 60-percent grade, which is the same thing (almost) and is a significantly steep hill to hike or drive up. A 100-percent grade would be a 45° angle (forward 100 feet, down or up 100 feet). Here are some approximate values: 5° = 9 percent; 10° = 18 percent; 15° = 27 percent; 20° = 36 percent; 25° = 47 percent; 30° = 58 percent; 35° = 70 percent; 40° = 84 percent.

Granny gear: An especially low gear in a manual transmission. It provides more low speed power than the usual first gear, or low gear.

GCWR: Gross combination weight rating. The total weight of a loaded vehicle together with a loaded trailer. The GCWR for a rig is approximately the basic curb weight (no cargo) plus the total towing capacity of the rig.

GVWR: Gross vehicle weight rating. This is the maximum amount a rig can weigh, including the basic curb weight of the vehicle plus the maximum allowable payload, including fuel, driver, passengers, such accessories as winches and the heavy bumpers supporting them, and cargo.

High-centered: This means a rig is hung up on a high obstacle between the front and rear wheels. For example, a front wheel makes it over a rock, but the frame comes down against it and keeps the front wheel from reaching the ground again.

Hooked up: This means the tires have traction on the ground. If your wheels are spinning, you aren't hooked up.

Horsepower: A unit of power defining force acting over time. A force of 1 pound-foot is the force that lifts a 1 pound object a distance of 1 foot without factoring in how long it takes. One horsepower is the energy required to lift an object weighing 550 pounds a distance of 1 foot in 1 second.

Hubs: This refers to the connection of the wheels to the axles and usually refers to the front wheels. With hubs unlocked, the front wheels freewheel, or spin freely. This reduces wear on the front differential. To engage 4WD, the hubs have to be "locked in." This can be done manually (with manual hubs) or automatically (with automatic locking hubs).

Hydraulic'd: Also hydrolocked. This means an engine has water inside the cylinders from water being sucked into the engine during an attempted water crossing. It's important not to try to start an engine in this condition, because the pistons can't compress the water and the connecting rods bend instead, ruining the engine.

IFS: Independent front suspension. A suspension system that allows each front wheel to move independently of the other one. It gives a smoother ride on-highway but is less desirable for off-road travel because as the wheel rises over an obstacle, ground clearance under the differential may actually decrease.

Insta-Trac: Chevrolet's name for its 4WD system, used in Blazers and Tahoes. It uses a chain-drive T-case with part-time 4WD, which should not be used on dry pavement. It allows shifting-on-the-fly to change between 2WD and 4WD Hi while moving. The T-case has 4WD Lo. Insta-Trac uses a thermally actuated front axle disconnect. The transfer cases used are the NV231 or the NV232 (push-button) on the Blazer and the NP241 on the Tahoe.

Jeep: Jeep is now a trademark of the Chrysler Corporation, and Chrysler's Jeep division produces Wranglers, Cherokees, and Grand Cherokees. The origin of the term Jeep is obscure. It probably comes from the character "Eugene the Jeep" in the Popeye comic strip of the 1930s. Jim Allen, writing in the March 1995 issue of *Four Wheeler*, investigates the history of the term in detail. During World War II, Jeep eventually came to mean the 1/4-ton Command Reconnaissance 4x4 truck, or 1/4-ton Military Truck, as it was later called. Jeep is often said to have been derived from the acronym GP for General Purpose Military Truck, but this is probably not the case. The 1/4-ton 4x4 was called Jeep before the designation GP came to be used. Right now, Mitsubishi is the only other company licensed to use the term Jeep for its 1/4-ton 4x4 vehicle, because it licensed the term from the Willis Corporation before Chrysler acquired the Jeep line. However, Mitsubishi can't use this term for vehicles sold in the United States.

Juicebox: Slang for automatic transmission.

L: The abbreviation for liter, a measure of engine displacement, as in a 4.0L engine. (See also *ci* and *displacement*.)

Lifted: Raising a rig to get more ground clearance. Lifting can be done by installing suspension lifts, which raise the frame and body higher off the axles, or with body lifts, which raise the body higher off the frame. Body and suspension lifts don't help the clearance of the differentials or steering mechanism, but installing larger tires does, making it the third way of gaining more ground clearance for your rig.

Limited-slip: See *posi*.

Locked-in: This refers to the locked position of manual front wheel hubs, so the front wheels are locked to the axles for 4WD.

Locked-up: This refers to engaging differentials that are equipped with locking devices (lockers) so both wheels turn as a single unit.

Lockers: A locking device placed in a differential to convert it from open (which allows the two wheels to turn at different speeds) to closed (which locks the wheels together so they turn as a single unit). There are also limited-slip differentials, which direct more of the torque to a wheel that still has traction when the other wheel is spinning. (See *posi*.)

Meats: Large, oversized tires.

Mondo: Very large.

Mudder: Tires specifically designed for use in deep mud or a rig specifically equipped to run through mud bogs.

Nerf bars: Metal tubes installed below the rocker panels to protect the lower part of the truck's sheet metal from rock damage. Running boards serve the same purpose. Some 'wheelers feel that nerf bars or running boards decrease the flexibility of the rig's frame to some degree. They also decrease ground clearance if installed hanging lower than the frame.

NMF: Net moving force. It's the final force of the tire against the ground and is the force that moves the vehicle along the ground. It's determined by the power of the engine and the gear ratios of the torque converter, the transmission, the T-case, and the differentials, as well as the size of the tires. In a Hummer it's also determined by the gear ratio in the geared hubs.

OBD: See *on-board diagnostics*.

OEM: Original equipment manufacturer. Refers to equipment manufactured or distributed by the original automobile manufacturer. Aftermarket equipment is produced and distributed by a variety of manufacturers other than the original manufacturer and offers hard-core 'wheelers great opportunities for beefing up their rigs in creative ways.

Off-camber: This refers to the slope of road in a curve in which the inside of the curve is higher than the outside. This tends to throw a rig toward the outside of the curve and sets up a rollover.

Off-highway: The politically correct version of the term off-road. Environmentalists are afraid off-roaders drive off existing trails and tear up the forests, meadows, and streambeds. Therefore, in response to this, sensitive New Age 'wheelers are adopting the term *off-highway*, implying they stay on existing trails or dirt roads. Responsible wheelers are concerned about the environment and don't go around tearing up off-trail real estate because of a basic reverence for and commitment to the land. Irresponsible 'wheelers shouldn't tear up the land either, because if they do, the regulators will come down on all of us and close off even larger chunks of public land to off-road use. Somehow, when it comes right down to it, off-highway just doesn't have the same romantic ring to it as off-road. I doubt it will ever completely replace off-road, which runs in the dusty blood of at least three generations of dedicated off-roaders.

Off-road: See *off-highway*.

On-board diagnostics: The Federal (Level I) and California (Level II) standards for emission control. They require that emission monitoring systems be guaranteed for 100,000 miles. Complying with these, manufacturers have developed very sophisticated ways of monitoring engine performance, making engines more economical and reliable. The monitoring systems gather data from five main groups of sensors: oxygen sensors in the exhaust manifold, RPM sensors, engine load sensors, throttle position sensors, and temperature sensors. These sensors control engine performance by servo (feedback) circuits, altering such things as fuel/air mixture in response to the data gathered. See the section on OBD systems in Chapter 7.

Open differential: See *differential.*

Overdrive: A transmission gear that decreases the engine speed necessary to move the vehicle at a certain speed by decreasing the power to the driveshaft. The higher the first number in a gear ratio, the lower the gear and the more power delivered to the driveshaft through the transmission. In a four-speed automatic transmission, low gear (first gear) might have a ratio of 2.45:1, second gear a ratio of 1.45:1, and high gear (third gear) 1.00:1. Then, to save gas and decrease wear and tear on the engine, overdrive (fourth gear) is available, which might have a ratio of 0.69:1. Overdrive is usually used on flat roads, where there's not a lot of demand on the engine.

Oversteer: The condition when a vehicle going around a curve tends to turn more than the driver is intending it to turn. This often occurs because the rear wheels are losing their grip and the rear end is swinging to the outside of the curve.

Part-time 4WD: A 4-wheel drive system allowing a vehicle to be in 4WD on surfaces with poor traction. The T-case has no differential or viscous coupling, and the front and rear driveshafts are locked together, rotating at the same speed. When driving on a highway with good traction in 2WD drive, the front wheels and rear wheels move at different speeds when the vehicle goes around a curve or turns a corner. Driving on a firm surface in part-time 4WD causes wear on the tires and drivetrain, because the front and rear wheels can't move at different speeds.

Portal axle: The offset geared hub that the AM General Hummer uses to increase ground clearance. The axle enters the hub above the hub's center, which raises the entire rig higher off the ground. The hub also contains gears that increase the force to the wheels by a factor of 1.92:1. This means the differentials can be smaller, since some of their work is done by the geared hubs. Smaller differentials mean more ground clearance.

Posi: A limited-slip differential that directs part of the power away from the spinning wheel to the wheel still with traction. It gets its name from the original limited-slip device, which GM called Posi-Traction. A posi does not direct 100 percent of the engine's torque to the wheel with traction like a locker does but has better handling characteristics for

highway driving than a locker. (See *locker.*) Land Rover uses a limited-slip system called ETC and the Mercedes M-Class SUV uses one called ETS. (See *ETC* and *ETS.*).

PTO: Power take-off. It's a connection off the transfer case or transmission that allows the attachment of power equipment directly to the drivetrain. An example would be a winch made for PTO operation, which would be more powerful and faster than an electric winch. PTOs are generally available only on heavier T-cases used in larger trucks, though there are winches being advertised now that run directly off the power-steering pump.

Pulley block: See *snatch block.*

Pumpkin: Slang for the inside gears of a differential. Same as *chunk.*

Quadra Drive: A sophisticated full-time permanent 4WD system available on the Jeep Grand Cherokee Limited model. It uses the Quadra-Trac II NV 247 T-case with a Gerotor coupling, along with traction-on-demand Gerodisc couplings in each Hydra-Lok (also called Vari-Lok) differential, front and rear.

RTI: Ramp Travel Index. *Four Wheeler* magazine's specific measurement of the flexibility of a rig's frame and suspension. Technically, RTI measures axle articulation. See Appendix B, 4xFacts, for a full description of RTI.

Redline: The maximum RPM at which an engine should be operated. Operating it over that level may cause failure of the engine. Also, what happens to my heart rate when I try to run a mile in under 10 minutes.

Rock-crawler: A vehicle specifically outfitted for rock crawling. Typically, it is lifted and has part-time 4WD, oversize tires, especially low gears in the differentials, and at least one locking differential. It may have an aftermarket add-on creating an extra low gear in the T-case. It probably has a manual transmission.

Rubber-side up: Upside down, as in a rig that has rolled over and has ended up with its tires facing the sky.

Selec-Trac: One of the Jeep 4WD systems. It allows selection of either full-time 4WD for driving on highway surfaces with good traction or part-time 4WD for maximum traction on surfaces with poor traction. It uses an NVG 242 T-case. It's available on certain Cherokee and Grand Cherokee models and soon will be available on TJ Wranglers as well.

Semifloating: A type of rear axle design that carries the weight of the vehicle against the outer section of the axle. If the axle breaks, the hub and wheel can come off the vehicle. This can't happen with a full-floating axle.

Shackle block: See *snatch block*.

Shiny-side down: Upside down. A rig is shiny-side down if it has rolled over and has ended up with its roof on the ground. (See *rubber-side up*.)

Sidehill: Traveling across the side of a hill, as opposed to driving directly uphill or downhill. A dangerous position because it can lead to a rollover.

Single-line: See *double-line*.

Siped: To increase the traction of tires used for snow-driving, tires can be siped, which involves creating a bunch of small, shallow cuts in the tread. In the snow, these little cuts open up and increase the bite of the tire against the snow.

SmartTrak: The 4WD system used by Oldsmobile in its Bravada sport-ute. It is a permanent 4WD system and uses viscous coupling in the T-case, allowing the front and rear wheels to turn at different speeds on firm surfaces. It has no low range and no 2WD. The transfer case is a BW 4472.

Snatch block: A pulley with a hook attached to it for use with a winch cable to increase the pull of the winch or to change the direction of the winch pull. Also called a shackle block or pulley block. (See *double-lining*.)

Submarining: Driving a rig through relatively deep water.

Sucking sand: Driving behind someone, especially in an off-road race.

Tailgunner: The last rig in an off-road convoy. Its driver is responsible for everyone's completing each section of the trail.

Tall gears: Gears set up for higher speed and lower power. They have smaller numbers than low gears. Third gear (high gear) in a transmission might have a ratio of 1.00:1. This gear is "taller" than first and second gears, which might have ratios of 2.45:1 and 1.45:1, respectively. Overdrive is taller than any of them, with a ratio of 0.69:1.

T-case: See *transfer case*.

Teeter-totter: As in "diagonal teeter-totter," Harry Lewellyn's term to describe slipping of opposite wheels of a vehicle in 4WD (e.g., right front and left rear).

Three-wheeling: When one wheel loses traction and lifts off the ground, the rig is three-wheeling. This usually happens when the diagonally opposite wheel falls over the rim of a hill or drops into a rut or pothole.

Torque: Technically, the force that acts on an object to start it rotating or that acts to alter the rotation of an object. The term torque as applied to gas and diesel engines defines the rotational force an engine can develop at a certain RPM (e.g., 300 lb-ft. at 2,400 RPM). For serious rock crawling, it's desirable to have an engine that reaches its peak torque at low RPM, giving maximum pull at slow crawling speeds. "Torque" also applies to other components of the drivetrain. Torque (represented by the Greek letter "tau" or "τ") equals the length of the lever arm ("r") times the component of force acting perpendicularly to the lever arm ($\sin\theta F$) where theta (θ) is the angle between the direction of force (F) and the lever arm. $\tau = r\sin\theta F$. For example, a tire encounters a certain resisting force as it tries to drive the vehicle forward. This resisting force has to be overcome by the axle as it drives the wheel and tire forward. The rotational force that the axle has to generate is expressed as "torque" by considering the length of the lever arm between the axle and the ground. The lever arm is equal to the radius of the tire and wheel. Since the force is acting at 90° to the radius of the tire, $\sin\theta = 1$, and $\tau = rF$. This shows that for larger tires (larger "r" value), the axle must generate more torque to move the vehicle ahead. That's why you may have to swap in heavier-duty differential gears if you lift your rig and put larger tires on it.

Tow strap: A heavy nylon strap, 20 or 30 feet long and 2 or 3 inches wide, used to pull a stuck vehicle

117

out of mud, sand, snow, etc. It's called a "yank strap" if the towing vehicle starts out with 5 or 6 feet of slack in the strap, then drives forward, using the elasticity of the nylon to help snap the stuck vehicle out of the mud or whatever it's stuck in. This is a dangerous technique and must be used with caution. See the section in the text on "Tow Straps."

Track: The distance between the centers of the two tires at the front or the two tires at the rear. The wider the track, the more stable the vehicle.

Trail boss: The driver of the lead vehicle in an off-road convoy.

Transfer-case: Also called a T-case. It's a cast-iron or aluminum case containing a system of gears transferring power from the transmission to the front and rear driveshafts. It can transfer power with gears (gear drive), through a heavy chain (chain drive), or through viscous coupling. Viscous coupling allows the front and rear driveshafts to turn at different speeds and allows the rig to be in 4WD on firm surfaces with good traction. Most T-cases allow you to select 2WD Hi, 4WD Hi, or 4WD Lo.

Trailer queen: A fancy rig, usually a modified 4x4 pickup, intricately painted, heavily chromed, and lifted to the sky, which looks great at a show but would probably tip over when it hits its first off-road pothole or off-camber curve. It's hauled from show to show on a trailer.

Tree hugger: A dedicated, well-meaning environmentalist. Many tree huggers seem to believe land and wildlife must be protected by governmental closure of public lands or restricted use of private lands rather than through education of the public.

Tree-saver: A heavy nylon strap wrapped around a tree to which a winch cable is anchored. It saves the tree from being damaged by the winch cable, and it saves the winch cable, because wrapping the cable around the tree and hooking it to itself kinks and ruins it. Also called a tree strap.

Turned turtle: Same as rubber-side up and shiny-side down.

Understeer: This occurs when a vehicle going around a curve tends to turn less than the driver intends it to. This typically occurs early in a curve, when the momentum of the vehicle tends to keep it going in a straight line. It also occurs when the front tires lose their grip on a slippery curve with the driver accelerating and throwing the weight of the rig onto the back wheels. Also called plowing or pushing in racing parlance. Most passenger vehicles are designed with a little bit of understeer.

Vehicle behavior point: The point in a curve when the natural tendency of a vehicle to understeer early in the curve changes to the tendency to oversteer later in the curve.

Viscous coupling: A system of connecting the front and rear driveshafts inside the T-case using a silicone medium that changes its consistency with changes in temperature. As it gets hot, it stiffens. When a rear wheel is spinning, for instance, the rear driveshaft moves faster, heating the silicone compound and making it stiffer. This transfers torque to the front wheels, which still have traction.

'Wheeler: Slang for 4-wheeler.

'Wheelin': Slang for 4-wheeling.

X-case: Another abbreviation besides T-case for transfer case.

Yank strap: See *Tow Strap.*

Zexel-Torsen: The limited-slip torque-biasing differential an AM General Hummer uses. (See *posi.*)

4xFACTS
ODDS AND ENDS TO HELP YOU CHOOSE AND USE YOUR 4X4

In this, the second edition of *4-Wheel Freedom*, we decided for several reasons to eliminate the tables with the specifications of the various sport-utes available. The main reason is the rapidity with which they change and become out of date. It's better to get the exact specs of the vehicles in which you're interested from the various automobile and 4x4 magazines, the manufacturer's web site, or from the manufacturer's brochures available from the dealer. By leaving out these tables, we could devote more space to the new tips and techniques we've put elsewhere in the book. We hope this will make it more readily available to a greater number of 4x4 enthusiasts.

We're including a few additional facts about 4x4s, 4WD systems, and locking or limited-slip differentials to help you interpret the information you get from the Internet, the dealer, or the 4x4 magazines.

RAMP TRAVEL INDEX

You may run across some unique specifications in some of the 4by magazines or on the various web sites. The Ramp Travel Index (RTI), for instance, is a specific measurement of the flexibility of a rig's frame and suspension carried out by *Four Wheeler* magazine. Technically, RTI measures axle articulation. The rig being tested is driven forward in 4WD, low range, so that its right front wheel goes up a special ramp, designed by *Four Wheeler*. The measurement is the distance the front wheel runs up the ramp without a rear wheel losing traction. That distance is divided by the wheelbase and the result multiplied by 1,000. An RTI of 500 means that the rig can drive up the ramp a distance equal to one-half the wheelbase before a rear

wheel loses traction. The higher the RTI, the more flexible the axle articulation and frame flexibility.

FORCES ON A MOVING VEHICLE

Tony Scotti, the creator of the Scotti School of Defensive Driving, uses his engineering background to study the forces on moving vehicles, expressed in units of gravity, or g's. One unit of gravity's pull equals one g and is simply a force equal to the standing weight of the vehicle. A vehicle weighing 4,000 pounds has a force of 4,000 pounds, or 1 g, pushing it toward the ground.

When a vehicle stops, the efficiency of the braking force is expressed in g's. When a vehicle turns a corner or goes around a curve, the sideways force on it is also expressed in g's. A vehicle generating a braking force close to 1 g can stop very efficiently. A vehicle that can withstand a sideways force (called lateral acceleration) of 1 g in a turn is a very stable vehicle.

BRAKES AND BRAKING

It's difficult to come by the exact specifications of the brakes on the various rigs. The ideal braking system, with current technology, would have large disc brakes front and back, driven by four-wheel, four-channel ABS. In its February 1996 issue, *Four Wheeler* magazine evaluated 10 SUVs and chose the '96 Jeep Grand Cherokee as the Four Wheeler of the Year. They included the distance and time required to brake from 30 mph to zero and from 55 mph to zero. The formula for calculating braking force is $B = V/(32.2t)$, where B is the braking force generated in g's, V is the velocity in feet per second (mph x 1.47), 32.2 is the acceleration of gravity in feet per second per second, and t is the time required in seconds to stop.

The Grand Cherokee and Range Rover 4.0SE braked the most efficiently. Both were able to go from 30 mph to zero in 30 feet and 1.5 seconds, generating a stopping force of 0.91 g's. Both have disc brakes front and back, and both have four-wheel ABS, three-channel on the Cherokee and four-channel on the Range Rover. The discs on the Range Rover are larger (about 12 inches compared to 11 for the Cherokee), but the Range Rover weighs more (curb weight 4,960 pounds compared to 3,931 for the Cherokee). A braking force of 0.91 g is very good.

In *Four Wheeler's* test, the Chevy Tahoe, coming in second to the Grand Cherokee for Four Wheeler of the Year, braked less efficiently than any of the other SUVs. It has 11.6 inch discs on the front and 10.0 inch drums on the rear, with a four-wheel, three-channel ABS. It was able to go from 30 mph to zero in 38 feet and 1.8 seconds, generating 0.76 g of braking force. It has a curb weight of 5,134 pounds.

LATERAL ACCELERATION

Lateral acceleration is the centrifugal force a vehicle can withstand as it turns a corner or curve before the wheels (usually the rear ones) lose their grip on the pavement, causing the rig to skid. If a vehicle could withstand a lateral force of 1 g, it could withstand a sideways force equal to its own weight. A 4,000-pound rig could withstand a lateral push of 4,000 pounds. Very few vehicles can withstand this much. Most high performance sports cars in a turn withstand a lateral acceleration of around 0.9 g.

The formula for lateral acceleration is: $LA = V^2/32.2r$, where *LA* is force of lateral acceleration in g's, *V* is the velocity in feet per second (mph x 1.47), 32.2 is the acceleration of gravity in feet per second per second, and *r* is the radius of the turn or curve. If V (velocity) is expressed in miles per hour, the formula becomes $LA = V^2/14.9r$.

Several of the automobile magazines evaluate this figure routinely for cars. A vehicle is driven centered on a circular line painted on a paved skidpad. *Motor Trend* uses a circle 200 feet in diameter (radius of 100 feet); *Car and Driver* uses one 300 feet across (150-foot radius). They've included some sport-utility vehicles, trucks, and vans in their testing.

Motor Trend's figures (October 1999) give the '95 Chevy Corvette ZR-1 holding a turn to 0.99, and the '97 Porsche 911 Turbo reaches a full 1.00. The '97 Ferrari F355 Berlinetta and the '98 Dodge Viper GTS both reach an amazing 1.01.

The SUVs tested come in between 0.62 and 0.76 g. Vehicles at both ends of the size spectrum tied for the low of 0.62 – the '99 RAV4 Soft Top and the '99 Lincoln Navigator. The massive Ford Excursion wasn't tested for lateral acceleration, though it's 60-0 braking distance of 172 feet took the prize for longest among the vehicles tested.

Lateral acceleration, called *roadholding* by *Car and Driver*, is an important figure, because it measures the stability of a particular rig, both on- and off-highway. Hopefully, it will become generally available for SUVs soon.

NEW SUVs

The demand for sport-utility vehicles hasn't peaked yet. The manufacturers keep bringing out new models and variations on the old ones. Within the last four years or so, we've seen the arrival of full-size models like the Chevrolet Tahoe, the GMC Yukon and Yukon Denali, the Ford Expedition and its corporate twin, the Lincoln Navigator. Chevy has upgraded the Suburban and GMC has renamed its version to the Yukon XL. Ford has brought out the massive Excursion to compete with the Suburban. The Toyota Land Cruiser's corporate twin as been upgraded to the Lexus LX 470. GM has brought out an upgraded version of the Tahoe as the Cadillac Escalade. The Dodge Durango is really a full-size rig, though some consider it midsize.

Relatively recent additions to the midsize class include the Mercedes M-Class SUV, both the V6 ML 320 and the V8 ML 430, the Mercury Mountaineer (an upgraded version of the Ford Explorer), the Infiniti QX4 (an upgraded Nissan Pathfinder), the Kia Sportage, the Mistubishi Montero Sport (a mid-price version of the standard Montero), the Oldsmobile Bravada, and the Subaru Forester (slightly smaller than the Subaru Outback, itself a recent addition). Lexus also has the RX 300, and the Nissan Xterra has just arrived on the scene. GMC has the Envoy, an upgraded Jimmy/Blazer. Land Rover has upgraded the Discovery to the Series II, with Hill Descent Control and a stabilization system called Active Cornering Enhancement (ACE). BMW has entered the SUV arena with the X5. The Honda CR-V is large enough to be considered midsize.

The Toyota RAV4 has arrived, and the Suzuki Sidekick has been revamped as the Grand Vitara with a V6 engine. Isuzu's VehiCROSS has been upgraded from a concept to a production model.

Some have come and gone. The Suzuki X-90 didn't make it, and the Acura SLX made only a short appearance. The rugged Land Rover Defender 90 is no longer available in the U.S. as a new vehicle.

CORPORATE TWINS

Several vehicles bearing different names are similar, made by one corporate division or manufacturer and licensed to be sold under a different name by another. The following vehicles are basically the same from the standpoint of underlying design, though there may be major differences in styling, suspension, and appointments. The automobile magazines refer to these vehicles as "corporate twins." Sometimes there are triplets.

Chevy Blazer, GMC Jimmy, and GMC Envoy.
Chevy Tahoe, GMC Yukon, GMC Yukon Denali, and Cadillac Escalade.
Chevy Suburban and GMC Yukon XL.
Toyota Land Cruiser and Lexus LX 470.
Ford Expedition and Lincoln Navigator.
Isuzu Rodeo and Honda Passport.
Nissan Pathfinder and Infiniti QX4.
Suzuki Grand Vitara (V6) and Geo Tracker

4X4 VANS

If you'll never be driving off-road and aren't concerned about having a vehicle that can extricate you from the aftermath of such disasters as floods, fires, and earthquakes, then consider buying one of the vans with a 4-wheel drive or all-wheel drive option. That at least gives you the security of better highway handling in bad weather. Vans offering a 4x4 option include the Chevrolet Astro, Dodge Grand Caravan, Eagle Summit Wagon, Ford Aerostar, GMC Safari, Mazda MPV, and Toyota Previa.

4WD SYSTEMS

The type of transfer case in a rig determines the nature of the 4-wheel drive system. This information is for those of you who really want to know what you're getting in a 4x4.

It's difficult to get this information from a lot of car salespeople. In my experience, many of them are more familiar with passenger cars than they are with 4x4s, and they simply don't understand what kind of 4WD system moves the rig they're trying to sell you. There are some notable exceptions, and I'm indebted to the many knowledgeable 4x4 dealers and salespeople who provided me with background information for this book.

In American vehicles, most current transfer cases come from one of three companies—New Venture Gear (NVG), Borg-Warner (BW), or Dana-Spicer.

Chrysler owned a company called New Process. GM and Chrysler teamed up and formed New Venture Gear (NVG). The NVG plant that makes T-cases and manual transmissions is located in Troy, Michigan. New Process is now a division of NVG. T-cases from the former New Process company carried the letters NP. When New Venture Gear was formed, the letters in front of the T-case numbers changed from NP to NV or NVG.

Basically, T-cases give you one of the five following 4WD options:

1) Part-time 4WD with a 2WD option and both Hi and Lo ranges in 4WD. The front and rear driveshafts are locked together so the front and rear wheels move at the same speeds. This type of T-case gives maximum traction, but you can only use part-time 4WD on slippery surfaces. Using it on dry pavements causes a lot of wear on drivetrain and tires. Examples: Chevy Tahoe's Insta-Trac with an NP 241 T-case, Chevy Blazer's Insta-Trac with the NV 231 T-case or the push-botton NV 233, and Jeep's Command-Trac with the NVG 231 T-case.

2) Part-time or full-time 4WD with a 2WD option and both Hi and Lo ranges in 4WD. In 4WD Hi, these T-cases let you choose either a mode that locks the front and rear driveshafts for maximum traction on slippery surfaces (part-time 4WD) or a mode that allows the front and rear wheels to turn at different speeds (full-time 4WD). Full-time 4WD doesn't give you as much traction as part-time 4WD, but you can use full-time 4WD on dry pavement or lightly graveled roads. This option is useful when traveling on mostly dry highways that have patches of snow and ice here and there. Examples: Jeep Cherokee's Selec-Trac and the Dodge Durango with the NVG 242 T-case. The Hummer uses a beefed-up version of this T-case without the 2WD option.

3) Full-time 4WD with a 2WD option and both Hi and Lo ranges in 4WD. This type of T-case doesn't let you lock the T-case in 4WD Hi, so there's always some slippage between the front and rear wheels. It doesn't let you choose the maximum traction the part-time 4WD option offers, but it's basically a minimal brainer and you don't have to think about

what kind of 4WD you need. Example: Chevy's Autotrac and Ford Explorer's Control-Trac, which use an electronic clutch to transfer torque between front and rear sets of wheels.

4) Full-time 4WD with no 2WD option, but both Hi and Lo ranges in 4WD. These systems are usually called Full-time 4-Wheel Drive or Permanent 4-Wheel Drive in the promotional literature for vehicles that have it. It's also a minimal brainer, since you never have to decide whether you want 2WD or 4WD; the vehicle is always in 4WD. Some of these systems use viscous coupling or a Gerotor in the T-case, which allows the T-case to decrease the degree of slippage between the front and rear driveshafts when either the front or rear wheels start to spin. This transfers power to the set of wheels still with traction. These systems still have 4WD Lo range for crawling power when you need it. Example: Jeep Grand Cherokee's Quadra-Trac II with the NV 247 Gerotor T-case. This system becomes Quadra Drive when used with Gerodisc Vari-Lok (Hydra-Lok) differentials front and rear.

5) Full-time 4WD with no 2WD option and no low range in the T-case. This is the ultimate no brainer, because the vehicle is always in 4WD Hi. These systems generally use viscous coupling or something similar to allow the transfer of power to the set of wheels with traction when the other set starts to slip. The off-road capabilities of these systems are diminished because you can't shift into 4WD Lo for rock crawling or hill climbing. Examples: Oldsmobile Bravada's SmartTrak with the BW 4472 T-case, and the Subaru Outback's 4WD system, which is basically front-wheel drive, transferring torque as needed to the rear wheels.

LIMITED SLIP DIFFERENTIALS (POSIS) AND LOCKERS

Limited slip differentials, called posis from the original GM Posi-Traction, and locking differentials direct torque to the wheel with traction when the opposite wheel is slipping. (See Chapter 3 for a detailed discussion of posis and lockers.) There's a confusing bunch of these devices out there. Here's a summary of what's available.

LIMITED SLIP DIFFERENTIALS (POSIS)

Device	Manufacturer	Type	Availability	Comments
Power-Lok	Dana/Spicer	Clutch	Optional on Dana axles.	More durable than Trac-Lok. Call Precision Gear.
Trac-Lok	Dana/Spicer	Clutch	Factory option on Dana axles	More available than Power-Lok.
Traction-Lok	Ford	Clutch	Factory option on Ford light trucks	
Torq-Line	US Gear	Clutch	Aftermarket for GM Corporate differentials	
Traction-Plus	Moroso Performance Products	Clutch	Aftermarket for GM trucks	Strongest clutch-type posi available.
Calmini	Calmini Products	Clutch	For Isuzu and Suzuki SUVs	
Nissan	Nissan Motorsport	Clutch	For Nissan light trucks and Pathfinders	
Top-Spec	Eaton	Clutch	Aftermarket clutch-type posi	
Gov-Lok	Eaton	Hybrid	Factory option on GM light trucks	Some features of a locker. Aftermarket on other vehicles. Combination posi and locker.
Sure-Grip HD	Auburn Gear	Cone	Aftermarket for GM, Ford,Chrysler,Toyota. Factory option for Ford light trucks	Available also from Mopar Performance for Chrysler axles.
Sure-Grip Pro	Auburn Gear	Cone	Aftermarket for GM, Ford,Chrysler,Toyota. Factory option for Ford light trucks.	50% more torque biasing than the HD model.
TrueTrac	Tractech	Gears	Aftermarket posi	Medium duty applications.

Zexel-Torsen	Zexel-Torsen	Gears	Factory option for Hummers	Torque-biasing pos.
Power Brute	Precision Gear	Gears	Aftermarket for Japanese light trucks	

LOCKERS, MANUAL AND AUTOMATIC

Device	Manufacturer	Type	Availability	Comments
ARB Air Locker	ARB	Manual, Electric and pneumatic	Aftermarket locker	Air compressor can be used to inflate tires.
Command Locker	PowerTrax	Manual, Electric	Aftermarket locker	Affordable.
Lock-Right	PowerTrax	Automatic	Aftermarket locker	Old standard automatic locker.
Performance Locker	PowerTrax	Automatic	Aftermarket locker	Heavier duty than the Lock-Right.
Detroit Locker	Tractech	Automatic	Aftermarket locker	Heavy duty. Old standard automatic locker.
Detroit SofLocker	Tractech	Automatic	Aftermarket locker	Smoother, lighter duty.
Detroit E-Z Locker	Tractech	Automatic	Aftermarket locker	Lighter duty.
Detroit C-Locker	Tractech	Automatic	Aftermarket locker	For C-clip axles.

RESOURCES
MAPS, SCHOOLS, AND EQUIPMENT

NOTE: The addresses and web site URLs listed below were current at the time of publication. Due to various restrictions, we have not included phone numbers.

MAPS

Allied Services, 966 N. Main Street, Orange, California 92667. U.S. Geological Survey topographical maps and other maps.

Sidekick Off Road Maps, 12475 Central Avenue, Suite 352, Chino, California 91710. Videos, maps, and trail guides.

Trails Illustrated, P.O. Box 3610, Evergreen, Colorado 80439-3425. Maps of national parks in western states.

USGS Information Services, P.O. Box 25286; Denver, Colorado 80225. U.S. Geological Survey topographical maps.

U.S. Department of Agriculture Forest Service Regional Offices

Alaska Region, Federal Office Building, 709 West Ninth Street, P.O. Box 21628, Juneau, Alaska 99802.

Eastern Region, 310 West Wisconsin Avenue, Room 500, Milwaukee, Wisconsin 53203.

Intermountain Region, Federal Building, 324 25th Street, Ogden, Utah 84401.

Northern Region, Federal Building, 200 East Broadway Street, P.O. Box 7669, Missoula, Montana 59807.

Pacific Northwest Region, 319 SW Pine Street, P.O. Box 3623, Portland, Oregon 97208.

Pacific Southwest Region, 630 Sansome Street, San Francisco, California 94111.

Rocky Mountain Region, 11177 West Eighth Avenue, P.O. Box 25127, Lakewood, Colorado 80225.

Southern Region, 1720 Peachtree Road NW, Atlanta, Georgia 30367.

Southwestern Region, Federal Building, 517 Gold Avenue SW, Albuquerque, New Mexico 87102.

U.S. Department of the Interior Bureau of Land Management State Offices

BLM Alaska State Office, 222 West 7th Avenue, Suite 13, Anchorage, Alaska 99513-7599.

BLM Arizona State Office, 3707 North 7th Street, P.O. Box 16563, Phoenix, Arizona 85011.

BLM California State Office, Federal Building, 2800 Cottage Way, Room E-2845, Sacramento, California 95825-1889.
BLM Colorado State Office, Attn: Public Room, 2850 Youngfield Street, Lakewood, Colorado 80215.

BLM Idaho State Office, 3380 Americana Terrace, Boise, Idaho 83706.

BLM Montana/North & South Dakota State Office, 222 North 32nd Street, P.O. Box 36800, Billings, Montana 59107-6800.

BLM Nevada State Office, Attn: Public Room, 850 Harvard Way, Reno, Nevada 89520-0006.

BLM New Mexico/Oklahoma/Texas State Office, 1474 Rodeo Road, P.O. Box 27115, Santa Fe, New Mexico 87502-0115.

BLM Oregon/Washington State Office, 1300 NE 44th Avenue, P.O. Box 2965, Portland, Oregon 97208-2965.

BLM Utah State Office, Attn: Public Room, 324 South State Street, Suite 301, P.O. Box 45155, Salt Lake City, Utah 84145-2303.

BLM Wyoming/Kansas/Nebraska State Office, 2515 Warren Avenue, P.O. Box 1828, Cheyenne, Wyoming 82003.

ORGANIZATIONS

BlueRibbon Coalition, Inc., P.O. Box 5449, Pocatello, Idaho 83202. Nationwide networking organization representing motorized recreationists working to keep public land open for motorized recreation. Membership is $20 a year.

Family Motor Coach Association, 4WD Chapter (FMCA 4-Wheelers), 1638 Scooter Lane, Fallbrook, California 92028. Organization for motorhomers who tow 4x4s behind them and go wheelin' once they settle into camp.

SEMA (Specialty Equipment Market Association), P.O. Box 4910, Diamond Bar, California 91765-0910.

Tread Lightly! Inc., 298 24th Street, Suite 325C, Ogden, Utah 84401. Private nonprofit corporation that interfaces between private users of public land and government agencies, such as the U.S. Forest Service and the BLM. Membership is $20 a year.

United 4-Wheel Drive Association, 4505 W 700 S, Shelbyville, Indiana 46176. National 4-wheeling group coordinating the networking activities of many of the local clubs. A good, basic 4-wheel group to join.

AUTOMOBILE MANUFACTURERS AND DISTRIBUTORS

AM General Corporation. Hummer. [http://www.hummer.com]

American Honda Motor Company. Passport. CR-V. [http://www.honda2000.com]

American Isuzu Motors. Amigo, Rodeo, Trooper, VehiCROSS. [http://www.isuzu.com]

American Suzuki Motor Corporation. Grand Vitara. [http://www.suzuki.com]

BMW AG. BMW X5. [http://www.bmw.com]

DaimlerChrysler Corporation. Wrangler, Cherokee, Grand Cherokee, Dodge Durango, Mercedes ML 320, Mercedes ML 430. [http://www.daimlerchrysler.com]

Europa International, Inc. Mercedes Gelaendewagen (G-wagon). [http://www.gwagen.com] (There's not much information on this site. Visit the main Mercedes G-wagon site: [http://www.mercedes-benz.com/e/cars/g-class/default.htm]

Ford Motor Company. Ford Explorer, Ford Expedition, Ford Excursion, Mercury Mountaineer, Lincoln Navigator. [http://www.ford.com]

General Motors Corporation. Chevy Blazer, Chevy Tahoe, Chevy Suburban, Chevy Tracker, Oldsmobile Bravada, Cadillac Escalade, GMC Jimmy, GMC Envoy, GMC Yukon, GMC Yukon Denali, GMC Yukon XL. [http://www.gm.com]

Kia Motors America, Inc. Sportage. [http://www.kia.com]

Land Rover North America, Inc. Land Rover Discovery Series II, Range Rover 4.0 SE, Range Rover 4.6 HSE. [http://www.landrover.com]

Lexus, a division of Toyota Motor Sales, U.S.A., Inc. LX 470, RX 300. [http://www.lexus.com]

Mistubishi Motor Sales of America. Montero, Montero Sport. [http://www.mitsubishicars.com]
Nissan Motor Corporation. Pathfinder. Xterra. [http://www.nissan-usa.com]

Quigley Motor Company, Inc. 4WD conversions of full-size Chevrolet/GMC and Ford vans and pickups. [http://www.quigley4x4.com]

Subaru of America, Inc. Legacy Outback, Forester. [http://www.subaru.com]

Toyota Motor Sales, U.S.A., Inc. 4Runner, Land Cruiser, RAV4. [http://www.toyota.com]

BOOKS, MAGAZINES, NEWSLETTERS AND WEB SITES

All-Wheel and Four-Wheel-Drive Vehicle Systems, by Wesley M. Dick, Dana Corporation, The Forty-First L. Ray Buckendale Lecture. Society of Automotive Engineers, Inc., 400 Commonwealth Drive, Warrendale, Pennsylvania 15096-0001. SAE publication SP-95/1063 (952600).

American Survival Guide, Y-Visionary Publishing L.P., 265 South Anita Drive, Suite 120, Orange, California 92868-3310. Articles on wilderness survival, off-road recreation, and driving.

Auto Math Handbook: Basic Calculations, Formulas, Equations and Theory for Automotive Enthusiasts, by John Lawlor. HP Books, Berkley Publishing Group, 200 Madison Avenue, New York, New York 10016.

Automobile, K-III Magazine Corporation, 888 Seventh Avenue, New York, New York 10106. Editorial offices: 120 East Liberty Street, Ann Arbor, Michigan 48104. Subscriptions: Automobile, P.O. Box 55752, Boulder, Colorado 80322.

Backroad Trips & Tips: Glovebox Guide to Unpaved Southern California, Second Edition 1993, by Harry Lewellyn. Glovebox Publications, P.O. Box 18615, Anaheim, California 92817. A guide to Southern California trails, it also contains a lot of pearls on off-roading in general.

Bushdriver Magazine, 25 Valley Park Crescent, Turramurra NSW 2074, Australia. Australian off-roading magazine. Airmail subscription AUS$55/year.

Car and Driver, Hachette Filipacchi Magazines, Inc., 1633 Broadway, New York, New York 10019. Editorial office: 2002 Hogback Road, Ann Arbor, Michigan 48105. Subscriptions: P.O. Box 52906, Boulder, Colorado 80322.

Chevrolet & GMC Light Truck Owner's Bible, by Moses Ludel. Robert Bentley, Inc., Automotive Publishers, 1000 Massachusetts Avenue, Cambridge, Massachusetts 02138. Advice on repairing, beefing up, and driving your Chevrolet 4x4.

A Comprehensive Guide to Land Navigation with GPS, by Noel J. Hotchkiss, Alexis Publishing, Alexis USA, Inc., 1037 Sterling Road, Suite 203, Herndon, Virginia 22070. A good text on navigating, with or without GPS.

Country Roads Series, Country Roads Press, P.O. Box 286, Castine, Maine 04421. Guides for country road trips to places of scenic and historical interest. There is a book for each of many states. (*Country Roads of Idaho, Country Roads of Ohio, Country Roads of Vermont,* etc.)

Developments for Drivelines in Four-Wheel Drive Systems. Society of Automotive Engineers, Inc., 400 Commonwealth Drive, Warrendale, Pennsylvania 15096-0001. SAE special publication SP-95/1127.

Do-It-Yourself Medicine, by Ragnar Benson. Paladin Press, P.O. Box 1307, Boulder, Colorado 80306. Excellent manual on medical treatment when you have no one to rely on but yourself.

Driving Techniques for the Professional and Non-Professional, by Anthony Scotti. PhotoGraphics Publishing, 629 Edgewater Avenue, Ridgefield, New Jersey 07657. Solid information on the theory and practice of staying alive behind the wheel. Aimed primarily at law enforcement, it has good advice for everyone. By the founder of the Scotti School of High-Performance Driving.

Ecological 4-Wheeling Adventures, 2925 College Avenue, Suite A7, Costa Mesa, California 92626. Editor: Harry Lewellyn. Newsletter, atlases, maps.

Federal Lands: Information on the Use and Impact of Off-Highway Vehicles. United States General Accounting Office Report to the Honorable Bruce F. Vento, House of Representatives. August 1995. Report to the House from the GAO on the implementation of Executive Orders 11644 and 11989 issued in the 1970s pertaining to use of off-road vehicles on public lands. Obtain free by calling the GAO at 202/512-6000. Ask for document GAO/RCED-95-209.

4x4Now.Com and 4x4Books.Com. URLs are: [http://www.4x4now.com] and [http://www.4x4

books.com]. A web site devoted to 4-wheeling. Videos of trails, articles on off-road driving technique, information about rigs, products, books, and videos. Also for sale: GPS devices, computerized USGS topographical map programs for use with GPS and laptop computers. Go to [http://www. 4x4now.com/4wht.htm] for experts' articles on various aspects of 4-wheel driving, including several by Brad DeLong.

4x4Road.Com. URL is: [http://www.4x4road.com]. This is the 4-Wheel Freedom website for this book. Visit it for additional tips on 4-wheel driving, including driving in snow and ice, mud, hills, water, handling vehicle fires. Valuable links to other 4x4 websites and other websites of interest.

4-Wheel Drive & Sport Utility Magazine, McMullen & Yee Publishing, Editorial offices: 774 S. Placentia Avenue, Placentia, California 92670. Subscriptions: P.O. Box 68033, Anaheim, California 92817.

Four Wheeler, Four Wheeler Publishing, Ltd., 227 Park Avenue, New York, New York 10172. Division of General Media Automotive Group. Editorial office: Four Wheeler, 3330 Ocean Park Blvd., Santa Monica, California 90405. Subscriptions: Four Wheeler, P.O. Box 420435, Palm Coast, Florida 32142.

Fundamentals of Vehicle Dynamics, by Thomas D. Gillespie. Society of Automotive Engineers, Inc., 400 Commonwealth Drive, Warrendale, Pennsylvania 15096-0001

Jeep Owner's Bible, by Moses Ludel. Robert Bentley, Inc., Automotive Publishers, 1000 Massachusetts Avenue, Cambridge, Massachusetts 02138. Repairing, beefing up, and driving your Jeep.

Jp Magazine. The Dobbs Publishing Group, 3816 Industry Blvd, Lakeland, Florida 33811.

The Land Rover Experience, 2nd edition, by Tom Sheppard. Land Rover, Lode Lane, Solihull, West Midlands B92 8NW, England.

The LandUse Network, email network of off-road recreationists oriented toward ecological, intelligent use of the outdoors. Email address is lun@off-road.com. Web site URL is http://www.off-road.com/landuse/landuse.htm.

Mark A. Smith's Guide to Safe, Common Sense Off-Road Driving. Mark A. Smith Off-Roading, Inc., P.O. Box 1601, Georgetown, California 95634. Good tips on 4-wheeling by one of the major gurus.

Medicine for Mountaineering, edited by James A. Wilkerson, M.D. The Mountaineers, 1011 SW Klickitat Way, Seattle, Washington 98134. Excellent all-around first-aid book for outdoor enthusiasts.

Military Vehicles Magazine, David Ahl, Editor. SBI, Inc., 12 Indian Head Road, Morristown, New Jersey 07960. The web site URL is http://members. aol.com/mvehicle/home.htm.

The Mining Company's 4-wheel drive section. Part of a large web site covering many topics. The 4-wheel drive pages contain a lot of useful information about 4x4s, with links to manufacturer's sites. The URL is http://4wheeldrive.miningco.com.

Motor Trend, Petersen Publishing Company, 6420 Wilshire Blvd., Los Angeles, California 90048.

Off Road, Argus Publishers Corporation, 12100 Wilshire Blvd., Suite 250, Los Angeles, California 90025. Editorial offices: P.O. Box 49659, Los Angeles, California 90049. Subscriptions: P.O. Box 451, Mount Morris, Illinois 61054.

The Off-Road 4-Wheel Drive Book, by Jack Jackson. Patrick Stephens Limited of Haynes Publishing, Nr Yeovil, Somerset, BA22 7JJ, England. An excellent description of the 4-wheeling scene in the United Kingdom, Middle East, and Sahara Desert, containing much good advice by veteran expedition leader and 4-wheeler Jack Jackson.

Off-Road.Com, URL is http://www.off-road.com. Extensive web site with much 4x4 information about trails, rigs, products, books, and videos. Host of the off-road.com email network, email address is offroad-request@off-road.com.

Off-Road Recovery Techniques: A Practical Handbook on Principle and Use of Equipment, by Nick Cole. Motor Racing Publications Ltd., Unit 6, The Pilton Estate, 46 Pitlake, Croydon CRO 3RY, England.

Paladin Press, P.O. Box 1307, Boulder, Colorado 80306. Large selection of books and videos on outdoor survival, personal freedom, evasive driving, and related topics. Visit the Paladin web site. The URL is http://www.paladin-press.com.

Petersen's 4-Wheel & Off-Road, Petersen Publishing Company, 6420 Wilshire Blvd., Los Angeles, California 90048.

Property Matters: How Property Rights Are Under Assault and Why You Should Care, by James V. DeLong, published by The Free Press. Excellent review of the current struggle between traditional property rights and radical environmentalism. For more information consult the author's web site. The URL is http://www.regpolicy.com.

Road & Track, P.O. Box 1757, Newport Beach, California, 92663.

Survival: A Manual That Could Save Your Life, by Chris & Gretchen Janowsky. Paladin Press, P.O. Box 1307, Boulder, Colorado 80306. Excellent manual on survival skills by Alaskan survival experts.

Survivalist's Medicine Chest, by Ragnar Benson. Paladin Press, P.O. Box 1307, Boulder, Colorado 80306. A practical do-it-yourself medical and surgical manual.

Tires, Suspension, and Handling, 2nd edition, by John C. Dixon. Society of Automotive Engineers, Inc., 400 Commonwealth Drive, Warrendale, Pennsylvania 15096-0001.

The Tread Lightly! Guide to Responsible Four-Wheeling and *Tread Lightly!'s Guide to Responsible Mountain Biking*. Tread Lightly! Inc., 298 24th Street, Suite 325C, Ogden, Utah 84401.

Unstuck, by Bill Burke's 4-Wheeling America, 2134 S. Humboldt Street, Denver, Colorado 80210-4619. Excellent video on winching techniques.

Why Skid? Modern Winter Driving Techniques. The Bridgestone Winter Driving School, P.O. Box 774167, Steamboat Springs, Colorado 80477. Books and videos on handling snow and ice.

SCHOOLS

The Adventure Company, 8855 Appian Way, Los Angeles, California 90046. Sierra Nevada and Baja California off-road trips and training with Harald Pietschmann.

Bill Burke's 4-Wheeling America, 2134 S. Humboldt Street, Denver, Colorado 80210-4619. Professional instruction in off-highway driving. Guided trips.

Bob Bondurant School of High Performance Driving, Firebird International Raceway, P.O. Box 60968, Phoenix, Arizona 85082.

David Bowyer's Off-Road Centre, East Foldhay, Zeal Monachorum, Crediton, Devon, EX17 6DH, England. Established in 1986, it is one of the oldest public off-road schools.

Bridgestone Winter Driving School, 1850 Ski Time Square Drive, P.O. Box 774167, Steamboat Springs, Colorado 80477. Hands-on training in handling snow and ice.

Esprit de Four 4-Wheel Drive Club, Hollister, California. Four-wheel driving instructional clinics twice a year for 30-40 vehicles at the Hollister Hills SVRA (State Vehicle Recreational Area), near San Jose.

Harry Lewellyn, 2925 College Avenue, Suite A7, Costa Mesa, California 92626. Ecological 4-Wheeling Adventures. Professional instruction in off-highway driving. Guided trips.

Rick Russell/Sidekick Off Road Maps, 12475 Central Avenue, Suite 352, Chino, California 91710. Professional instruction in off-highway driving. Guided trips.

San Bernadino Sheriff's Department EVOC (Emergency Vehicle Operations Center) Training Program, P.O. Box 1456, San Bernadino, California 92402. EVOC training, 4x4 off-road courses.

Scotti School of Defensive Driving, 10 High Street, Suite 15, Medford, Massachusetts 02155. Evasive and counterterrorist driving.

Skip Barber Racing School, 29 Brook Street, P.O. Box 1629, Lakeville, Connecticut 06039. Racing and corporate driving courses.

EQUIPMENT

Batteries and Electrical Equipment

Custom Electrical Specialists, 6245 Bristol Parkway, Suite 229, Culver City, California 90230-6983. Good Samaritan Dual Battery System.

Optima Batteries. Nonliquid, nonspillable, heavy-duty batteries. [http://www.optimabatteries.se/ett.htm]

Wrangler NW Power Products. Dual battery installation kit and other electrical products. [http://www.WranglerNW.com]

Camping, Hunting, and Sporting Goods

Coleman Company, 250 N. St. Francis, Wichita, Kansas 67202. Camping equipment.

R & M Specialty Products, P.O. Box 1683, Windsor, California 95492. Under-the-hood hot water shower.

Sportsman's Guide. 411 Farwell Avenue, So. St. Paul, Minnesota 55075. Ammunition, camping, hunting, and shooting supplies.

CB Radios

Uniden America Corporation, 8700 North By Northwest Blvd., Indianapolis, Indiana 46250. Uniden CB radios and Bearcat scanners.

Chain Saws

Husqvarna Forest & Garden Company, 9006-J Perimeter Woods Drive, Charlotte, North Carolina 28216. Husky chain saws.

Stihl Company. Andreas Stihl, D-7050 Waiblingen, Germany. Consult the Yellow Pages for the dealer nearest you. Chain saws.

Drivetrain Conversions, Axles, Engines, T-cases, and Transmissions

Advance Adapters, Inc., 335 Santa Bella Avenue, P.O. Box 247, Paso Robles, California 93446. Equipment and instructional manuals for drivetrain conversions in many makes of 4x4s.

Currie Enterprises, 1480-B N. Tustin Ave., Anaheim, California 92807. Drivetrain conversions, axles, lockers. Electromotive, Inc., 14004-J Willard Road, Chantilly, Virginia 22021. JFI fuel injection modification for Jeep 6 cylinder 4.2L engines.

Hicks 4x4 Specialists, 1321 S. Garey Ave, Pomona, California 91766. Transmissions, axles, T-cases.

Howell Engine Developments, Inc., 6201 Industrial Way, Marine City, Michigan 48039. Fuel injection systems for the Jeep 258 cid inline 6-cylinder and all V8 engines.

Mopar Performance, P.O. Box 215020, Auburn Hills, Michigan 48321-5020. Ported fuel injection systems for the Jeep 258 cid inline 6-cylinder engine.

New Venture Gear, Inc., 1775 Research Drive, Troy, Michigan 48083. Manufacturer of transfer cases and manual transmissions. T-cases made by New Process Gear, a division of NVG.

Six States Distributors, Inc., 1112 West 33rd South, Ogden, Utah 84401. Custom driveshafts, universal joints, CV (constant velocity) joints.

Tri-County Gear, 1143 W. Second Street, Pomona, California 91766. Transfer cases and transmissions.

General Equipment

Con-Ferr Mfg. Company, Inc., 123 South Front Street, Burbank, California 91502-1983. Off-road equipment manufacturer and distributer.

Dick Cepek, Inc., 17000 Kingsview Avenue, Carson, California 90746. Off-road equipment manufacturer and distributer.

Forrest Tool Company, 44250 Gordon Lane, P.O. Box 768, Mendocino, California 95460. Max Multipurpose Tool ("Max-ax").

4WD Hardware, Inc., P.O. Box 57, 44488 State Route 14, Columbiana, Ohio 44408. Off-road Jeep equipment through catalog ordering.

Gempler's, P.O. Box 270, 211 Blue Mounds Road, Mt. Horeb, Wisconsin 53572. General agricultural equipment, including work clothes and boots, camping supplies, first aid material, Safety Seal tire repair kits, safety equipment, and tools.

Harbor Freight Tools, 3491 Mission Oaks Blvd, Camarillo, California 93011. Miscellaneous hardware, winching supplies, tow straps, wrenches, welding equipment.

KC Hilites, Inc., P.O. Box 155, Williams, Arizona 86046. Off-road lights.

Leon Rosser Think Jeep, P.O. Box 1185, Bessemer, Alabama 35021. Off-road equipment distributer.

Northern, Inc., P.O. Box 1499, Burnsville, Minnesota

55337. Miscellaneous hardware, winching supplies, tow straps, wrenches, welding equipment.

Performance Products: for Toyota Trucks, 4Runners, Tacomas, T100s & Landcruisers, 7658 Haskell Avenue, Van Nuys, California 91406. Off-road equipment for Toyotas.

Quadratec, 5125 West Chester Pike, Newtown Square, Pennsylvania 19073. Catalog supplier of off-road Jeep equipment.

Q-Weld Company, 5230 W. 16th Street, Suite 349, Indianapolis, Indiana 46224. Epoxy repair putty.

Smittybilt, Inc., 2090 California Avenue, Corona, California 91719. Off-road equipment manufacturer and distributer.

Tomken Machine, 36580 US Hwy, 24 No., Buena Vista, Colorado 81211. Heavy-duty off-road equipment, including bumpers, rocker skids, and spare tire carriers.

Global Positioning Systems (GPS)

Eagle Electronics, P.O. Box 669, Catoosa, Oklahoma 74015. Eagle AccuNav Sport.

Garmin, 9875 Widmer Road, Lenexa, Kansas 66215. Garmin GPS devices.

Magellan Systems, 960 Overland Court, San Dimas, California 91773. Magellan Trailblazer XL.

Micrologic, 9174 Deering Avenue, Chatsworth, California 91311. Micrologic Sportsman.

Trimble Navigation, 9020-II Capital of Texas Highway North, Suite 400, Austin, Texas 78759. Trimble Scout and Trimble ScoutMaster.

Lockers

Air Locker, Inc. ARB-USA, 1425 Elliott Avenue, West, Seattle, Washington 98109. Locking differentials, under-the-hood air compressor, 4x4 accessories.

Al's Repair, Al Yenney, 900 N. Avery, Pasco, Washington 99301. ARB locker sales and installation, 4x4 drivetrain conversions.

Auburn Gear Inc., 400 East Auburn Drive, Auburn, Indiana 46706, Aftermarket limited-slip differential (posi).

Dana/Spicer. Phone 800-729-3262 for the distributor nearest you. Power-Lok and Trac-Lok aftermarket limited-slip differentials (posis).

Eaton Corporation, Torque Control Products Division, 26101 Northwestern Highway, Southfield, Michigan 48076. Aftermarket automatic locking differential.

Moroso Performance Products, 80 Carter Drive, P.O. Box 1470, Guilford, Connecticut 06437. Aftermarket limited-slip differential (posi) for GM trucks. Strongest clutch-type posi available.

PowerTrax Lock-Right, 245 Fleischer Avenue, Costa Mesa, California 92626. Aftermarket Lock-Right and Performance Locker automatic locking differentials.

Tractech (formerly Dyneer), 11445 Stephens Drive, P.O. Box 882, Warren, Michigan 48090. Detroit Locker, C-Locker, SofLocker, E-Z locker, aftermarket automatic locking differentials, TrueTrac limited-slip differential (posi).

Shocks and Suspension

Bilstein Corporation of America, 8845 Rehco Road, San Diego, California 92121. Shock absorbers.

Rancho Suspension, 6925 Atlantic Avenue, Long Beach, California 90805. Lift kits and shock absorbers.

Superlift Suspension Systems, 211 Horn Lane, West Monroe, Louisiana 71292. Lift kits.

Tires, Wheels, and Tire Equipment

Alcoa Company of America, Wheel Products International, 1600 Harvard Avenue, Cleveland, Ohio 44105. One-piece hot-forged aluminum wheels.

BF Goodrich, 600 S. Main Street, Akron, Ohio 44387. Tires.

Bridgestone, One Bridgestone Park, P.O. Box 140991, Nashville, Tennessee 37214-0991. Blizzak snow tires.

Dick Cepek, Inc., 17000 Kingsview Avenue, Carson, California 90746. Off-road and performance tires.

Goodyear Tire & Rubber Company, 1144 E Market Street, Akron, Ohio 44316. Wrangler tires.

Interco Tire Corporation, P.O. Box 486, Rayne, Louisiana 70578. Super Swamper Boggers.

Mickey Thompson Performance Tires, 4670 Allen Road, Stow, Ohio 44224. One-piece, hot-forged aluminum wheels and performance tires. Mickey Thompson Baja Belted Sidebiters and Sportsman Pro.

Quadra-Flate, 29913 Westlink Drive, Suite 10, Menifee, California 92584. System for airing down or reinflating all four tires at once.

Safety Seal. North Shore Labs Corp, P.O. Box 568, Peabody, MA 01960. Professional-level tire-repair kits with self-vulcanizing tire-sealing repair strips.

Welding

Hornell Speedglas, Inc., 2347 Edison Blvd., Twinsburg, Ohio 44087. Welding helmet.

Premier Power Welder. Under-the-hood welding system and high-amperage alternator. [http://www.premierpowerwelder.com]

Winches, Jacks, Ground Anchors, and Winch Equipment

Harbor Freight Tools, 3491 Mission Oaks Blvd., Camarillo, California 93011. Winching supplies, tow straps.

Hi-Lift Jack Co., 46 W. Spring Street, P.O. Box 228, Bloomfield, Indiana 47424. Hi-Lift jack.

Jackall 8000, New-Form Mfg. Company, 25 Whaley Street, Milverton, Ontario N0K 1M0, Canada. Canadian version of high-lift jack.

Mesa Industries, 2687 Orange Avenue, Suite A, Costa Mesa, California 92627. SureClaw wheel anchors.

Mile Marker, Inc. Mile Marker hydraulic 2-speed hydraulic winch. [http://www.milemarker.com]

Northern, Inc., P.O. Box 1499, Burnsville, Minnesota 55337. Winching supplies, tow straps.

Pull-Pal Inc., P.O. Box 639, Carbondale, Colorado 81623. Ground anchor.

Ramsey Winch Company, 1600 N. Garnet, P.O. Box 581510, Tulsa, Oklahoma 74158-1510. Winches.

Superwinch, Inc., 45 Danco Road, Putnam, Connecticut 06260. Winches.

Warn Industries, Inc. Winches, lights, other accessories. [http://www.warn.com]

INDEX

ABOUT THE AUTHOR

Dr. Brad DeLong lives in Idaho along with his wife, Irene Lamberti, and their four "fur" children, Hershey, Arthur, Sadie, and Bailey. They are outdoor enthusiasts and use 4-wheeling to gain access to the beautiful land they love. The author is a neurosurgical spine specialist, and Irene is a chiropractor and video producer. They've created the Orofino Spine Center, where they practice together. Contact the author in care of the publisher for information about workshops and seminars on off-roading.

The author, his wife, their dog Hershey, and their Jeep Wrangler in the snow.